the
Holocaust
and
Catholic Conscience

the Holocaust and Catholic Conscience

Cardinal Aloisius Muench and the Guilt Question in Germany

Suzanne Brown-Fleming

Published in association with the United States
Holocaust Memorial Museum

University of Notre Dame Press
Notre Dame, Indiana

Published in Association with the United States Holocaust Memorial Museum

*The views as expressed are the author's alone and do not necessarily
represent those of the United States Holocaust Memorial Museum
or any other organization.*

Library of Congress Cataloging-in-Publication Data

Brown-Fleming, Suzanne.
    The Holocaust and Catholic conscience: Cardinal Aloisius Muench and the
guilt question in Germany / Suzanne Brown-Fleming.
        p.   cm.
    "Published in association with the United States Holocaust Memorial
Museum."
    Includes bibliographical references and index.
    ISBN 0-268-02186-4 (cloth : alk. paper)
    ISBN 0-268-02187-2 (pbk. : alk. paper)
    1. Muench, Aloisius J. (Aloisius Joseph), 1889–1962.   2. Holocaust, Jewish
(1939–1945)—Moral and ethical aspects.   3. World War, 1939–1945—Religious
aspects—Catholic Church.   4. Catholic church—Foreign relations—Germany.
5. Germany—Foreign relations—Catholic Church.   6. Christianity and
antisemitism—History—20th century.   7. Germany—History—1945–1955.
I. United States Holocaust Memorial Museum.   II. Title.
    BX4705.M755B76 2005 2006
    261.2'6'094309044—dc22

                                                                            2005025264

for Klara Lenz, Annemarie Stadler, and Margaret Stadler

Contents

Acknowledgments

This project has benefited enormously from the support of the United States Holocaust Memorial Museum. I am grateful to have been a fellow at the Museum's Center for Advanced Holocaust Studies in 2000 and to have been a participant in the Center's June 2001 summer research workshop, "The Churches and the Holocaust: The Response of Laity, Clergy, and Church Authorities." Both experiences significantly shaped this book. In August 2001, I was privileged to join the professional staff of the Center for Advanced Holocaust Studies. My colleagues at the Center and at the Museum at large supplied the resources and positive environment necessary to write this book, and they continue to provide a dignified, upstanding, superior, and ever-challenging intellectual forum for my scholarship. I thank especially Robert M. Ehrenreich, director of the Center's University Programs Division, and Paul A. Shapiro, director of the Center for Advanced Holocaust Studies. Their consistent support for my work has been a great gift. Others who especially gave of their time to ensure the completion of this book include Benton Arnovitz, Michael Gelb, and Laura Brahm in the Center's Academic Publications Division; Wendy Lower, director of the Center's Visiting Scholars Program; Margaret Obrecht, staff director of the Museum's Committee on Church Relations and the Holocaust; and Severin Hochberg in the Center's Division of the Senior Historian.

I feel a great sense of pride and accomplishment to have published this book with the University of Notre Dame Press, in association with the United States Holocaust Memorial Museum. I am thankful for the encouragement and support I have received from Barbara Hanrahan, director of the University of Notre Dame Press. Thanks also to Jack Kirshbaum, who edited the manuscript; Michael Gelb, for his editorial comments; as well as Lowell Francis, Rebecca DeBoer, and all the staff of UND Press, who have made the publishing process a consistent pleasure. It seems highly appropriate to bring this story to the public record under the auspices of one of the finest presses at a Roman Catholic institution of higher education in the United States. Its publication by such a press is made doubly meaningful by the involvement of the Museum.

A number of other institutions provided crucial support for this project, and must be thanked. The Center for German and European Studies at the University of California-Berkeley and the German Academic Exchange Service supported this project in 1996. A five-month fellowship from the *Friedrich-Ebert-Stiftung* in Bonn, Germany, supported exploratory research in Munich in 1997. A grant from the history department at the University of Maryland at College Park made travel to Munich possible. The German-American Center for Visiting Scholars in Washington, D.C., the German Historical Institute's Washington office, and the University of Maryland's Mary Savage Snouffer Fellowship provided financial support for research during 1998 and 1999. The Holocaust Education Foundation hosted the first presentation of my work at Northwestern University during the "Lessons and Legacies" conference in 2000. I especially wish to thank my friend and mentor Zev Weiss, president of the Holocaust Educational Foundation, Peter Hayes, chair of the "Lessons and Legacies" conference series and member of the United States Holocaust Memorial Council's Academic Committee, and Geoffrey Giles, director of the Holocaust Educational Foundation's Eastern Europe Study Seminar and 2000–2001 J.B. and Maurice C. Shapiro Senior Scholar-in-Residence at the Center for Advanced Holocaust Studies. The Holocaust Educational Foundation's 1999 Summer Institute on the Holocaust and Jewish Civilization as well as the 2001 and 2003 Eastern Europe Study Seminars were key formative experiences for me. The University of Maryland's Joseph and Rebecca Meyerhoff Center for Jewish Studies, chaired by Marsha Rozenblit, provided matching funds for my 2001 visit to the extermination camps in Poland. For me, this trip encapsulated the everlasting necessity of scholarly work on the Holocaust.

Several individuals lent expertise, time, and energy to this project. First and foremost, I thank my doctoral advisor and mentor, James F. Harris, for his integrity, patience, good advice, exacting standards, and unquenchable faith in me. Marsha Rozenblit at the University of Maryland and Richard Wetzell at the German Historical Institute provided sound, constructive critiques and a kind ear for many years. For their cheerful labors on my behalf during my final year in graduate school, I thank Peter Beicken in the University of Maryland–College Park's German department, Rebecca Boehling at the University of Maryland–Baltimore County, and Jeffrey Herf, professor of history at the University of Maryland–College Park and 2004 Charles H. Revson Foundation Fellow at the Center for Advanced Holocaust Studies. Dr. Timothy Maher, Heather Morgan, John Shepherd, and the friendly staff at the Catholic University of America were always eager to help throughout my work with the Muench collection. I thank them for making my research experience a pleasant one.

I thank also my professional colleagues who took much time and effort to read my work over the last several years, especially Doris Bergen, professor of history at the University of Notre Dame and a member of the United States Holocaust Memorial Council's Academic Committee; Michael Berkowitz, reader in modern Jewish history at University College London and 2002 Charles H. Revson Foundation Fellow at the Center for Advanced Holocaust Studies; and Frank Buscher, professor of history at Christian Brothers University. My thanks also go to Robert P. Ericksen, professor of history at Pacific Lutheran University and member of the United States Holocaust Memorial Council's Committee on Church Relations and the Holocaust; Susannah Heschel, Eli Black Professor of Jewish Studies at Dartmouth College and member of the United States Holocaust Memorial Council's Academic Committee; and Michael Marrus, Chancellor Rose and Ray Wolfe Professor of Holocaust Studies at the University of Toronto and also a member of the United States Holocaust Memorial Council's Academic Committee. I owe much to John T. Pawlikowski, O.S.M., professor of ethics and director of Catholic-Jewish Studies at Catholic Theological Union and chair of the United States Holocaust Memorial Council's Committee on Church Relations and the Holocaust; Michael Phayer, professor emeritus of history at Marquette University and 2001 Fellow at the Center for Advanced Holocaust Studies; Elias Fuellenbach of the Dominican Courent in Düsseldorf; and Kevin Spicer, C.S.C., professor of history at Stonehill College and member of the United States Holocaust Memorial Council's Committee on Church Relations and the Holocaust. Finally, I thank James Waller, Edward B. Lindaman Chair and professor of psychology at Whitworth College, for his support of my work.

Most of all, I thank my husband, Mark Richard Fleming, who has enthusiastically supported my scholarly endeavors over the last fifteen years. Nothing I accomplish is possible—or of value—without him. I hope I have written a book that will someday make Madison Anna and Eleanor Margaret Fleming—our daughters—proud of their mother.

Abbreviations

ACHA	American Catholic Historical Association
ACUA	Archives, The Catholic University of America
CAN	*Catholic Action News* (Fargo, North Dakota)
CC	Central Committee; short for DPCC
CC/M or C	Chancery Correspondence Files/organized under M or C
CCVA	Catholic Central Verein of America
CGCPA	Classified General Correspondence of the Political Advisor
CIC	Counterintelligence Corps, U.S. Army
CUA	Catholic University of America
DP	Displaced Persons
DPCC	Displaced Persons Central Committee
ECR	Education & Religious Affairs division, U.S. Army
Einsatzgruppen	Special Task Groups

Gestapo	Secret State Police (*Geheime Staatspolizei*)
HM	Aloisius Muench Papers
ICCJ	International Council of Christians and Jews, Geneva
ICD	Information Control Division, U.S. Army
IMT	International Military Tribunal
KKGH	Church Committee for Prisoners' Aid (*Komitee für kirchliche Gefangenenhilfe*)
Msgr.	Monsignor
NA	National Archives, College Park, Maryland
NCCJ	National Conference of Christians and Jews, New York
NCWC	National Catholic Welfare Conference
NCWC-WRS	National Catholic Welfare Conference-War Relief Services
NSDAP	National Socialist German Workers' Party (*Nationalsozialistische Deutsche Arbeiterpartei*)
NZ	*Neue Zeitung*, Munich
OMGUS	Office of Military Government, United States Zone
OPAG-B	Office of the U.S. Political Advisor to Germany-Berlin
RA	Religious Affairs office, OMGUS
RG	Record Group
SHAEF	Supreme Headquarters, Allied Expeditionary Force
SS	Guard Corps (*Schutzstaffel*)
UNRRA	United Nations Relief and Rehabilitation Administration
USAREUR	United States Army Europe (beginning August 1952)
USFET	United States Forces European Theater (July 1945–March 1947)
USHMM	United States Holocaust Memorial Museum, Washington

Introduction

Aloisius Muench and the Question of Guilt and Responsibility

During a private audience in May 1957, the leader of the universal Roman Catholic Church, Pope Pius XII (1939–58), told a "story . . . with a great deal of delight" to Archbishop Aloisius Muench, who was then Vatican papal nuncio to Germany. "Hitler died and somehow got into heaven," began the pope. "There, he met the Old Testament prophet Moses. Hitler apologized to Moses for his treatment of the European Jews. Moses replied that such things were forgiven and forgotten here in heaven." "Hitler [was] relieved," continued the pope, and "said to Moses that he always wished to meet him in order to ask him an important question. Did Moses set fire to the burning bush?" "Our Holy Father told me the story with a big laugh," Archbishop Muench told Monsignor Joseph Adams of Chicago in a subsequent letter.[1]

The "delight" and "laughter" described by Archbishop Muench indicates that neither he nor Pope Pius XII appeared to understand the inappropriateness of telling a joke relating to the murder of six million European Jews. Nor did either man appear uncomfortable with attributing similar motivation between Moses' arbitration of the Ten Commandments after an angel of God appeared to him in a burning bush and Adolf Hitler's rumored involvement in the 1933 Reichstag fire, an event that facilitated consolidation of his dictatorial powers. This exchange—perhaps more than any other appearing in the papers of Aloisius Cardinal Muench—encapsulates how little importance either man appeared to place on the Jewish experience under National Socialism. It captures the failure of the institutional Roman Catholic Church to undertake a strong and public position of sensitivity, respect, and positive action toward Jews and Judaism during the papacy of Pius XII.

American-born Aloisius Cardinal Muench (1889–1962) was a key and heretofore ignored figure in internal German Catholic discussion about the Holocaust, Jews, and Judaism between 1946 and 1959. (Hereafter, as is common practice, I adopt the order "Cardinal Aloisius Muench" for Muench and other cardinals.) He was the most powerful American Catholic figure and influential Vatican representative in occupied Germany and subsequent West Germany during this period. German-American bishop of the diocese of Fargo, North Dakota (1935–59), Muench held five key positions in Germany in these years. He was the Catholic liaison representative between the U.S. Office of Military Government and the German Catholic Church in the American zone of occupied Germany (1946–49), Pope Pius XII's apostolic visitor to Germany (1946–47), Vatican relief officer in Kronberg, near Frankfurt am Main (1947–49), Vatican regent in Kronberg (1949–51), and Vatican nuncio to Germany from the new seat in Bad Godesberg, outside Bonn (1951–59).

This book tells the story of German Catholic consideration—and ultimate rejection—of guilt and responsibility for Catholicism's relationship to Nazism in general and to the persecution of European Jewry specifically in the first decade and a half following World War II. This book tells the story of lingering anti-Semitism, in Germany and in the United States, in the postwar years. Muench was an important player in the candid and uncensored dialogue about the Nazi period among members of a large and often prominent circle of contemporary Germans and Americans. Within this self-selected and yet broad and powerful circle, Muench's philo-German, anti-Jewish notions mirrored and at times influenced or inspired postwar actions and views of Jews and culpability for the Holocaust.

Spanning his stay in Germany between 1946 and 1959, Muench received tens of thousands of letters from German Catholics. Some

requested help with immigration to the United States, others wanted
help to obtain a revision of their denazification sentence, and still others needed extra rations of food or clothing. A small number wrote
hoping to have their imprisonment for war crimes commuted. Still
more were trying to locate lost relatives, or wished to fend off restitution claims from Jewish survivors, or sought the release of family
members retained as prisoners of war by American, British, French,
or Russian authorities. German Catholics wrote for aid in resisting
the requisitioning of their homes by American GIs, or sometimes
sent philosophical reactions to Muench's annual pastoral letter.
Some penned their political reactions to Allied policies, especially the
Potsdam Agreement (1945); others reflected on their social reactions to
displaced persons, including Jews.

"I always wished to meet and make the acquaintance of a non-
German of good will who holds a position of weight and influence,"
Elisabeth Baumgart of Selingen told Muench after reading his pastoral
letter *One World in Charity* (1946).[2] At a time when only "cries of hate"
could be heard toward Germans, argued Theodor Lebeda of Limburg in
1947, Muench's pastoral letter calling for charity and mercy toward
Germans was a welcome change.[3] Thea Brack, wife of SS-Oberführer
(and Catholic) Viktor Brack, wrote to Muench seeking his help in obtaining clemency for her husband, who had been tried as a war criminal and convicted for his integral part in the Nazi euthanasia program.
In it, she referred to Muench as "the highest Roman Catholic American
dignitary in Germany."[4] Muench received these letters because of his
position within the Catholic hierarchy in the United States and in
Vatican City, and because he was the American liaison to the German
Catholic Church for U.S. occupation authorities. A major theme that
emerges in the letters is the denial of any significant level of ideological
and practical participation in the National Socialist regime by German
Catholics.

Although largely overlooked by historians, Muench's papers are a
valuable resource for studying discussions about World War II and the
Holocaust in postwar Germany. Letters from German Catholics, numbering in the thousands, describe their own "victimization," be it via
expulsion, bombing, the denazification process, material need, losing
sons and fathers to the front or to imprisonment, or becoming a people
shamed in the eyes of the post-Holocaust world.[5] Of special value are
those letters to Muench commenting directly and unambiguously on

crimes against Jews or which describe the (few) surviving Jews in their communities. Roughly 300 Germans wrote letters to Muench commenting directly on the Holocaust. They included lay Catholics; convicted Catholic war criminals involved in Holocaust-related crimes, their families, or their champions; members of the German Catholic clerical upper hierarchy; priests and nuns; Catholic politicians; ethnic German expellees; German prisoners of war; and German Jews. Muench's German correspondence numbered 15,000 letters in 1956, and he received many more by 1959.[6] That among more than 15,000 letters only 300 addressed the Holocaust indicates just how unusual direct commentary by Germans about the persecution of European Jewry was in the immediate postwar decade.

The general absence of specific discourse on Jews, anti-Semitism, or the Holocaust makes these 300 letters all the more valuable. Muench's pastoral letter *One World in Charity* appeared in religious and secular publications alongside statements denying Germans' complicity in Nazi crimes. Letters to him commenting on *One World* confirmed that German Catholics (and some non-Catholics) considered him a figure of German descent, one who especially understood German "suffering." For this reason, they wrote to Muench on Holocaust-related topics in unusually frank and telling ways, allowing the historian to carefully reconstruct a lively dialogue concerning who should be assigned guilt or responsibility for the murder of approximately six million European Jews during World War II, and in what manifestations anti-Jewish notions still lingered postwar.

This dialogue linked not only Muench and German Catholics but also Muench and American Catholics and clergy, Vatican prelates, and American occupation officials. In addition to 300 letters from Germans, Muench received more than 100 letters from U.S. Catholics and military government personnel commenting frankly on the taboo issues of anti-Semitism, surviving Jews, and the Holocaust. What emerges is a disturbing picture of anti-Jewish prejudices that influenced not only German Catholics but also the highest offices of American Catholicism and American military personnel.

_____

In January 1946, the first installment of *One World in Charity* appeared in the United States. It surfaced in occupied Germany one year later. *One World* called Allied authorities "other Hitlers in disguise, who would make of [the German] nation a crawling [Bergen-] Belsen."[7] Only a few criminals perpetrated the inhuman crimes carried out under the Nazi regime, argued *One World.* Why, then, asked Muench, should women and children suffer, because "some policy makers in top levels revived the Mosaic idea of an eye for an eye?"[8] Muench's imagined "one world" would "never be built by those who hate, and in hating take their inspiration from the hard teaching of an eye for an eye and a tooth for a tooth. It will have to be built by those who believe in Christ's law of love,"[9] juxtaposing the Old Testament laws of Moses and Israel—the laws of Judaism—to those of Christ, of love, of the New Testament, of Christians.

Muench's open sympathy toward Germans in word was confirmed in deed by his active participation in the sweeping, Vatican-supported, postwar clemency campaign on behalf of convicted war criminals. When, in 1953, Muench heard that Konstantin von Neurath, Erich Räder, Karl Dönitz, Walther Funk, Baldur von Schirach, Albert Speer, and Rudolf Hess purportedly had "no bed during the day, chairs without a back, lights [on] at night . . . [and] poor meals" while incarcerated in Spandau prison,[10] he called the imprisonment of these leading Third Reich personalities "another terrible blotch on our record for decent, humane treatment toward war criminals." Referring to these men—among whom were the former Reich foreign minister; the former commander-in-chief of the German naval forces; the former head of the Hitler Youth; the former Reich minister for armaments; Adolf Hitler's former deputy; and former Reich press secretary, president of the Reichsbank, and general plenipotentiary for the war economy—Muench wrote in his diary, "mercy toward criminals—if they were that—is still a Christian virtue."[11]

One World, as well as the very particular language about "Christian virtue" used by Muench about clemency, exemplified the tie between the political language and religious language used by prominent postwar figures, language that juxtaposed "mercy" or "love"—usually associated with Christianity—and "vengeance," commonly associated with Jews and Judaism.[12] More than a decade after the pastoral letter's appearance in occupied Germany, some German Catholics still recalled the principles of "love" and "mercy" versus "vengeance" featured in *One World.* In one letter, former Nazi party member and prison guard Josef Hering of Amberg wrote Muench to complain about his treatment under American internment. He cited a passage from *One World* to repudiate the behavior of the Americans: "Let us not become party to the crimes of Hitler, in that we now do what we so harshly judged and fought the Nazis for doing . . . no double-standard should be applied to the law of justice," Hering quoted.[13]

Focus on "love" and "mercy" versus "vengeance" was a theme appearing in the arguments made by Pope Pius XII, Bishop Muench, and German bishops, clerics, and lay Catholics pressing for amnesty for convicted war criminals in the late 1940s and early 1950s. In January 1951, Bishop Joseph Freundorfer of Augsburg (Bavaria) sent an urgent telegram to American High Commissioner John J. McCloy. "As bishop of the diocese in which Landsberg prison lies, I submit the following plea to the American high commissioner and American authorities. I ask that you re-examine the death sentences for Landsberg criminals, now so prominently discussed again. It would be a merciful, Christian, and humane deed to fully re-examine these death sentences. The prisoners already atone by experiencing the agony of uncertainty. Such an act of mercy would prove American willingness to act on humanitarian grounds, an idea recently under attack."[14] Freundorfer's statement captured the essence of the Catholic clemency argument: association of "the spirit of reconciliation," of "mercy," of "humanitarianism," and of forgiveness, with Christianity. The dark underside of Catholic appeals for "love" and "mercy" was a lingering anti-Semitism and easy references to stereotypes painting Jews as vengeful, excessively influential, or motivated by greed or material gain.

Further, letters and recollected conversations recorded by Muench in his diary describe Jewish Germans who escaped Nazi Germany and became American citizens as "alien" or "recent" Americans, unfamiliar with "American" standards of fairness and incapable of true loyalty to the United States, "in control" of American policy-making in Germany, and as "avengers" who wished to harm Germans. Muench himself referred repeatedly to "Thirty-Niners, those who fled Hitler's Germany around 1933 and 1934, took out citizen papers around 1939, and then reappeared in an American uniform in Germany to wreak their vengeance in every way possible on the defeated foe."[15]

In January and February 1948, a number of accused German war criminals tried in the U.S. *versus* Valentin Bersin ("Malmedy") Army Trial claimed they suffered vicious beatings and inhuman deprivations at the hands of their American captors during pretrial interrogations. Cardinal Josef Frings of Cologne was the conduit by which the 1948

Malmedy affidavits claiming abuse reached American military governor General Lucius Clay. In mid-November 1948, Frings sent a petition to Clay including what he called "new" documents (the Malmedy affidavits) indicating that "a number of innocent men [were] being executed at Landsberg."[16]

Frings sent Muench a copy of the materials as well.[17] Muench replied that he himself had been in touch with Malmedy defense counsel Willis Everett earlier that summer.[18] Contacted by a Father Franz Lövenstein of Erlangen in September 1948 and asked to give Lövenstein several addresses, including Everett's, one of Muench's secretaries replied, "with regard to the names and addresses requested, His Excellency wishes to submit the following, with the understanding, of course, that you are not to use his name in connection with any letters or briefs that will be sent to those gentlemen. The enclosed newspaper clipping regarding . . . appeals will interest you . . . The names and addresses referred to above are on a separate slip of paper enclosed herewith.[19] Enclosed was the promised slip of paper, in long-hand and in Muench's handwriting, recording the name of "Colonel Everett."[20] Two months later, Muench commented to Frings, "one should really be ashamed of the way [interrogations] played out. The one satisfaction in this whole affair is the fact that true Americans did not conduct the pretrial interrogations, as is evidenced by their names. One can assume they learned such methods in the concentration camps before immigrating to the United States."[21] To Everett, he wrote that he "hung his head in shame" upon reading about the original trial, but "raised it again with pride when [Muench] saw what [Everett] did to rehabilitate our good name."[22]

Aloisius Muench disliked what he perceived as the "vengeful" influence of Jews in general and of German émigré Jews in particular on American juridical procedure in Germany. An example of Muench's dislike for Jews in general was his chance meeting with Jewish Pole Marimpolski,[23] described by Muench as a "Warsaw Jew, about thirty-eight years old, well educated, and in Germany to obtain extradition papers for Germans who committed atrocities while in Poland."[24] In a letter to his sister Terry, Muench referred specifically to Marimpolski's Jewishness and work for the Polish War Crimes Commission, and also to Marimpolski's "connections to the Communist Warsaw government"—in Muench's mind, another mark against him. In early January 1946, the two men, coincidentally seated together on a train from Berlin to Frankfurt, had a lengthy conversation about war crimes. During the course of the conversation, Muench acknowledged "stories of German concentration camps, particularly Maidanek [Majdanek] and Auschwitz, were horrible and quite well-known to American newspaper readers." But Muench then told a "taken aback" Marimpolski that "all criminals who are guilty of atrocities, including those in Russia, Poland, and Czechoslovakia, should be punished."[25]

To Muench, crimes committed by Russians, Poles, and Czechs against Germans did not differ from those committed against Jews in death camps like Auschwitz and Majdanek. "These people have distorted notions of justice," he wrote his sister. He conflated "Jewishness" with communism and "vengefulness" and recognized but downplayed the question of German atrocities in extermination camps. Muench found it easy to slide into arguments about "vengeful" Jews allegedly controlling the American prosecution. This occurred in a number of specific cases, for instance that of Ernst Baron von Weizsäcker. Weizsäcker served as head of the political section in the Nazi Foreign Ministry, state secretary in the Foreign Ministry, and German ambassador to the Holy See. He was the main defendant in the so-called Wilhelmstrasse trial (Case Eleven), named for the accused who had served in the German Foreign Office. On 11 April 1949, U.S. Military Court V sentenced Weizsäcker to seven years in prison, reduced to five years on 2 December 1949.[26] U.S. High Commissioner John J. McCloy pardoned him in October 1950.[27]

Muench knew Weizsäcker's defense attorney, American jurist Warren Magee, and considered him a friend.[28] Muench had such high regard for Magee that he petitioned Vatican Undersecretary of State Monsignor Giovanni Battista Montini (who would become Pope Paul VI) to arrange a meeting between the jurist and Pope Pius XII.[29] In 1948, Muench wrote of his private conversation with Magee and German jurist Helmuth Becker. The three men discussed the Nuremberg successor trials grimly. Muench made the following notes in his diary about their conversation: "trials without precedent—contrary to all American traditions. Eighty Jews—émigrés—[work for] the prosecution staff . . . American name [is] blackened in history."[30] Muench and Magee discussed this on at least two other occasions. Magee visited Muench in late April 1948 and reported what Muench called "depressing news about the Nuremberg trials, [in which] there was a disregard for American standards of jurisprudence."[31] Later that June, a disgruntled Magee apparently told Muench that "Thirty-Niners" ran the Wilhelmstrasse trial.[32]

Years later, Muench's negativity toward Jews' alleged influence in the United States remained strong. Take, for example, his comment about the Society for the Prevention of World War III,[33] a U.S.-based nonprofit group that identified Germany as a threat to world peace, advocated a "hard peace" for Germany in 1944–45, and acted as a "watchdog" group postwar. In late 1955, Muench described the society as a "hate group financed by a wealthy Jew named Lipschnetz."[34] Muench received letters that mirrored and even went beyond his own prejudices. One, written by German Catholic Otto Kling of Munich in 1947, expressed the belief that "the American generals [Lucius] Clay and [Walter] Muller" were "Jews." Kling implied that former U.S. president Franklin D. Roosevelt was murdered at Jewish hands, writing to Cardinal Michael Faulhaber of Munich, "a few weeks before the war's end, the merciful President Roosevelt allegedly died of a 'stroke,'" but the cardinal should recall "the Talmud saying 'the Gentile is like the sacrificial animal—you must murder the most noble among him.'"[35] Former president Herbert Hoover purportedly told Muench, "no émigrés who were not citizens for at least twenty years should be permitted to shape and execute policies in Germany."[36]

Muench, as well as some American prelates, clerics, lay Catholics, and U.S. occupation personnel, believed Jews in general and Jewish displaced persons specifically to be greedy, willfully destructive, sexual predators, thieves, and anarchists involved in leftist activities. In a 1950 letter to Monsignor Paul Tanner, Muench acknowledged "some growth of Anti-Semitism." "But as elsewhere," wrote Muench, it was "a reaction to Semitism—the requisitioning of hundreds of homes for Jewish displaced persons, the damage done to the property during the occupancy, the exorbitant claims that are now being made under the restitution law, black marketeering, the defense of smutty publications by Jewish printers and publishers etc."[37]

In a letter to Muench, Anton Rupert Sittl of Munich went even further; "KZ (*Konzentrationslager*) Jews possessed coupons that allowed them to buy new Mercedes Benz and Opel cars straight off the factory lot, for a mere 4,000 to 6,000 deutschmarks. [They] turned around and sold the cars for 100,000 deutschmarks."[38] Monsignor Walter Fasnacht of Chicago complained about the allegedly "communistic and pro-Semitic" press in Chicago.[39] According to the cardinal's recollections in his diary, Army major and Catholic John McHugh believed that "Jews in the army sought positions of influence," such as in the Information Control or Education divisions, "where they could control thought."[40]

When appointed nuncio, Muench remarked on the "fact that [he was] in the same post of duty in which [Eugene Pacelli, now Pius XII] distinguished himself with great honor."[41] Some German Catholics also connected their careers. Johannes B. Dietl of Regensburg remarked that Muench was "the only Vatican representative to enjoy popularity equal to that of former Nuncio Pacelli."[42] Curate Alfons Haslberger of Bad Adelholzen agreed: "like so many Germans, we are overjoyed that Germany has once again received a nuncio like Pacelli, who has a command of the German language and knows of Germany's situation, which is even more difficult than it was after the First World War."[43]

Many indicators point to a genuine camaraderie between Muench and Pius XII. During their second audience in Rome on 12 July 1946, they conversed in German, a habit that became a hallmark of all their future audiences.[44] In 1953, after the dedication of the North American College in Rome, Pius XII singled out Muench among all the attendees. Pius XII "walked along nodding to the various cardinals and bishops and stopped suddenly as he spied Archbishop Muench," wrote Father Gerald Weber, also in attendance. According to Father Weber, Pius said to Muench, "I am so happy you are present in Rome for the dedication. Don't forget to see me before you leave." It was "the only stop the pope made and the only person he talked to."[45] When Pope Pius XII died in October 1958, Muench mourned him, telling friends Helen and Jack Crowley that the pope "treated him with the affection and love of a father to his son."[46]

Between 1946 and 1958, Muench related information about events in Germany to the pope in written reports. In 1950, Muench told his mother, Theresa Kraus Muench, that Pius XII admitted to reading each of Muench's reports on Germany personally.[47] This was still the case in 1953, despite the pope's deteriorating health.[48] Muench's written reports to the Holy See focused on issues of immediate concern to the Church or German Catholics: material needs, Catholic education/school reform, upholding the Concordat as well as a Vatican diplomatic presence in all of Germany, structural rebuilding of physically destroyed Catholic communities, or assimilating and meeting the needs of large Catholic populations expelled to the western zones of occupied Germany under the Potsdam accords. They also spoke about the pope's concern regarding the spread of communism. In one example among several, after a 1954 audience, Muench noted Pius XII's "worries and anxieties about the onward march of Communism . . . in the Western world."[49]

Commenting to Archbishop Samuel Stritch of Chicago about his 1948 visit with the pontiff, Muench wrote that Pius XII was "intensely interested in the Church in Germany, manifesting an amazing grasp of the whole situation."[50] Muench's perspective on Pius XII's "grasp of the German situation" changed subtly a year later, and, privately at least, Muench was willing to say so. After their annual audience in the fall of 1949, Muench commented in his diary, "the Holy Father is more interested in the affairs of the Church in Germany than in any other part of the Church." But the pope "looked back to his experiences in Germany" and expected these experiences to serve as precedents for contemporary decisions, added Muench. Muench thought the pope did not seem to "fully grasp" the implications of the loss of German sovereignty, occupation, lack of independent political status in the various Länder (states), and the increasing secularization of German culture.[51]

Regarding the issues of anti-Semitism, Nazi crimes, and the Church's wartime relationship to the Nazi government or to persecuted European Jewry, little written correspondence between Pope Pius XII and Muench exists. They conducted a great deal of their business and shared their opinions, concerns, and even levity within the confines of private oral audiences in Rome. One exception was Muench's denial in the face of evidence that Pope Pius XII ignored the genocidal killing of Orthodox Serbs in Croatia. The background was this: philosopher and educator Friedrich Wilhelm Foerster,[52] whose work Muench was acquainted with, planned a new edition of his book *Authority and Freedom* with the Vita Nova publishing house in Lucerne, Switzerland.[53] In the new edition, Foerster planned to detail negotiations between the Holy See and the Croat fascist leader Ante Pavelic.

Pavelic acted as head of the new state of Croatia in the spring of 1941, after the Nazi dismemberment of Yugoslavia. A Catholic, Pavelic intended to make Croatia a Catholic state. To achieve this, he planned to murder half of the Serbian Orthodox population and to force the remaining half to become Catholic or emigrate. Archbishop Alojzije Stepinac, chosen by the Holy See to head the national Catholic Church in Croatia, arranged an audience between Pope Pius XII and Pavelic in May 1941. The Vatican stopped short of formal recognition of Croatia, instead sending Croatia an apostolic visitor who acted, in reality, as a nuncio.[54] Pavelic was responsible for the murder of some 600,000 Orthodox Serbs. Foerster wrote pointedly, "now one sees why Pope Pius XII was forced to stand back from any clear condemnation of Nazi crimes, both during and after the war."[55]

Muench heard of Foerster's study and its contents via their mutual acquaintance F. W. Schuchard. "A German priest who knows Professor Foerster well told me it is probably senility that caused him to fall into such a trap," Muench wrote to Schuchard. "You are correct: [Foerster] is often influenced by so-called false friends, as evidenced by the fact that he would believe this 'white book' of Yugoslavia to be genuine. He should certainly know that the Communists are not shy about telling lies when it suits their purposes. In my audience with the Holy Father, which lasted over an hour, not one word about politics was uttered, though I hear plenty of political talk here in Germany. I really can't understand why some let themselves be beguiled by the slogan 'Vatican Politics,'" Muench concluded.[56]

In addition to a genuine camaraderie with Pope Pius XII, Muench enjoyed close relationships with a number of German Catholic bishops. He wrote to Monsignor Sebastian Bernard of Milwaukee that he felt as "much at home" with the German hierarchy as he did with the bishops of the United States.[57] To Monsignor Edward Kersting of Burlington, Wisconsin, Muench wrote, "I have won the good will of the German bishops, priests, and people. It is making my work easy."[58] Such feelings were not a figment of Muench's imagination. During a February 1947 audience with Pope Pius XII, the pope confirmed that several German bishops wrote to Rome in praise of Muench.[59] Former head of the German Center Party and close confidant to the pope Monsignor Ludwig Kaas told Muench that the bishops of Germany noted their "good fortune to have an apostolic visitor [in Muench] who knew German history and traditions and showed sympathetic understanding for grave German needs and problems."[60] When the archbishop of Berlin, Konrad von Preysing, visited Muench's mother during his 1947 tour in the United States, he delivered a personal message from her son.[61] When Muench received the title of apostolic regent in 1949, auxiliary bishop of Munich Johannes Neuhäusler told him, "Catholic Germany rejoiced at the Holy See's expression of confidence in their best friend."[62]

It was Cardinal Josef Frings of Cologne who told Muench that he [Muench] would be named as apostolic nuncio in 1951.[63] Frings considered Muench "a fellow-brother in the German episcopate," a feeling Muench shared.[64] In 1947, indignant that military government censors opened a letter from the cardinal, Muench called Frings "an outspoken opponent of Hitler" who did not deserve to have his letters censored. Muench castigated Religious Affairs Division officials, telling them that "the pope rewarded [Frings] with the cardinalate [in 1945] for his opposition to Hitlerism. [Frings's] brother died a victim of Hitlerism. Yet the cardinal is subject to such humiliating treatment by men who do not know even recent historical events, or are so utterly indifferent to the high policies of their own government."[65]

Muench was particularly close to Cardinal Michael Faulhaber of Munich. When the cardinal died, he bequeathed to Muench an amethyst ring decorated with eighteen diamonds. The cardinal's sister told Muench that it was Faulhaber's favorite ring, and that he considered "Muench and the Holy Father" his "best friends."[66] "I shall never forget this favor of friendship—we have come close to each other," Muench said of Faulhaber.[67] Perhaps the best hallmark of Muench's acceptance by the German hierarchy was Auxiliary Bishop Walter Kampe of Limburg's proposal that a foundation be established on the occasion of Muench's retirement as nuncio in December 1959. The foundation's purpose would be "to keep the name of Aloisius Cardinal Muench alive in our grateful memory."[68]

Exchanges between Muench and his contemporaries reflected on-going dialogue about World War II and National Socialism in the late 1940s and 1950s.[69] When Muench first arrived in Germany in 1946, both victors and vanquished wrestled with the phenomenon of National Socialism and all that it had wrought. They tried to explain how it happened, how it should be understood, how to assess blame for it, how to regulate its punishment, and how to learn from it, a process described by scholars as *Vergangenheitsbewältigung*, literally, "mastering the past." One strand in early discussions of *Vergangenheitsbewältigung* was the notion of "collective" guilt.

Contemporaries understood "collective" guilt to mean that "all" Germans bore culpability or guilt for Nazism and its crimes. Hence, "collective" guilt implied wrongdoing on the part of "all" Germans. The notion of collective "responsibility," on the other hand, implied moral accountability: individual Germans who may not have supported the Nazi regime (and hence did not bear "guilt") still had the obligation to help Nazism's victims. The concept of German "collective" responsibility, then, meant that Germany as a nation bore the obligation to help Nazi victims after the war, regardless of variations in degree of "guilt" within the German population itself. Hannah Arendt described collective responsibility as follows: "every government assumes political responsibility for the deeds and misdeeds of its predecessors and every nation for the deeds and misdeeds of the past."[70]

The onset of the Cold War dramatically revised America's relationship to its former German foe. The Cold War "transformed old enemies into Allies and old Allies into sworn enemies," writes Omer Bartov.[71] The perceived need of Americans, Germans, and the West as a whole to unite against Communism meant that reconstruction in Germany (and elsewhere in the West) became tied to representing World War II as a site of a shared and ultimately unifying "victimhood."[72] The postwar Christian Democratic Union (CDU) emerged in this particular international and domestic context. The immensely popular Christian Democratic politician Konrad Adenauer sensed that his political success rested on under-emphasizing German guilt and focusing instead on economic recovery and political democratization.[73] Prior to 1949, Adenauer avoided the Jewish issue, sensing that emphasis on it would alienate a bloc of voters essential to a CDU electoral majority.[74] But after becoming West German chancellor in 1949, Adenauer shifted his position and spoke publicly about Nazi persecution of European Jewry.

Adenauer's political efforts were a part of *Vergangenheitspolitik,* the political process that from approximately 1949 to 1953 dealt with the Nazi past. Recognized and widely accepted by the West German public, it lifted the pre-1949 social, professional, and political restrictions and punishments the Western Allies had placed upon millions of former Nazi party members, reintegrating them into the status quo. Simultaneously, the new state defined itself in opposition to the ideology of National Socialism.[75] On 27 September 1951, Adenauer told *Bundestag* members,

> in an overwhelming majority, the German people abhorred the crimes committed against the Jews and did not participate in them. During the period of National Socialism there were many Germans,

acting on the basis of religious belief, the call of conscience, and shame at the disgrace of Germany's name, who were willing to assist their Jewish fellow citizens. In the name of the German people, however, unspeakable crimes were committed which require moral and material restitution. . . . The government of the Federal Republic will support the rapid conclusion of a law regarding restitution and its just implementation. A portion of identifiable Jewish property is to be returned. Further restitution will follow."[76]

Adenauer exonerated "most" Germans while still acknowledging the enormity of Nazi crimes against Jews and a need for the West German state to accept responsibility for them, implying a broader policy that rejected collective guilt but accepted collective responsibility.[77]

In United States circles, the issue of "collective" guilt first came to the fore in 1943, when Secretary of the Treasury Henry Morgenthau discovered that the European Advisory Commission (EAC) and Supreme Headquarters Allied Expeditionary Forces (SHAEF) in London planned for the economic rehabilitation of Germany after her defeat. Perceiving such a policy as politically irresponsible, Secretary Morgenthau proposed his "Program to Prevent Germany from Starting a World War III," coined the Morgenthau Plan, which stipulated that Germany should become a non-industrial, agrarian "pastureland." Over the course of the final war years and early postwar years, the Morgenthau Plan—which never became policy—was understood by many as anti-German, "vengeful," and as carrying a tacit assumption of German "collective" guilt.[78]

Through the end of the war and until the beginning of the International Military Tribunal (IMT) held in Nuremberg in October 1945, the U.S. Army understood itself as operating according to the notion of "collective" guilt and the leitmotiv that "there are no good Germans." The theme of "punishment" characterized the tenor and direction of American military government's information to the German people.[79] Internal memoranda indicate that the IMT (which lasted until October 1946) significantly reshaped the American army's position toward collective guilt.[80] By the fall of 1945, occupation procedures became informed by the principle of punishing guilty individuals, not by notions of "collective" punishment or guilt.

In a January 1946 memorandum for army units stationed in occupied Germany, General Robert A. McClure directly quoted the American chief prosecutor at Nuremberg, Supreme Court justice Robert H. Jackson, to argue that the suspension of civil liberties and the use of terror meant the Nazis had silenced all democratic opposition. Creating guilt feelings among Germans was not constructive, according to McClure's memo. The army should approach Germans not on the basis of "guilt" and "punishment," but rather on the basis of "cause" and "consequence." If Germans could be made to think of their "individual (rather than collective) records," the "indifference, hostility and moral apathy" that stood in the way of "rebuilding a democratic Germany" might lessen. But, on the other hand, McClure cautioned against "absolving . . . the whole German people . . . of all blame for what happened."[81]

The U.S. army did not view all Germans as "guilty of crimes," but it did wish to instill in them a sense of responsibility for Nazism. "Most Germans must bear a share of the responsibility for the Nazi regime and the war. Otherwise, the destruction of political parties and labor organizations would not have been accomplished so swiftly and easily, the ranks of the Nazi party would not have swelled so rapidly, the deprivation of civil liberties would not have been accepted so meekly," stated McClure's memo.[82] In summary, notions of individual, political, and moral responsibility informed Allied decision-making.[83] But discussions about "collective" guilt still continued, because as long as Germans could argue that Allied victors accused the German population of "collective" guilt, Germans could (and did) feel unjustly treated, and, conveniently, cast aside questions of personal guilt. In reality, the Allies never handed down an official document postulating "collective" guilt.[84]

Like the U.S. Army in 1944–45, the German Protestant (Evangelical) Churches adopted the stance of accepting "collective" guilt as an initial strategy. At the Evangelical Church Provisional Council meeting in Stuttgart (18–19 October 1945), Protestant leaders issued a statement to the World Council of Churches later termed the "Stuttgart Declaration of Guilt." It read in part, "we, with our people, know ourselves to be not only in a community of suffering but also a solidarity of guilt. With great anguish we state: Through us inestimable suffering was inflicted on many peoples and lands . . . We now declare in the name of the whole church: indeed we . . . fought for long years in the name of Jesus Christ against the spirit that found horrible expression in National Social[ism] . . . but we charge ourselves for not having borne testimony with greater courage."[85] In this statement, Protestant leaders acknowl-edged "solidarity" of guilt, but allowed individual perpetrators the comfort of anonymity, their singular deeds subsumed within the "com-munity" of the German people.[86]

Catholic bishops in Germany took the opposite stance. They de-nied collective German participation in Nazism while emphasizing the deeds of a few especially conspicuous offenders. The first postwar pas-toral letter of the Bavarian bishops' conference, issued on 28 June 1945 from the location of Eichstätt, claimed, "with few exceptions, the Ger-man people had no knowledge of the atrocities committed against in-nocent persons . . . in the concentration camps. Therefore it was all the more deeply shocking when the news became public."[87] By August 1945, when the German bishops collectively issued a pastoral letter from their annual bishops' conference in Fulda, the text expressed a bit more awareness about complicity. The pertinent paragraph read, "we profoundly deplore the fact that many Germans, even in our own ranks, allowed themselves to be deceived by the false teachings of National Socialism, [and] remained indifferent to the crimes against hu-man freedom and dignity; many by their attitude lent support to the crimes, many became criminals themselves. A heavy responsibility falls upon those who, because of their influence, could have prevented such crimes and did not do so but made these crimes possible and in this way associated themselves with the criminals."[88]

But the remainder of the five-page Fulda pastoral letter praised Catholics at large. It thanked the Catholic clergy and dioceses for the "loyalty" shown to their church during "hard times" via their circula-tion of "pastoral words from [the German bishops] that countered the errors and crimes of Nazism." The pastoral letter credited the German bishops with repelling the state's encroachment into religious life and raising their voices against race hatred (*Rassendunkel und Völkerhass*)." Catholics at large were unblemished: "we are happy to say that in such great numbers you kept free from the idolatry of brutal power. We are happy that so many believers never bowed before Baal. We are happy that the godless and inhumane teachings were rejected across the great range of Catholic brethren," wrote the bishops.[89]

The German bishops may well have taken their cue from one of their greatest champions, Pope Pius XII. On 2 June 1945, he gave a radio address from Rome rejecting "collective" guilt. In his address entitled "The Church and National Socialism," he described Nazi oppression of

Catholics, praised the "millions of Catholics who . . . never ceased to raise their voices" against Nazism, and defended the Concordat.[90] The Church could not be held accountable for the few individual Catholics who cooperated with the Nazis, argued Pius XII, adding that the encyclical *Mit brennender Sorge* demonstrated the Church's understanding of the dangers of National Socialism. Aside from repudiating so-called collective guilt in his June radio address, Pope Pius XII sent more than 900 railroad cars of foodstuffs, clothing, and medicine to Germany during the postwar years.[91]

Muench fully and unequivocally agreed with Pope Pius XII's position, and he would cite it publicly in the years to come. He repeatedly rejected both collective guilt and collective responsibility throughout his years in Germany, with absolutely no change in his position. In his first address as dean of diplomatic corps and papal nuncio to West Germany, on 4 April 1951, Muench said in a public statement to the president of the Federal Republic, Theodor Heuss, "was it not my high sovereign, His Holiness Pope Pius XII, who openly espoused the cause of the German people in a broadcast to the world on 2 June 1945? [This] only a few weeks after the capitulation of the German Reich, in the midst of the rising flood of hate and defamation of the German name? By this action he was the first . . . to draw . . . a clear line of distinction between your people and that political system which in the years from 1933 to 1945 persecuted . . . first and foremost, what was best in the nature of the German people themselves . . . the Catholic Church . . . every genuine expression of Christianity . . . and the freedom and dignity of other nations."[92]

Catholics, Bishop Muench argued, were either victimized by Nazism or resisted it, citing the "war against Nazism" fought by the German Catholic clergy and the papal support it received in the form of Pius XI's *Mit brennender Sorge.* Subsequently, argued Muench, Pius XII issued "many declarations . . . on the errors of Nazism." German bishops provided "good leadership" in this regard, and defections to Nazism among the Catholic clergy were few, claimed Muench.[93] He viewed collective guilt as a "poison" in German political life that was largely the product of misinformation.[94] In a report to Cardinal Samuel Stritch of Chicago, Muench wrote,

> In view of the record of Catholic resistance to Nazism, Catholic Church authorities have not felt they ought to make a public pronouncement on collective guilt as some of the Protestant Church

leaders have done. It would be hypocrisy to do so. Furthermore, the good people who were in opposition to Nazism from the very beginning would resent it, as did many Protestants when some of their clergy made an avowal of collective guilt. Generally speaking, they say that they had no choice under Gestapo methods [or] they had no knowledge of atrocities committed in concentration camps. Finally, powerful governments cooperated with the Nazis politically, financially, and commercially until the very outbreak of the war. In consequence, they declare that they are not any more guilty than these governments and . . . peoples.[95]

In actuality, the record shows Catholics defending their Church only within the structures defined under the 1933 Concordat. There were few documented exceptions outside of Bishop August Clemens von Galen's public protest against Nazi euthanasia practices.[96] The popular argument adopted by Muench and many others that Catholicism acted as a bulwark against Nazism does not apply to the persecution of European Jewry, for neither the Holy See nor the body of German Catholic bishops publicly opposed anti-Semitism or publicly condemned Hitler's war against the Jews.[97]

To date, very few collections of the papers of contemporary German, American, or Vatican Catholic dignitaries are fully accessible to historians. The Muench papers constitute an unusual exception. According to his biographer, Father Colman Barry, Muench took his papers with him to Rome when he retired from the German nunciature in December 1959. After his death in 1962, "Muench's papers, covering the years 1946 to 1962, were returned from Rome to his diocesan archives. Their express weight was 2,500 pounds," writes Barry.[98] In addition, Muench, who kept an archive at the Bad Godesberg nunciature, transferred at least some materials directly to Fargo prior to his assignment in Rome.[99]

As early as June 1956, Muench assigned his secretary, Father Gerald Weber, the task of sending files back to Fargo. The bulk of them consisted of then-inactive personal correspondence, including his German correspondence. Muench directed that his German correspondence, already numbering 15,000 letters by 1956, be organized by four German nuns: Sisters Ilga Braun, Fridburga Gumbert, Genovefa Schwert, and Cäcelia Rieger of Saint Lioba convent in Freiburg/Breisgau.[100] Muench continued to send records directly to Fargo until his departure from Germany in December 1959. In February 1960, now in Rome as a member of the College of Cardinals, Muench wrote a letter of thanks to the president of Allen Silk Mills in New York, coincidentally named Charlie Muench,[101] for "getting boxes with personal belongings, diplomatic archives . . . into the United States . . . without custom difficulties." Muench added that other boxes were "on the way." "For the greatest part they are historical archives . . . a record of my activity in Germany . . . of great value and inestimable worth to this humble third bishop of Fargo."[102]

After Muench's death on 15 February 1962, the first person to see his papers in Fargo was Sister Ilga Braun, secretary to the Bonn nunciature since 1951. Muench's successor in Fargo, Bishop Leo Dworschak, invited Sister Braun to his diocese that February. She took a one-year leave of absence from Bad Godesberg, where she was in the service of its new nuncio, Archbishop Corrado Bafile, and stayed in Fargo until 1963 to organize the Muench papers.[103]

Muench's reason for ensuring that his papers could be openly accessed in Fargo soon became apparent. In 1961, while a cardinal in the Roman curia, Muench commissioned Father Colman Barry to write his biography.[104] Father Barry became acquainted with Muench in 1953. Monsignor John Tracy Ellis, managing editor of the *Catholic Historical Review*,[105] asked Muench to review Barry's first book, an adaptation of the young priest's dissertation (written under his advisor, Monsignor Ellis), entitled *The Catholic Church and German Americans*.[106] Muench expressed reservations given his lack of formal historical training.[107] Nonetheless, he agreed to the task, loved the book, and produced a glowing review of it.[108] Barry thanked Muench for his positive review and Muench's suggestion that Barry seek a publisher willing to translate the book into German.[109]

Muench tracked Barry's later projects, telling a colleague in 1957 that Barry's most recent work, a history of Saint John's Abbey in Collegeville, was "fascinating," and the product of a "well-trained historian."[110] Surely, it was this admiration that led Muench to request that Barry write his biography.[111] At Muench's request, Barry conversed with the cardinal in Fargo during the summer of 1961 and began interviewing Muench's family, friends, colleagues, and acquaintances in Milwaukee, Fargo, Germany, and Rome.[112] Eight years later, in 1969, Barry produced *American Nuncio; Cardinal Aloisius Muensch,* which is still the only existing biography of Muench.[113]

In September 1972, Bishop Justin A. Driscoll of Fargo presented the Cardinal Muench papers to the archives of the Catholic University of America (CUA) in Washington, D.C.[114] Professor John Zeender, then chairman of the CUA department of history, assigned graduate student James Oswald the task of indexing the papers.[115] Oswald finished the finding guide in 1976. Written nearly twenty-five years ago, this document is still the operating guide for the papers.

Barry's recapitulation of Muench's years in Germany charts three main areas. The first is Muench's major success as head of the Vatican mission for Catholic displaced persons and prisoners of war (1947–49). Muench brokered donations, primarily from the Vatican and American Catholics, amounting to nearly five million dollars. The second is Muench's involvement, at the behest of Pius XII, in maintaining the validity of the 1933 Concordat signed by Pope Pius XI and Adolf Hitler, then chancellor of Nazi Germany. A third issue was maintaining the autonomy of Catholic schools. Church jurisdiction over Catholic schools was agreed upon in the 1933 Concordat, and is a specific example of why the standing Concordat remained important to both the German Catholic Church and the Vatican.[116] Significantly, Barry does not treat exchanges between Muench, American Catholics and occupiers, Vatican officials, and Germans on guilt and responsibility for the Holocaust in any lengthy or systematic way.[117] My book addresses this vital gap.

Reviews of Barry's book appeared in two cross-denominational publications, the *Journal of Ecumenical Studies* and *Church History.* In *Church History,* David O'Brien of Holy Cross College in Worcester, Massachusetts, offered little criticism of Barry's study. He noted only that Muench "shared the myopia of the Cold War" and therefore supported the policies promoted by Konrad Adenauer, Pope Pius XII, and American occupiers, to the exclusion of "other options" for German, American, and universal Catholicism.[118] Several Catholic journals and newspapers also reviewed Barry's book, including the *Catholic Historical Review,* the *Catholic Messenger,* the *American Benedictine Review,* and *Our Sunday Visitor.* All were uncritical.[119]

Only the *Journal of Ecumenical Studies* published critical commentary. Professor Franklin H. Littell of Temple University, while praising certain aspects of Barry's study, pointed out that it lacked objectivity. Littell wrote, "if [Muench] displayed the strengths of the German-American Catholic tradition, Cardinal Muench also shared its weaknesses."

Barry missed "the meaning of the Holocaust in Christian as well as Jewish history," noted Littell—at that time, a lone voice.[120]

This book is the first since Barry's biography to assess Muench's career during his years in Germany. As liaison representative between the German Catholic Church and U.S. occupation forces in Germany, Pope Pius XII's apostolic visitor to Germany, relief officer in Kronberg, regent, and finally nuncio to Germany, Muench was a key participant in internal German Catholic discussion and reflection about Jews, anti-Semitism, and the Holocaust.

Muench's own anti-guilt stance and anti-Jewish prejudices mirrored those of many German and American Catholics around him. But by publicly announcing his philo-German and anti-guilt worldview (and privately agreeing with and reinforcing anti-Jewish stereotypes), he legitimized, gave added weight to, and in some cases created this particular interpretation of the German Catholic relationship to Nazism and the Holocaust. His standing and influence in U.S., German, and Vatican hierarchies gave sanction to the idea that German Catholics needed no examination of conscience. In this way, he was emblematic of the Catholic Church's failure during this period to confront its own complicity in Nazism's anti-Jewish ideology.

1

The Life and Career of
Aloisius Muench

n 1948, Father John LaFarge approached Bishop Muench, Vatican relief officer in Kronberg and Catholic liaison representative to the U.S. occupation forces in Germany, to ask for his help in the case of Alfred Haas. A German Jew forced to immigrate to New York in November 1938, Haas had lost his medical practice and two homes under so-called "Aryanization" of German Jewish property.

American Jesuit John LaFarge was an important figure among American Catholic leaders for several reasons. First, he was co-author of the encyclical *Humani Generis Unitas,* commissioned by Pope Pius XI in August 1938. The encyclical condemned racism and racial anti-Semitism specifically, but was never published.[1] LaFarge was also the most influential Catholic spokesman on black-white race relations in the United States. He was on the editorial staff of the weekly Catholic journal *America* from 1926 until his death in 1963, and was its editor-in-chief between 1944 and 1948.[2] From 1933 onward, *America* was one of the few American Catholic journals to provide continuous critical coverage of Nazi anti-Semitism and the Holocaust, publishing fifty-six articles and forty editorials on the subject.[3]

At LaFarge's urging, Haas wrote to Muench for advice on the restitution process.[4] Muench, feigning ignorance, replied to Haas, "gladly
I would be of service to you but property matters are entirely outside my
competence. In affairs such as you propose I am lost like a babe in the
woods. Because of the very complicated system of military government,
it is not easy to find one's way around. Could you give me some ideas
on how I could help, or whom I ought to contact in the matter? My
competence lies purely in the religious field. In his eagerness to help,
Father LaFarge, I suppose, thought that I am competent in any matters
pertaining to the military government. I wish this were the case. I derive
much pleasure from being able to help people in need."[5] Muench also
wrote to LaFarge, including his reply to Haas. "I wish that I could help,
but really I do not know how. Such matters are absolutely strange to me,
and to begin to deal with them would be so time-robbing that I would
have to neglect the work assigned to me by the Holy Father and the
bishops of the United States. This, of course, I could not do."[6]

More likely, Muench was unwilling to help because Hass was
Jewish. On at least four separate occasions, Muench became directly and
deeply involved in property dispute cases, in each instance aiding
Catholic Germans in danger of losing "their" property to former Jewish
owners. In these instances, Muench contacted highly placed German and
American officials and, in the case of German Catholic Joseph
Weishäupl of Munich, even the American Catholic hierarchy.[7] Muench
discussed his efforts on behalf of Weishäupl in a 1955 diary entry: "I met
Dr. Lansing, Bavarian [*Bundestag*] representative in Bonn, [and] discussed a restitution case with him. [There is] little outlook of success—
pressure of Jewish immigrant groups who sold property under duress
during Hitler regime now demand restitution. Present owners are com-
pensated, but 1 [*Deutsch*]mark for 10 [*Reichsmarks* due to] currency
reform. Much dissatisfaction. Some bought property on a fair basis, gave
money to the emigrant—saved life and property. [This] creates anti-
Semitism.[8] Muench's sympathies (and antipathies) were clear enough:
Jewish "immigrant groups . . . demanded" restitution at the expense of
Germans, who, thought Muench, "bought property on a fair basis" and
in doing so "saved [the] life" of the former Jewish owner.

In a fourth instance involving close acquaintances, Muench was even
less careful to hide his distaste for Jews, nor did his German acquaintances
and some U.S. occupation personnel hide their own prejudices. For long
generations, the Methschnabel family of Kemnath, Bavaria, owned a

textile business, *Hans Methschnabel Textilwaren,* specializing in cloth, woolens, and ready-made clothing. Muench first met Hans Methschnabel in 1939 when he and his mother vacationed in Kemnath, which was his mother's childhood home.[9] In mid-August 1946, American occupation officials confiscated *Hans Methschnabel Textilwaren* and placed a Jewish displaced person from Warsaw named Hoglich in charge of its management. A second Polish-Jewish displaced person was assigned there as well. According to Anthony Schuller, Hans Methschnabel's son-in-law and heir, the citizens of Kemnath were outraged at the idea that the business was now under the management of two Jewish displaced persons. Eight days after confiscation of the firm, Schuller received judgment on his status from the local Spruchkammer (Appeals Board). The board assigned former National Socialists not accused of war crimes into five categories depending on their offenses. It classified Schuller, a Nazi party member since 1935, as a fellow traveler (*Mitläufer*), the least serious category other than exoneration. Though this judgment enabled Schuller to petition for the return of his business, he feared the Jewish trustee would not be easily dismissed. "That a former Polish journalist is not the suitable man for my extensive textile business, and that he could do me great damage, is plain to see," Schuller wrote in a letter to Muench. "When this type manages to cling to something, it is nearly impossible to extract him."[10]

Muench received Schuller's letter in early September 1946 and acted immediately. He wrote to a Father Henderson, Catholic chaplain at the 1st Infantry Division army headquarters in Regensburg. Muench asked Father Henderson to "get information about the past" of the two men now managing Schuller's business. "Some of these gents exploit the fact that they were in concentration camps for their own benefit, although some were there because of an unsavory past," Muench warned.[11] Henderson in turn contacted John F. Orzel, Catholic chaplain for the 6th Constabulary Regiment in Bayreuth. In October 1946, Father Orzel visited the Schullers in order to hear their accounting of events. He then tried to reach the American property control officer in charge of the Methschnabel's business, an Officer Kidder, stationed in the town of Weiden. After a number of unsuccessful attempts, Orzel theorized that Kidder avoided him due to a (suspected) Jewish background. "Every time I call Mr. Kidder's office, his secretary answers the phone and asks me who I am," Officer Orzel wrote to Muench. "Then she tells me to hold the line until she informs Mr. Kidder that I would like to talk to him. Each time she comes back with "I'm sorry, but he's not in." I sometimes wonder, Bishop, if this Mr. Kidder is Jewish.

If he is, then it is obvious why he is postponing the disposition of [*Hans Methschnabel Textilwaren*] as long as he possibly can. He no doubt intends to keep his two fellow countrymen employed just as long as it is in his power to do so. What do you think, Bishop?"[12]

Father John Orzel was not the only one to cast aspersions on property control officer Kidder. Anni Schuller insinuated that Kidder was a "good friend of the Jewish *Treuhander* Hoglich," though she had no reliable basis for this assumption.[13] On 26 October, Anthony and Anni Schuller visited Muench in Kronberg to ask his continued help in getting the business back. During their conversation, the three remarked that Kidder must be responsible for the delay. They called Kidder a plague, a "pestilence" (*Pestbeule*). The three blamed their sentiments on Kidder himself. "Such men are responsible for increasing anti-Semitism," wrote Muench in his diary.[14]

When Property Control in Kemnath and Weiden did not release the business, Muench wrote to J. M. Ferguson of Property Control-Munich.[15] He must have been effective, for by late November 1946 the Schullers reacquired their business.[16] By 1950, it was thriving again.[17] Her prosperity did not soften Anni Schuller's attitude toward Jews. In 1954, she wrote Muench to tell him of a department store in Regensburg "owned by Jews, just like everywhere." She noted that its construction cost over 1 million deutschmarks, a "trifle for Jews." "Jews take all they can from reparations," she complained. And in no case was the profiteer the expelled German Jew who had actually owned the business, she said, implying that German Jews were at least preferable to Polish ones. In the town of Weiden, she reported, a former Polish shoemaker now owned the local department store. And, to add insult to injury, the Federal Republic granted Jewish business owners tax advantages.[18] Her stereotypes about Jews as profiteering, dishonest, excessively rich, sly, and ingratiating remained strong nine years after the Allies defeated Nazism.

Muench's response in these property dispute cases raises a number of important questions. Where did his extreme philo-German sensitivities come from? And how had his reactions to those Jews he encountered in postwar Germany (reactions ranging from indifference to open hostility) been informed and formulated prior to his work in Germany?

Aloisius Muench was born in Milwaukee, Wisconsin, on 18 February 1889. "Allie" was the first of seven surviving children born to Joseph

Muench and Theresa Kraus. Joseph descended from generations of Catholic farmers in Sankt Katharina, a village in the Bohemian Forest on the Austrian side of the Bavarian-Austrian border. He immigrated to Milwaukee in 1882 at the age of eighteen. Theresa was born in Kemnath, a town northwest of Sankt Katharina in the Upper Palatinate region of Bavaria and also close to the Bavarian-Austrian (now Czech) border. Her father was a baker. Her family immigrated to Milwaukee in 1882, when Theresa was fourteen. Six years later, she married Joseph.[19]

In Milwaukee, Joseph worked as a master carpenter at the Northwestern Furniture Company. Theresa worked in the home, sewing, knitting, cooking, and raising the seven children. The family lived on the north side of Milwaukee, among other German Catholic immigrants. Religion was a strong force in their family life. Young Allie's parents spoke only German at home, though he and his siblings answered in English.[20] Muench began to train for the priesthood at the age of fourteen. In 1904, he entered Saint Francis Seminary, an institution with predominantly German traditions and cultural emphases. In June 1913, Allie was ordained Father Aloisius Muench and appointed to Saint Michael's parish, which was composed of German immigrants.[21] He remained in Milwaukee until 1917, when he became assistant chaplain of Saint Paul's University Chapel at the University of Wisconsin–Madison. While in Madison, Muench obtained a master's degree in economics from the University of Wisconsin (1918).[22]

In 1919, at the age of thirty, Muench entered the University of Fribourg in Switzerland, where he pursued a doctorate in social sciences, specializing in the theological disciplines of economics, social morality, and social ethics.[23] That summer, Muench visited Munich as a student representative of the Catholic Central Verein of America (CCVA). There he met the apostolic nuncio to Bavaria, Eugenio Pacelli, the future Pope Pius XII, for the first time.[24] Muench earned his doctorate in social sciences, magna cum laude, in July 1921. Due to his academic aptitude, the archbishop of Milwaukee, Sebastian Messmer, granted Muench permission to remain in Europe for additional study at the Universities of Louvain (Belgium), Cambridge, Oxford, the London School of Economics, the Collège de France, and the Sorbonne. At these universities, he studied the economic and social rehabilitation of post–World War I Europe.[25]

Dr. Muench returned to St. Francis Seminary in 1922 to begin his career as a professor. He taught fledgling seminarians social science,

Catholic catechetics and apologetics, and dogma classes. In 1929, at age forty, Muench set aside his teaching duties to become rector.[26] It was during this period that Muench met Samuel Stritch, Messmer's successor as archbishop of Milwaukee.[27] Muench reached the rank of monsignor in September 1934. On 10 August 1935, at Stritch's recommendation, Pope Pius XI named Muench bishop of the diocese of Fargo, North Dakota. Apostolic nuncio to the United States (Archbishop) Amleto Cicognani consecrated Muench in the *Jesu* Church of Milwaukee on 15 October.[28] The diocese of Fargo became one of several Sees with large German-American Catholic populations and bishops of German descent, the others being Saint Louis, Dubuque, and Saint Cloud.[29] Muench remained in Fargo until Pope Pius XII appointed him apostolic visitor to Germany in 1946.[30]

Aloisius Muench's worldview was profoundly shaped by the teachings and tendencies of the universal Roman Catholic Church during the late nineteenth to mid twentieth centuries in general and by the midwestern German-American Catholic tradition in particular. At the turn of the twentieth century, German Americans constituted a powerful force in the American Catholic Church. Strong German-American Catholic communities existed in the Chicago, Saint Paul, and Milwaukee vicinities.[31] German-American Catholicism in the United States was deeply nationalistic and conservative prior to 1900 but became more liberal and progressive in the twentieth century, as evidenced by its leadership in social reform.[32] Muench was involved in two prominent German-American Catholic social movements. One was the Rural Life Movement based in Collegeville, Minnesota.[33] The other was the Catholic Central Verein of America (CCVA).[34] Despite support for such social movements, twentieth-century German-American Catholicism remained, on the whole, conservative,[35] and its adherents remained leery of other religious traditions.[36]

In his monthly column "The Bishop Writes," which Muench published in the Fargo diocesan newspaper *Catholic Action News,*[37] Muench demonstrated himself to be firmly anti-socialist and anti-communist. His views fell in line with Catholic dogma laid out in Pope Pius IX's encyclical *Quanta cura* (1864), denouncing the First International launched that year in London by Karl Marx, and with Pope Leo XIII's anti-socialist encyclical *Rerum Novarum* (1891), which insisted on the right to private property.[38] Communism was "atheistic, destructive, oppressive," Muench warned Catholics.[39] "Communism has a group of determined policy-makers who know clearly what they want and why they want it."[40] In July 1942, after nearly three years of bloodshed in Europe at the hands of the Nazis, and after the United States had entered the war against Hitler as an ally of the Soviet Union, Muench still warned diocesans about the dark future that would come of "unconditionally victorious Russian armies." He bemoaned the possibility of "communistic Russia dictating the peace" at war's end.[41]

The fate of European Jewry under Nazism was not an issue Muench chose to emphasize. Muench referred to crimes against Jews only in a general way, never using the word "Jew" specifically. Here again, Muench fit into the pattern established by his Church—to desist from any public condemnation, verbal or written, specifically referring to Nazi mass murder of European Jewry—best demonstrated in Pope Pius XII's vaguely worded Christmas message of 24 December 1942. Vatican Radio broadcast his homily, which amounted to 5,000 words that filled twenty-six pages of text and took approximately forty-five minutes to deliver. Its broad theme was human rights and the social order. Toward the end of the homily, the pope said, "humanity owes this vow [to return society to divine Law] to hundreds of thousands of people, who through no fault of their own and solely because of their nation or descent (*stirpe*), have been condemned to death or progressive extinction."[42]

This phrase could apply to many wartime injustices, for example the deportation of Poles and Lithuanians under Soviet occupation; the starvation of Soviet POWs at German hands in 1941–42; or German plans to "resettle" ethnic Germans in occupied eastern territories while either murdering the indigenous Slavic population or relegating them to positions of servitude. It might also apply to Nazi sterilization policy. Further, church officials in Germany and Rome remained concerned about Jewish converts to Catholicism, still considered "Jewish" under the Nuremberg Laws and therefore subject to the same fate. Probably, the pope had all of these things, including the mass murder of European Jewry, on his mind when he spoke these words. But in no way is it clear that these few sentences, buried in lengthy and dense text, referred especially to European Jewry.[43] In his own commentary on the pope's 1942 address, Muench emphasized only the social and economic turbulence that contributed to war and the manner in which Catholics should navigate it.[44]

In October 1943, referring to "Communism in Russia, Fascism in Italy, and Nazism in Germany," Muench wrote, "minorities and racial groups were treated with ruthless and savage contempt. Concentration camps, put in the charge of harsh and cruel men, were established for the imprisonment of those who still had the courage to assert their rights against tyranny. The black deeds of evil men caused much blood to flow in assassinations and massacres, purges and liquidations."[45] At the time that he wrote this column, Muench had access to widely distributed newspaper reports concerning Nazi persecution and deportation of European Jews as well as to reports on Nazi concentration camps, including even extermination camps in Poland.[46] In other words, Muench demonstrated awareness of the bitter fate of European Jews, though, like his pontiff, he never used the word "Jew" specifically. In 1943, Muench commented obliquely about Nazi extermination of European Jewry (again, without using the word "Jew" or "Jewry"), writing, "men who consider themselves a superior race will not hesitate to exterminate an inferior race if they conceive it to be to their advantage. Strong Nations will dominate over weak nations. The upper classes will exploit the lower classes."[47] As was the case in other published materials, Muench's critique of Nazism was also a critique of communism. In January 1944, Muench would repeat to *CAN* readers Pope Pius XII's claim that the papacy "gave support to a great number of refugees, homeless, and emigrants, including also non-Aryans."[48]

Muench was a severe critic of fascism, though his published materials tended to conflate what he considered the fallacies of communism with those of fascism. He described the Nazi state as "ugly and malformed," in that it "either heaped ridicule on century-old doctrines or subtly sought to use Christian ideas and Christian terms to confuse Christian minds and . . . hearts."[49] And yet, even before writing *One World* in December 1945 and arriving in Germany in August 1946, Muench differentiated between "government by a small clique of Nazis" and unblemished Germans at large.[50] He demonstrated beliefs that would make him an attractive candidate for selection as papal emissary to Germany: a clear rejection of Nazism based on its anti-Catholic ideologies, combined with sympathy for Germans themselves and a belief that German Catholics were, in general, victims of Nazism, not participants in it. These were exactly the sentiments that Pope Pius XII had expressed in his June 1945 radio address "The Church and National Socialism."

Fascism, wrote Muench, "denied man his inherent, natural rights." Italian fascism, German Nazism, and Russian communism meant individuals had "only such rights as the state accord[ed] him," wrote Muench.[51] Muench believed that both communism and Nazism were essentially fascism "in its worst form, two branches from the same poisonous tree of tyrannical dictatorship."[52] In clear terms, Muench criticized Nazi Germany in particular and fascism in general on numerous occasions. He was not unlike many German Catholics who openly defied Nazism on the basis of its anti-Catholicism, *not* on the basis of its anti-Jewish policy. "Fascism cannot be reconciled with Catholic teaching," asserted Muench, principally because of the fascist belief in "super-races." "We would not be worthy of the name of Christians if we would allow contempt to arise in our hearts for others because blood that is different from theirs flows in our veins," he wrote in 1940.[53] In his essay "The Church, Fascism, and Peace" (1944), Muench condemned what he called "the fascist tenet of master races." He did not use the more specific word "Nazi," important for analytical purposes in that Muench's use of the term "fascism" could mean Nazism, Russian communism, or Italian fascism. He decried fascism's end result, the "subjugation or even extermination of races and nations of inferior status." Muench called it "a great wrong" to "oppress, persecute, and kill people on account of their race." In this essay, Muench used the more specific term "anti-Semitism," calling anti-Semitism "full of inequity." He cited as positive and truthful Pius XI's famous statement that Christians were "all Semites in spirit." Catholicism and the Nazi "myth of blood and race" were incompatible, wrote Muench.[54]

Muench's rejection of Nazi racial theory, even as it pertained to Jews, did not exclude the possibility of his harboring other deadly anti-Jewish stereotypes that surfaced during his career in Germany. For example, this rejection of Nazi racial theory and simultaneous antipathy toward Jews for other reasons was certainly true of Swiss Lutheran theologian Adolf Schlatter, one of Dietrich Bonhoeffer's former professors. Schlatter, distinguished professor of theology at Tübingen, set himself in opposition to the Nazis' antidemocratic, nationalistic, and racist goals. Using language similar to that used by Muench, Schlatter argued in 1933 that "freedom makes a people . . . a mass of slaves is not a people . . . we Germans are not a product of race, but of history, over which . . . God

stands." Schlatter went so far as to say that "Jew hate" was a manifestation of "enmity toward God."

But the absence of racial ideology, James E. McNutt argues persuasively, "did not mean that Schlatter lacked convictions that boded ill for
Jewish Germans." Schlatter viewed contemporary Jewish influence in
German society and politics as overwhelmingly negative. He equated
Judaism with legalism; referred to the "Jewish banker" and "Jewish
rabbi" as the "pillars of Jewry;" believed that Jews "walked according to
the flesh;" and concluded that Jesus of Nazareth was an Aryan. His 1935
strongly anti-Nazi pamphlet "Shall the Jew Be Victorious Over Us? A
Word for the Christmas Season," which depicted Nazism and Judaism as
an intimately connected evil, sold 50,000 copies.[55]

Let us look at a different passage from Muench's "The Church,
Fascism, and Peace":

> The Jewish race is singularly honored by Catholic beliefs and by the
> things Catholics revere. We Catholics believe that the God-man and
> the Savior of the world sprang from the Jewish race. His mother,
> whom we hold in higher reverence than any other human being, was
> a Jewess. The Apostles and the first Christians were Jews. The
> Gospel was first preached to the Jews, and Jewish converts to the
> Faith became the first members of the Church almost everywhere in
> the Greek and Roman world. With a Jew who has religion, all
> Christians have much in common—belief in God, belief in the same
> Ten Commandments, and belief in the Old Testament. . . . It is true
> as stated in the New Testament, that a Jewish mob, led by a Jewish
> high priest, persuaded a Roman governor to condemn Christ to
> death . . . The Church does not blame the Jews of today but rather
> sees the sins of men through all time as responsible.[56]

Muench was not what Daniel Goldhagen coins an "eliminationist anti-
Semite," one who calls for the elimination of Jewish influence or of Jews
themselves from a particular society, or even for their death.[57] But
Muench still shared the common and historically deadly Catholic conception that Jews were so-called Christ-killers. In this way, he was not
unlike many in his generation of Christian theologians who rejected the
racial ideology of Nazism but still held fast to many other deadly forms
of anti-Jewish prejudice.

In 1935, Muench had a telling exchange with fellow Catholic priest Father Charles Edward Coughlin, founder of the National Union for Social Justice and of the Christian Front. On Sundays, from 1928 to 1942, Coughlin broadcast his radio program, "The Golden Hour of the Shrine of the Little Flower" (Coughlin's church) from Royal Oak, Michigan. He also published the incendiary tabloid newspaper *Social Justice*. Donald Warren describes Coughlin as "a right-wing anti-Semitic extremist" who blamed the Depression, and later World War II, on so-called "banksters, plutocrats, atheistic Marxists, and international financiers," Coughlin's coded words for Jews. Warren points out that Coughlin was a well-connected man, attracting the support of important Americans such as Franklin Delano Roosevelt and Joseph Kennedy (until 1934), Clare Booth Luce, Douglas MacArthur, and Henry Ford. Unsurprisingly, he gained the attention of Benito Mussolini and Adolf Hitler in Europe.[58] By 1938, forty-six radio stations in major cities across the United States carried his Sunday program.[59] Neither the Vatican nor the American Catholic hierarchy supported Coughlin, with the exception of Bishop Michael Gallagher of Detroit.[60]

In the April 1935 issue of the Catholic journal *Salesianum*, Bishop Muench publicly refuted Coughlin's economic theories while admiring some of his critiques and his oratorical gifts. Entitled "Father Coughlin's Money Program," Muench's article praised Coughlin for his, in Muench's view, positive role as a "prophet" rooting out evil influences on U.S. economic life. "[Coughlin] gives expression to what is in . . . hearts when with unexcelled oratory he cracks down on money changers and international bankers whom he blames for the world's woes. One may disagree with his views but it must be conceded that by his broadcasts he has diverted attention away from socialistic and communistic agitators, created interest in social problems, and made people read . . . the encyclicals of [Popes] Leo XIII and . . . Pius XI."[61] Bishop Muench did not object to, and seemed to agree with, Coughlin's thesis that "money changers" and "international bankers" were partially to blame for the Depression. Muench merely objected to the notion that Jews, in the form of "money lenders" and "international bankers," were the sole cause of the Depression. Coughlin's scapegoating of Jews in this way did not strike Muench as problematic; indeed, Muench believed it had positive effects.

In his *Salesianum* article, Muench strongly criticized the "Radio Priest" for espousing specific financial programs, for example bimetallism and the nationalization of all banking, credit, and money. In the field of economics, argued Muench, Coughlin had no training, and ventured into a field in which he had "neither the mission nor the equipment." Citing the U.S. monetary system as the sole cause of the Depression made Coughlin "a monomaniac reformer."[62] Muench was not perturbed by Coughlin's expressions of anti-Semitism, but by his promotion of bimetallism and Coughlin's unbecoming demagoguery.

One month after the publication of the *Salesianum* article, Muench gave a public lecture at the Saint Rose Home and School Association of Milwaukee, where he denounced Coughlin's broadcasts as "imprudent" and his economic theories as "unsound." On 18 May, the *Milwaukee Sentinel* published a full-page summary of Muench's *Salesianum* article.[63] On 24 May, the *Chicago Daily News* published an extract of the *Salesianum* article as well.[64] In the midst of this controversy, Archbishop Stritch recommended that Muench be named bishop of the diocese of Fargo, North Dakota. According to Barry, Coughlin's weekly newspaper, *Social Justice,* announced that Muench "had been sent to the wilds of North Dakota." The *Detroit Free Press* interpreted Muench's new assignment differently, noting in a 13 August article that Muench labeled Coughlin's financial theories "contrary to Catholic philosophy" and was rewarded for it with a bishopric. Again according to Barry, Muench wrote to Coughlin directly, telling him that they could freely disagree with one another without bad feeling between them. Coughlin purportedly replied with a polite note congratulating him on his new appointment and making no mention of their disagreement.[65]

Well settled in Fargo, it was a twist of fate that uprooted Muench from his diocese and brought him to occupied Germany. In late December 1945, Pope Pius XII named thirty-two new members to the College of Cardinals in Rome. One prelate selected was Archbishop Samuel A. Stritch, former archbishop of Milwaukee, now of Chicago. Stritch received many letters of congratulations, including one from Bishop Muench. "I should like to purchase your red hat as a gift from me in gratitude for all the nice things you have done for me, and I should very much like the privilege of joining you on your trip to the Eternal City [Rome]."[66] Stritch replied that "of course" Muench should be a member

of his party.[67] Stritch, Muench, and thirteen others departed Chicago for
Rome on 12 February. On 22 February, Muench watched Stritch receive
his red hat (purchased by Muench) in Saint Peter's basilica with no
notion that his life would soon drastically change through a papal appointment.

During Nazi rule, the Holy See's nunciature to Germany was located in the capital of Berlin and headed by Archbishop Cesare Orsenigo, an Italian national.[68] A separate nunciature to the state of Bavaria existed in Munich because of its peculiar status dating back to
1871. Prior to the end of the war, on 8 February 1945, Orsenigo moved
what remained of his household to Eichstätt, a town located in the
middle-Franconian region of central Bavaria.[69] German defeat in May
1945 meant that the nunciature lost its official status. What had once
been Germany was now an occupied, non-sovereign territory. The
Allied Control Council in Berlin, consisting of American, British,
French, and Soviet deputies, determined that Orsenigo could nonetheless remain in Eichstätt. The Allied Control Council's decision pleased
Pope Pius XII, who desired the continuity of the "nunciature" in
Germany, even if unofficially. But Orsenigo died on 1 April 1946, leav-
ing only Monsignor Carlo Colli, his aide de camp, to maintain the link
between Pius XII and the German Catholic Church. In January 1947,
Colli, too, died, leaving the "nunciature's" secretary, Monsignor Bernard
Hack of Berlin, alone in Eichstätt.[70]

Pope Pius XII had been papal nuncio to Bavaria and the German
Weimar Republic and, thereafter, Vatican secretary of state. During his
papacy, Pius XII was known in Vatican circles as *il papa tedesco*, "the
German Pope," due to his love for the German people. Pius XII
remained a stout Germanophile before, during, and after the Third
Reich.[71] After his contact with the German episcopate was interrupted
by the Allied capture of Rome in March 1944, Pius XII sought ways to
keep up with the situation of the Catholic Church in increasingly devas-
tated Germany. To this end, he dispatched what is dubbed the "first
Vatican mission" to Germany in early June 1945, with American
Monsignor Walter Carroll at its helm. In September 1945, the pope
ordered the "second Vatican mission" to Germany, and in October 1945,
the "third Vatican mission," headed by Archbishop Carlo Chiarlo. The
end result of the third Vatican mission was its establishment as a permanent fixture in occupied Germany. The Vatican relief mission set up
household in Kronberg, on the outskirts of Frankfurt am Main. The aim

of the Kronberg mission, officially established at the Villa Grosch (Gartenstrasse 1), was to alleviate the suffering of Catholic displaced persons and prisoners of war.[72] The Kronberg mission catered to several national groups of Catholic displaced persons, providing each with its own priest-delegate.[73]

Chiarlo's experience with the United States Army commander of SHAEF, Major General Dwight D. Eisenhower, and his chief of staff, General Bedell Smith, made it clear that the head of the Kronberg mission must be an American. In early November 1945, the three men met at Army headquarters in Frankfurt. Polish Archbishop Joseph Gawlina, acquainted with Chiarlo since the Italian archbishop's days as nuncio to Poland, acted as an interpreter for him. During this meeting, Eisenhower outlined the operating guidelines for the soon-to-be-established permanent mission in Kronberg. Eisenhower emphasized that it was to be of a "strictly religious and moral" (as opposed to diplomatic) character. After the interview Smith took Gawlina aside to berate him concerning the Holy See's choice of Chiarlo as mission head. Smith told Gawlina, "those Italians don't understand a thing about their position in the world. The [head] can only be an American . . . but never an Italian or German."[74] Some in the Vatican secretariat of state also viewed Chiarlo as an inappropriate choice. Archbishop Filippo Bernardini, nuncio to Switzerland, had this to say about Chiarlo in a conversation with Muench: "Chiarlo—a mistake. No interest in Germany—no German."[75]

These sentiments and incidents would help to determine Bishop Muench's selection as a replacement for the deceased nuncio and head of the Kronberg mission. When he traveled to Rome three months later (February 1946), Muench expected only to see Stritch consecrated cardinal. Following the ceremonies in Saint Peter's basilica, on 22 February, Stritch paid a courtesy call to Pope Pius XII.[76] He found the pope troubled about the Holy See's situation in Germany. The pope was worried, despite the fact that "nuncio" Orsenigo had been allowed to remain at the Eichstätt "nunciature" and Pius XII's trusted advisor, Father Ivo Zeiger, now resided at the Villa Grosch in Kronberg. Orsenigo got on well with Pius XII, but was disliked by the German bishops.[77] Zeiger was a German national, and therefore not able to provide official leadership as head of the Kronberg relief mission for displaced persons.[78] The three Vatican Relief Missions dispatched by Pius XII pointed to the need for an American to head the newly established Kronberg mission. Furthermore, a number of German bishops, including Bishop Konrad

Preysing of Berlin, requested an American bishop as mission head.[79] And so, during their audience, Pius XII turned to Stritch for his advice on an American to head the Kronberg mission. According to a later account by Muench, Cardinal Stritch replied that Muench, then in Rome, would be ideal. Muench had "sympathy" for the suffering German people, Stritch assured Pius XII. He might be the solution to the pope's troubles.[80]

Muench was at a sidewalk café talking with American journalists when Stritch sought him out to tell him about his audience with Pius XII. The following day, 23 February, Muench had his first audience with Pius XII, during which the pope informed him that his appointment as apostolic visitor was under consideration.[81] Two days before the Stritch party left Rome, Muench received an "urgent call" from Undersecretary of State Montini. Montini explained what Muench termed "the situation in Germany" and formally asked Muench to go to Germany as apostolic visitor. Muench understood his assignment to mean that he would "represent the Holy See in Germany [since] Germany [had] no national government, [meaning] the present nunciature . . . in Eichstätt [was] not able to function properly."[82] On 3 March, the day Muench returned to the United States from Rome, Montini notified Muench to again confirm that Pius XII had indeed chosen him as papal visitor.[83] Muench told his sister that he was obliged to secrecy until the appointment became official.[84]

Muench soon found himself in the unique position of serving both Pope Pius XII *and* the U.S. military government in the American-occupied zone of Germany. In late March 1946, Secretary of War Robert Patterson wrote to Monsignor Howard J. Carroll, general secretary of the National Catholic Welfare Conference (NCWC) in Washington, D.C. Patterson asked Carroll to nominate a Catholic religious leader "who [was] thoroughly familiar" with the history of the German Catholic Church, had the capability to confer with its leaders, could obtain the support of its agencies, and could serve as a liaison between it and the military government.[85] Carroll was already aware of the need for a nominee. In January, Methodist Bishop G. Bromley Oxnam requested that President Harry Truman appoint a civilian as liaison representative between the U.S. military government and the Protestant Churches in Germany. Truman agreed, as long as similar arrangements were made for representatives of the Catholic and Jewish faiths.

On February 20, Oxnam approached the NCWC and the Synagogue Council of America. Carroll consulted with the members of the NCWC board, who nominated Monsignor Anthony Strauss of Saint Louis, but, in early April, Strauss declined.[86] After returning from Rome, and thus knowing that Muench would soon become the Vatican's papal visitor to Germany, newly minted Cardinal Stritch, chairman of the NCWC's administrative board, requested that the liaison representative be Muench. For his part, Muench expressed reluctance, thinking that becoming liaison representative might interfere with his work as Vatican papal visitor. But Muench agreed after Stritch assured him that he would have the aid of a secretary, Father Stanley Bertke, to "act as [his] deputy whenever it would be impossible for [Muench] to be near [Army] headquarters," which had moved from Frankfurt to Berlin.[87]

On the advice of Stritch, then, Monsignor Carroll replied to Patterson on 10 April with a nomination. "The Most Reverend Aloisius J. Muench, Bishop of Fargo, North Dakota," was to act as the liaison representative between the Catholic Church authorities and the office of military government in Germany.[88] What Carroll knew in March–April about Muench's commitment to Pope Pius XII and Undersecretary of State Montini is unclear, though Muench remained under the impression that no one in the American hierarchy save Stritch knew of his assignment as Vatican papal visitor. On 7 May, Muench wrote to Carroll that civil affairs division Captain Roy E. May had contacted Muench "about his going to Germany on behalf of the N.C.W.C." as liaison representative between the German Catholic Church and the U.S. military government in Germany. Muench, "in a quandary," did not give Captain May a "definite acceptance." His next words to Carroll indicated that in early May, Muench's mission as papal visitor still remained top secret:

Here is the reason . . . *strictly confidential.* In Rome Monsignor Montini asked me to go to Germany as Apostolic Delegate ad interim. I accepted. He thought that there would be no difficulty in getting clearance from the Allied authorities, except such as might be made by the Russians. Whether or not this has happened I do not know. At least I have no further word. Cardinal Stritch, whom I called today, said that he would telephone the Apostolic delegate [Nuncio] in Washington [Amleto Cicognani], to learn about my mission for the Holy See. It would be highly embarrassing to go to Germany as a representative of the N.C.W.C. without having definite word . . . regarding the other mission. I could not give Captain May a definite answer until I talked to Cardinal Stritch. Will you kindly telephone Captain May and inform him that Bishop Muench has accepted but that a certain important matter must be cleared first before arrangements for the trip can be made.[89]

On 16 May, Muench received a radiogram from Cicognani in Washington, confirming that he was indeed to go to Germany as Pius XII's papal visitor.[90] A week later, on 22 May, Secretary of War Robert Patterson told Muench that the War Department had accepted the NCWC's nomination of him as liaison representative. During their conversation, they discussed the purpose of Muench's mission to Germany. Muench apparently did not tell Patterson about his prior commitment to the Holy See. In a letter, Patterson spelled out the War Department's expectations of Muench. "As you know, one of the most important objectives of Military Government in Germany is the development of democratic ideas. It is recognized that the church must play a leading role in the reeducation of Germany and the building of a spiritual basis on which a free society can be constructed. With this objective in mind, the War Department has asked each of the three leading faiths to nominate a well-qualified representative to go to Germany for the purpose of conferring with their respective German church leaders and to serve as liaison between those churches and General [Lucius] Clay's headquarters."[91]

As liaison representative to the Office of Military Government, United States Zone (OMGUS), Muench was to aid in the general area of spiritual reconstruction. He was *not* to serve as a "special pleader" to the military government on behalf of the German Catholic Church. Neither he nor his Protestant or Jewish counterparts were considered actual employees of the military government. Rather, they were "functionally responsible to the United States agencies which paid their salaries," and in Muench's case, this agency was the NCWC. Between summer 1946 and the end of occupation in 1949, Muench kept two offices, one in Kronberg (for his Vatican duties) and one in Berlin (for his military government duties).[92] Muench and his cohorts received billet, travel, and mess privileges, office space and equipment, and a direct line of communication to the chief of the Religious Affairs Branch of OMGUS.[93] Muench had one additional, and important, privilege. In compliance with Muench's request, in August 1946 Deputy Military Governor of

Germany Lucius E. Clay agreed to grant "the privilege of uncensored communication" to Muench and his (approved) assistant, Father Stanley Bertke. This meant that Muench could freely contact either Msgr. Howard Carroll, general secretary of the NCWC in Washington, or, alternatively, Msgr. Walter Carroll in Rome, in the format of either a diplomatic pouch or cable code messages.[94]

U.S. occupation statutes made it clear that Muench and his two counterparts were not to "assume responsibilities in the functional fields of operation directed and supervised by religious affairs officers of military government." They were "not attached to the office of military government" in the sense that they were "representatives of their respective faiths in the United States and functionally responsible to the United States agencies that paid their salaries. They shall not operate within the framework of nor under the functional direction of Military Government," noted one report.[95] In short, Muench, technically under the employ of the NCWC, did not have the power to make occupation policy. But German church officials and even occupation officers were not always aware of these regulations, and perceived Muench and his two counterparts as having strong influence with American policy-makers.

For example, in November 1947, occupation officer Karl Arndt, chief of the Religious Affairs office in Stuttgart, wrote to the director of Internal Affairs and Communications in Berlin concerning the status of Protestant liaison appointee Bodensieck and Catholic liaison appointee Muench. "In view of the fact that official publications of the Evangelical Church are referring to the Protestant Liaison Appointee Dr. Bodensieck as 'the personal representative of President Truman to the Evangelical Church in Germany (den persönlichen Beauftragten Präsident Trumans bei der Evangelischen Kirche in Deutschland),' and because official church circles seem to regard him as personal observer of the President of the United States in this area, we wish to be informed officially regarding his status in order that proper protocol may be observed should he be a personal emissary of the President of the United States," wrote Arndt. "This office would be grateful for a similar clarification of the position of Bishop Muench."[96]

As Catholic liaison representative, Muench had plentiful and regular access to the Religious Affairs Branch (part of the Education and Religious Affairs Division in Berlin) and other branch and division officers, and to General Clay and his political advisor, Robert Murphy, in particular.[97] Murphy actually studied German and at one point served as the American consul in Munich.[98] One of Muench's first conversations with Murphy and Clay involved the problem of "alien Americans hurting U.S. interests."[99] Muench forged a good relationship with Murphy, a fellow Catholic. Muench told Bishop Vincent Ryan of Bismarck, North Dakota, as early as November 1946, "planners were making a fiasco over here," that "the bureaucracy was terrible," but "fortunately, [Muench] got good help from Ambassador Murphy."[100]

Muench gathered information that he passed on to key German Catholic prelates on issues such as denazification, school reform, and Concordat policy. There is abundant evidence that Muench's undue influence on Germans was a source of frustration to occupation officers, especially in the Publications Control Branch (which fell under the Information Control Division). For example, during the fall of 1946, Muench approached publications control officers Lawrence Dalcher and Henry Siemer to request removal of the youth magazine *Lilliput's* license to publish. Muench complained that *Lilliput* was "communistic." In reporting to General Robert McClure about the incident, branch chief Douglas Waples had to clarify the incident itself and go into some detail on what Muench's position as liaison representative entailed, details apparently unclear to McClure.[101] Muench was meant to engage in religious activity only, but he interpreted this broadly, as to encompass more than spiritual development, interfering, for example, in publications policy, school policy, restitution, and clemency policy.[102]

Muench's dual role—as the NCWC's liaison representative to the American occupiers and as Pius XII's apostolic visitor—caused friction instantly, even before he arrived in Germany. The first ruffled feathers appeared when Muench requested permission from OMGUS officials to bring two secretaries with him to Germany. In addition to Father Stanley Bertke, Muench asked that Father Howard Smith accompany him to help with Vatican relief work. Clay refused Muench's request and told a colleague that he "already had to advise the Vatican that Bishop Muench is liaison representative for American Catholics and not for [the] Vatican."[103]

Clay did not appear to have any knowledge about Bishop Muench's commitment to the Holy See. When Muench arrived in Berlin in early August 1946 and met with Clay personally for the first time, he "assured" Clay that he was "not a Vatican representative" [!].[104] But to his superiors in the Holy See, Muench made it clear that he was first and foremost a Vatican emissary. Muench told Cicognani that he "should not want to have the work of the Papal Mission suffer because [he] had to function in dual capacity." Stritch "agreed with him," wrote Muench, "that the tasks of the Papal Mission take precedence over those of the War Department Mission." But he would "do [his] utmost" to prevent serious conflict between the two missions.[105]

In these new capacities, Muench toured the French, British, and American zones of Germany from September to December 1946 in order to converse with German bishops about the state of the Catholic Church in Germany. Muench's stint as apostolic visitor neared its end in January 1947, coinciding with Monsignor Carlo Colli's death and the resulting collapse of the Eichstätt "nunciature." Under an Allied occupation statute, Pope Pius XII could not appoint a new nuncio until Germany's political status changed.[106] He solved this dilemma by keeping Muench in Germany. Apostolic visitor Muench personally presented his findings to the Holy Father in February 1947, thereafter expecting to return home to Fargo. But by the end of their audience, Muench sensed the pope's desire that he remain in Germany "for an indefinite period."[107] To keep Muench in Germany, Pius XII named him head of the Vatican's mission for Catholic displaced persons and prisoners of war in Kronberg. As an American, Muench met the standard expressed by General Smith during his November 1945 audience with Archbishop Chiarlo.

The Kronberg Mission was financed through the United States National Catholic Welfare Conference War Relief Services Committee (NCWC–WRS) and by donations from American Catholics. It relied only partly on Vatican monies.[108] Muench was to fill the gap in the Eichstätt "nunciature" caused by the deaths of Orsenigo and Colli— unofficially, as the Kronberg Vatican mission had no diplomatic recognition. The Allied powers authorized its existence strictly for relief purposes. But Pius XII used the Villa Grosch in Kronberg as an unofficial and makeshift "nunciature" until a permanent one could be reestablished.[109] Secretary of the Eichstätt "nunciature," Monsignor Hack, traveled weekly from Eichstätt to Kronberg with documents and correspondence to be signed and approved by Muench.[110] All the while, Muench advised Religious Affairs officers on American policy toward the German Catholic Church.

In May 1949, the Basic Law formed the constitutional basis for the new Federal Republic of Germany, which convened its first operating parliament in September 1949. This meant the end of military occupation, and hence terminated Muench's status as liaison representative mediating American occupation forces and German Catholic prelates. The first chancellor of the new Federal Republic, Konrad Adenauer, a Catholic and a former member of the Center Party and now the leader of the CDU, soon became a strong and pro-western leader. In accordance with the Federal Republic's new status as an autonomous nation-state, Pope Pius XII designated Muench apostolic regent to Germany in October 1949. Muench told his good friend Martin Salm, back in Wisconsin, that his appointment as regent "did not involve any change of title or address," but rather gave Eichstätt the official status it lacked after the deaths of Orsenigo and Colli. But the "nunciature" had always continued to function, noted Muench. "We [in Kronberg] took over the work," Muench told Salm.[111] Eighteen months later, in March 1951, the Allied High Commission permitted the Federal Republic to form an independently operating Foreign Affairs ministry. Now Pius XII could officially name a nuncio to Germany again. On 12 March 1951, the nunciature moved from Eichstätt to Bad Godesberg, a suburb of Bonn, seat of the new West German government. Muench's office and residence was called Turmhof. On 4 April 1951, now-Archbishop Aloisius Muench became the dean of the German diplomatic corps, the first diplomat to be accredited to the Federal Republic.[112] He would remain nuncio until December 1959, when Pope John XXIII officially appointed him to the College of Cardinals in Rome.[113]

2

Excusing the Holocaust

The Sensation of One World in Charity

When appointed bishop of the diocese of Fargo in 1935, Aloisius Muench began the practice of preparing an annual pastoral letter to be read from pulpits across the diocese in five installments, beginning on the Sunday following Shrove Tuesday and ending on Passion (Palm) Sunday. Muench, who remained bishop of the diocese of Fargo until 1959, kept up this practice even through his tenure in Germany. In December 1945, in preparation for the Lent season of 1946, Muench drafted a pastoral letter entitled *One World in Charity*.[1] In it Muench took a strong position against "collective" German guilt and responsibility and equated Nazi crimes to Allied "crimes." He did so prior to any knowledge of either his imminent appointment as papal visitor or as the National Catholic Welfare Conference's choice as liaison representative between U.S. occupation officials and the German Catholic Church. Available documentation indicates that multiple, truncated versions of *One World* appeared in occupied Germany without Muench's intervention or consent. Even so, Muench never publicly recanted the anti-Allied and pro-German position he took in *One World*. In private, he even expressed satisfaction over its popular dissemination.

German-American readers thought *One World* made Muench particularly well suited to his new duties in ministering to a beleaguered (in their view) German society. For example, in response to Muench's appointment as apostolic visitor, the German-American newspaper *Der Wanderer* stated "Bishop Muench . . . knows Europe, the German people and their language, [and] understands the almost hopelessly muddled problems confronting them. He is imbued with a high and courageous sense of responsibility . . . [and] is a man of understanding and compassion . . . He stands revealed [as such a man] particularly in his recent Lenten pastoral, *One World in Charity.*[2] German readers, too, took note of *One World,* mimeographed it for wider distribution or requested additional copies (which the nunciature provided), and used it to justify the all too common argument that Germans were neither guilty nor responsible for Nazi crimes. *One World* resonated strongly with prevailing attitudes that German Catholics had "done nothing wrong" and hence ensured his popularity among them. Historians have ignored *One World,*[3] but it was an important part of the imagined community of victimization in postwar Germany. It is impossible to understand the public fame and career of Aloisius Muench in Germany apart from *One World.*

One World became a sensation in Germany by 1947, so it bears close scrutiny and analysis. In the opening paragraphs, Muench voiced a general appeal for the practice of "Christian charity" toward the defeated German and Japanese foes. The term "charity" has a long history in Catholic theology. The Latin root of "charity," *caritas,* means "love." Charity is the third and most important of the three theological virtues (faith, hope, and charity). Theologians define it as the highest form of Christian love. In essence, charity means love directed toward God and neighbor as the highest purpose of any Catholic.[4] Muench's focus on the term "charity," meaning (Christian) love, raises the issue of its opposite, hate or contempt toward God and neighbor. Alleged Jewish contempt for and rejection of the Son of God manifested in his human form, Jesus Christ, has been the basis of Christian anti-Judaism, as Christians believed that Jesus was the Messiah sent by God and rejected by the Jewish people.[5]

While important and necessary, distinctions between (religion-based) anti-Judaism and Nazi anti-Semitism, or, for that matter, any new nineteenth-century strain of anti-Semitism (racial, economic, political, or even Goldhagen's "eliminationist") distract from evaluating Christian accountability for the Holocaust. Former priest-turned-author and theologian James Carroll's reflections on his seminary training (1960s) are worth noting. "There was no escaping the source of conflict." "Jesus was the Messiah, and Jews as Jews rejected him. I knew, by the time I was a seminarian, *to say no in principle to antisemitism, with its crude sweeping racism, but Christian religious opposition to Jews was something else* [emphasis mine]. In Scripture class, we were taught to distinguish between antisemitism and anti-Judaism, with the clear meaning that the latter was an appropriate part of the faith. Love sinner but hate the sin—hate the sin, that is, of the Jews' rejection of the Lord."[6] Muench's essay "The Church, Fascism, and Peace," his pastoral letter *One World in Charity*, and Pius XI's *Mit Brennender Sorge* reject racism in clear language, but ignore the fact that Christian anti-Judaism had and has similar consequences to those of "crude" racism.[7] Also, use of the term "Christian" charity implies that virtues such as "love," "mercy," "forgiveness," and "justice," are strictly Christian virtues. It is no accident that many anti-Semitic stereotypes, calling Jews "vengeful," "greedy," "mercantile," "secular," or "materialistic," are the opposites of "Christian" principles implied in the virtue of "charity."

Given the silence of the Catholic Church in the face of the Holocaust, Muench's plea on behalf of defeated Germans and Japanese in *One World* is ironic. "We can no longer be silent. If we Christians do not raise our voices in behalf of mercy, compassion, and charity, will the pagans in our midst do so? In these hate-laden times we must dare to be brave, and fearlessly voice our convictions, lest fear become the parent of cruelty," wrote Muench.[8] Muench designated the virtues of "mercy, compassion, and charity" as specifically Christian virtues, as opposed to universal values shared by many religions. "Let us rise to the full stature of Christ and with Him proclaim the Lord's great law of love," wrote Muench. "Peace has never yet been built on hatred and revenge. Charity has been civilization's most successful builder. Nations long to create One World. By Christ's all-powerful law of love the goal can be achieved—One World in Charity." In Muench's view, "Christianity, charity, and love" were the opposites of "hatred and revenge." The law of love was the law of Jesus Christ, which by definition excluded Jews.

Muench entitled the first section of *One World,* "An Eye for an Eye." Muench commented on the "barbaric cruelties" conducted during

World War II, and deemed the atrocities carried out during the war unique—"no age record[ed] similar brutalities." He condemned a variety of disparate actions and events, so that German crimes appeared heinous, but no more so than acts committed by the Allies or even by the Catholic Church. "Let no one venture even as much as to mention again the Inquisition or Bartholomew's Night," wrote Muench. "Maidanek, Belsen[,] Buchenwald, Lidice, Hiroshima, and Nagasaki will cry out to their victims to arise and tell their story of horrible bestialities," thus equating the United States atomic attacks on Japan in the last month of the war with the Nazi concentration and death camp systems. Muench made no reference to the fact that Nazis targeted Jews for gassing in the prisoner-of-war and extermination camp Majdanek, nor did he cite the especially low value placed on the lives of Jewish prisoners in the concentration camps Buchenwald and Bergen-Belsen. In fact, Muench described Buchenwald as a place where "Germans tortured Germans," making no mention of any other national group incarcerated there.[9]

Muench proceeded to describe "the bombing of civilians in unfortified cities, the holocausts in [cities] of defenseless men, women, and children [and] the forced migration of millions from their homes and lands," a reference to ethnic Germans (and others) affected by the Potsdam Agreement (August 1945).[10] Citing the case of Soviet-occupied Lithuania (June 1940–June 1941), Muench detailed the deportation of 40,000 Lithuanians under Soviet occupation on 14–17 June 1941. "Children and old people, women and men, were crammed into cattle cars without food or water. Large numbers died in the railroad stations before the trains even moved. Nothing more was ever heard of those who were deported."[11] Though Lithuanian Jews also endured deportation by rail (often cattle) car under German occupation of Lithuania (late June 1941 to July 1944), and in greater numbers, Muench never mentioned Jews by name. Jews, approximately one-third of the Lithuanian population in 1939, were especially concentrated in Vilna (Vilnius) and Kovno (Kaunas).[12] A world center of *halakha* (rabbinic law), Vilna's Jewish community was second in importance in Europe only to the Warsaw community. In Vilna alone, Jews numbered about 57,000. The Lithuanian Jewish community was the first target of the Final Solution, and it fared the worst. As early as the end of 1941, 80 percent of Lithuanian Jews had been killed, and the death toll reached 96 percent by the end of the war.[13] Yet Muench ignored the fate of Jews in wartime Lithuania.

"Hundreds of thousands of Poles" suffered a fate "just as tragic" as that of Lithuanians under Soviet occupation, wrote Muench. "Wives were separated from their husbands, and children from their parents . . . the dispersal of Polish refugees is one of the most horrifying episodes in the historical annals of nations. . . . What terrible things befell civilian populations through bombing from Warsaw to Rotterdam, from Coventry, London, Cologne, Berlin and Dresden to Hiroshima and Nagasaki, need not be told," declared the bishop. "Hundreds of thousands" are "forced to work in [Soviet] mines and factories under conditions of slavery not much different from that practiced [under the] Roman [Empire]." Worse off, were the "approximately 20,000" Poles, Hungarians, Baltic nationals, and ethnic Germans expelled westward under the Potsdam accords.[14]

The second section of Muench's pastoral letter dealt with the topic of mercy.[15] "In some quarters it is not popular to make a plea for mercy. It may be difficult to put aside the pagan within us with his hard and cruel law of an eye for an eye and a tooth for a tooth, and put on Christ with His law of mercy, kindness, and love, but we have no option. We have to be either for or against Christ" he told his diocese. Though he did not specify which "quarters" decried "mercy," his listeners could easily infer that Jews were among them. By constructing sharp opposites that wove through centuries of familiar anti-Jewish teaching (love versus hate, mercy versus vengeance, kindness versus cold-heartedness), Muench did not have to speak the word "Jew" for his listeners to hear it.

"As Christians and as Americans we raise our voice in indignation against an official inhumanity which does not permit the United Nations Relief and Rehabilitation Administration (UNRRA) to ship relief supplies either to Germany or to Japan," said Muench. Here he expanded the circle of "merciful" to include not just Christians, but "Americans." "Having condemned the atrocities of the Nazis we can not now make ourselves guilty of similar atrocities."[16] "Shall we not sit in judgement now of the atrocities that are being committed in the name of retributive justice, which in actual fact, however, is not justice but plain revenge. We condemn, too, a conspiracy of silence on the part of a large influential segment of our press for not making known to the American people the real plight of the European peoples. Our people are generous: they would respond with full hands."[17] Again, he did not name the imagined enemy with undue influence in the American press. He left this to the imagination of his listeners.

In the third section of *One World*, "Bread on the Waters," Muench pursued the theme of guilt, focusing on Germans specifically. Muench denied the validity of "collective" guilt, stating, "the indictment of an entire nation can not be justified in the light of principles of democracy."[18] To bolster his defense of Germans, Muench cited a portion of U.S. Chief Justice Robert H. Jackson's opening commentary at the Nuremberg Trial repudiating the notion of "collective" guilt, the same passage used by General Robert McClure in his memorandum to U.S. Army units on the subject of German guilt. The National Socialist party, Jackson argued, had not earned a majority vote. Instead it came to power by way of an alliance between "the most extreme of the Nazi revolutionaries, the most unrestrained of the German reactionaries, and the most aggressive of the German militarists."[19] Muench was correct to understand that Jackson repudiated "collective" guilt. But neither Jackson nor the American military government repudiated notions of German *responsibility* for their crimes.

Muench, not stopping at the rejection of "collective" guilt, went further and claimed that "countless" anti-Nazis, many more than "the American people generally knew," including representatives of the Catholic Church, suffered under the regime. Here, he took the tack already being perpetuated in German Catholic circles and by the pope himself in his June radio address. Muench cited a 1945 edition of *Petrusblatt*, a Berlin Catholic newspaper, claiming that prior to its abolition by the Nazi regime in 1938, it "did not bow before the spiritual terror of National Socialism. For five long years, from 1933 to 1938, we waged a journalistic battle against race-hatred, lies, and injustice. Persecutions of Christians, oral and written warnings, interrogations, threats—nothing deflected us from the course charted for us by our bishops," the editorial claimed.[20] If applied to Catholic resistance efforts based on Nazi anti-Catholic policy, the *Petrusblatt* editorial rang true. Catholic resistance to Nazi measures curtailing Catholic schools, newspapers, associations, politics, and institutions is a historical fact, as is the Catholic outcry against Nazi slander of Catholic clerics, and, perhaps best known, resistance to euthanasia policy in the sermons of Clemens August von Galen, the so-called Lion of Muenster. Aware of this record, Muench wrote in *One World* that "an amazing story" of Catholic resistance to Nazism would be told in years to come.[21]

But Muench's focus on resistance to Nazis' anti-Catholic measures was and is highly misleading. For Muench did not separate those Catholic anti-Nazis who were also rabid anti-Semites from the (few) Catholic anti-Nazis motivated in part by opposition to Nazi crimes against Jews. This problem appears not only in *One World*, but in much of the literature exonerating Catholics on the premise of their "resistance" record. The crucial question is not whether some Catholics resisted (they did), but why they resisted. The major issues that motivated most Catholics determined to take risks in a potentially life-threatening regime did not include a high priority concern for the fate of Jewish Germans.

Muench finished the third section of *One World* with barely veiled references to the Morgenthau school of postwar planning, which called for territorial losses, harsh reparations policy, de-industrialization, and "pastoralization" of Germany. "To strip a people, not only of its house-hold goods, but also of its tools and machinery of production impov-erishes them."[22] "Mr. [Bernard] Baruch's plan to make Germany a nation of goat-herders and foresters" is "immoral, uneconomic, and unworkable," Muench said, quoting from the *London Economist*.[23] Treasury Secretary Henry Morgenthau Jr. and Bernard Baruch were Jew-ish Americans who initially advocated a harsh peace for Germany.

In the fourth section of *One World*, Muench again juxtaposed ideas of revenge with those of love and mercy, but portrayed mercy as a Judeo-Christian tradition by the tenth century B.C.E.: "To the Jews of old the Lord said: If thy enemy be hungry, give him to eat; if he thirsts; give him water to drink, for thou shalt heap hot coals upon his head, and the Lord will reward thee."[24] Victor nations, wrote Muench, needed to heed the words of the Old Testament (Jewish) Psalmists. "To Christians, too, come commands of mercy and love to a fallen foe," Muench wrote sev-eral paragraphs later. He cited Christ in the New Testament to bolster his point: "'But I say to you who are listening,' cried out Christ in his sermon on the Mount, 'love your enemies, do good to those who hate you.'"[25] Muench concluded "Happily few in numbers [were] those who reject this teaching of the God of Israel and of His Christ." In this passage, Muench clearly associated both Judaism *and* Christianity with mercy and love.[26] However, those in the United States "advocating the decimation of the German population" by means of starvation and pastoralization "could certainly not be called Christians, nor even Americans," argued Muench, likely referring again to Morgenthau and Baruch.

In this fourth section, Muench continued to argue against the notion that Germans in general should be held responsible for "Nazi" atrocities conducted by a "few." "Propaganda has done its deadly work. On the one hand, it has fixed on entire nations collective responsibility and war-guilt, and, on the other, it has created in the victor nations a *pharisaical* [emphasis mine] attitude of righteousness. The Lord's parable of the Pharisee and the publican (tax collector) who went up to the temple to pray, the one proud and boastful, the other meek and humble, could well be applied to the present-day international situation," wrote Muench. If seen in its biblical context, Muench's negative allusion to the Pharisee, who would have been Jewish, was not directed against Jews as such. But, due to the negative connotation attached to "Jewish" Pharisees in Catholic theology centuries later, it again created a binary relationship between the "good" Christian and the "wicked" Jew.

"As Christians, we have no choice but to be on the side of Christ, and we may be confident of this, that being on His side we are on the right side," Muench wrote. He tied being "Christian" to being "on the right side," again, by definition, excluding Jews. Christ taught "meekness, kindness, mercy, and charity," argued Muench. Adolf Hitler scorned such attributes, teaching instead "arrogance, pride, hatred, ill will, malice."[27] Muench's dividing line was religious, not racial, political, or economic. Christians and practicing Jews could be "just." Atheists and "pagans," be they Jewish or not, were "unjust."

In the fifth and final section of *One World,* called "The New Order in Christ," Muench returned to his pre-December 1941 pacifist sentiments. He criticized the current American administration for "putting to work a powerful machine of propaganda urging the maintenance of armies and navies on a scale larger than ever before." The alternative being, he argued, "taking the leadership among nations to bring about progressive disarmament and abolition of peacetime military training."[28] "Balance of power" arrangements such as those now taking place in the Truman administration sacrificed small nations "such as Finland, Lithuania, Estonia, Latvia, or the Balkan states" on what Muench called "the altar of expediency." Poland, "partitioned by her own Allies," could not call her soul "her own."[29] Financial resources should go to churches, schools, justice, and charity, not toward developing atomic weapons, he wrote. The small minorities of Catholics in Russia, Lithuania, Latvia, and Estonia, and the Church in Poland, were given no consideration in "Big Power" conferences, and suffered under totalitarianism. Muench finished this section in characteristic language, with a final plea that all men "submit themselves to the law of love of God and of neighbor."[30]

To conclude this analysis of *One World,* two points bear mentioning. First, Muench only acknowledged the mass murder of European Jewry twice in the entire twenty-five-page text, and never directly. In one of two examples, Muench wrote, "in Europe and Asia gangsters of a new type, pitiless and savage, rose to positions of power. They boasted of their totalitarian power with reason, for they controlled not only a strong secret police but also military might of unheard of proportions. These overlords set up concentration camps, the real horrors of which came to light only after the war, exterminated millions of persons because of theories of race inferiority and dragged into slave labor men whose countries they overran with lightning invasion."[31] Muench claimed that Hitler found criminal Germans to carry out the Final Solution based on planning no different in its nature from those postwar occupation policies that allowed for starvation or communist infiltration in Europe. Muench did not differentiate between ghettoization, mass shooting, gassing, and cremation, major Nazi tactics used to murder at least six million European Jews, and food rationing by the Allies in postwar Germany. In a second example, and the only time Muench referred to Jews by name in the context of victimization, Muench argued for mercy toward *Germans.* "We expressed our horror when the Nazis proclaimed the doctrine of racial guilt against all the Jews. Rightly we condemned such a doctrine. Shall we now profess it in the kind of peace we are making?"[32]

The most popular passage extracted from *One World* by Germans and repeated time and again between the appearance of *One World* in Germany in 1947 and Muench's retirement in 1959, was this: "Are we not making ourselves partners in the crimes of Hitler by now doing the very thing we once condemned and fought against? The hypocrisy is colossal. The fact that this forced labor goes now under the name of human reparations does not alter the fact that it is nothing less than labor slavery. We are wretched hypocrites if we do not denounce as a crime what we were quick to denounce when done by the enemy. The law of justice has no double yardstick for measuring misdeeds of friend and foe."[33] Germans cited this passage to remember the Nazi past in a particular way: as *regrettable but fully comparable* to acts committed by the Allies, especially the expulsion of ethnic Germans from eastern territories and denazification and war crimes procedures. And, inevitably, German accountability tended to become lost in these comparisons to Allied acts.

Muench divided his Easter 1946 pastoral letter, originally some 10,200 words in length, into five relatively equal segments, each constituting a separate weekly installment. After priests read it from the diocese of Fargo's pulpits on the five Sundays between Shrove Tuesday and Passion Sunday, *One World* was translated into German and printed in its entirety in at least two, and probably three, German-language newspapers in the United States. The first reprint appeared in the monthly *Familienblatt* (Techny, Illinois) in 1946. When Muench visited his mentor Archbishop Samuel Stritch in Chicago in June 1946, Father Markert of the Mission Press in Techny thanked Muench for his "kindness of some time ago to make it possible to have [his] excellent pastoral letter reprinted in the *Familienblatt.*" Markert's comments appear to indicate that he reprinted *One World* in its entirety. He claimed that *One World* elicited quite a response from the German-American readership, and he received a "number of letters" praising it. An unspecified number of priests requested extra copies, and concerned midwestern Catholics forwarded "considerable" donations "for the starving people in Germany and Austria" to the *Familienblatt* offices.[34]

At least two other translations also appeared in U.S. publications. The first of the five installments of *One World* appeared in .the German language *Nord-Dakota Herold* on 8 March 1946.[35] *Herold* editor Cornelius Sittard translated the text for *Herold* readers, and considered this task "an honor and a privilege." A German American with sisters and brothers in Aachen, he was convinced that "a willful order" was behind delays in the packages he sent to Aachen. It was Sittard's opinion that "a mentality just as despicable as the motives and actions of the former enemy [Axis] leaders" existed now in the United States. He agreed with *One World*'s argument that Germans should not be burdened with guilt, telling Muench that "a burden of hate" still "rests heavily on millions of innocent people under the pretext that [Nazism must be] eradicat[ed]."[36]

One year later, German-language newspapers in the United States remained interested in *One World.* The periodical *Der Wanderer* in Saint Paul, Minnesota, expressed interest in publishing the letter in April 1947.[37] Sudeten German priest Emmanuel J. Reichenberger (then in Chicago) approached *Wanderer* editor Alphonse J. Matt to suggest that "hundreds of thousands of copies be translated and distributed in Germany." According to Matt, Reichenberger wished to give "moral and spiritual comfort to a people driven to . . . despair . . . by physical suffering but even more by the feeling of being abandoned . . . by their fellow Christians around the world."[38] The Saint Josefsblatt in Mount Angel, Oregon, also reprinted a full translation in five installments.[39] A number of Muench's personal acquaintances in the United States distributed One World as well. William H. Regnery Sr., a Chicago industrialist and publisher, may have disseminated thirty thousand copies of it.[40] Mary Filser Lohr, president of the CCVA division for women, told Muench that his pastoral was "one of the most outstanding documents ever written," and that she "happily" distributed them in much of her correspondence.[41]

Some time between its appearance in the Familienblatt, Nord Dakota Herold, and Saint Josefsblatt and the first months of 1947, One World migrated across the Atlantic Ocean. What circulated in Germany was not a reprint of One World as already distributed in the United States, but multiple truncated versions of it. The circulating versions differed in length, but all had four features in common. First, they retained Muench's comments exonerating the majority of Germans of guilt or responsibility; second, they also retained the lengthy passages on the suffering of ethnic Germans and the German civilian population; and, third, the equation of Allied and Nazi so-called "crimes." Last, they all omitted Muench's brief references to the Nazi extermination campaign against European Jewry.

Cardinal Josef Frings, archbishop of Cologne, mentioned one version of the circulating pastoral letter in January 1947, noting to Muench that it "wandered through Germany like a ghost."[42] Other sources also trace its distribution back to the city of Cologne. One World was available there as early as 2 January 1947. Old friend to Muench and economist Franz Lauter wrote him, "a pastoral letter is circulating here, titled Die Einwelt in der Liebe, and you are showed to be its author. I too have a copy of it, sixteen single-spaced pages."[43] Lauter traced its dissemination in Germany to von Galen, noting that "talk went around last year [in 1946], that Bishop von Galen got hold of [One World] in Rome, though later this [rumor] proved to be false."[44]

Another of Muench's old friends hinted as to how it might have appeared in Cologne. Father Gabriel Vollmar relayed to Muench an exchange between himself and the director of the Catholic Borromäus

Verein in Bonn. According to Vollmar, the director asked him whether Muench had granted him permission to publish *One World*. Vollmar replied that as of January 1947, Muench had not, but conjectured that perhaps Muench granted his permission after January, due to the growing problem of hunger in the Rhineland.[45] The *Verein* director then relayed a bit of hearsay: rumor had it that a priest "with a Polish-sounding name" had approached the archiepiscopal vicar general's office in Cologne, asking that *One World* be granted imprimatur.[46] At first the office expressed reservations. The "Polish sounding" priest then presented a letter, supposedly signed by Muench, granting authorization. Upon seeing this alleged letter of permission, the Cologne office granted imprimatur.[47] Muench wrote back to Vollmar, denying the story. "I have never granted permission for the publication of this pastoral letter, and I ask that you tell this to the director of the *Borromäus Verein*." "Nor will I grant it in the future," continued Muench. "I discussed this matter with you once earlier."[48] As Muench did indeed grant permission to the *Familienblatt* in the spring of 1946, we can assume that Muench referred here only to the "sixteen single-spaced" version Lauter saw in Cologne and supposedly distributed by the archiepiscopal vicar general's office.

Muench acknowledged that "newspapers report[ed] on a pastoral by him discussing conditions in Germany" in a February 1947 interview with National Catholic Welfare Conference correspondent Max Jordan. He thought the mistaken impression that *One World* was a new publication might have been created because Vatican radio had referred to it recently. By February 1947, military government officials were aware of its existence and distribution without the necessary approval from the Information Control division's publications branch.[49] A version of it already circulated in the states of Württemburg-Baden and Hesse. Religious Affairs branch chief in Stuttgart Karl Arndt became concerned enough to contact John O. Riedl, acting head of Religious Affairs in Berlin. Upon investigation, Riedl could discern only that the *Familienblatt* reprinted it in 1946, and this version "somehow" reached Germany.[50]

Evidence shows that the dissemination of *One World* in Germany was a grass roots movement among German Catholic clergy and laity, a fact of great importance to the question of how German Catholics understood their own culpability for the Holocaust. According to *One World,* they seemed to have no culpability. In 1952, Father Vollmar wrote to Muench, "how happy I am today to have distributed your wonderful pastoral letter of February 1946."[51] Monsignor Joseph Kamps kept a borrowed copy obtained from a priest of the *Gesellschaft Jesu* in Beuren, Westphalia.[52] In April 1947, Sister Maura of the Mission for the Poor and Sick (*Missionare der Armen und Kranken*) in Dortmund, read *One World* while hospitalized in St. Joseph's hospital, Dortmund-Hörde. Struck by it, she asked her fellow nuns "to pray for Muench every day, so that his great work on behalf of Germans would be supported." After showing it to her doctor, she ordered it to be copied and distributed in "academic circles."[53] Sister Alodia of the *Missionare* told Muench, "her friends and acquaintances read Muench's pastoral with great interest and wonderment." The *Missionare* "had the pastoral copied again, for the poor German people were no longer used to such understanding and deeply shared sympathy."[54] A Munich schoolteacher claimed she got the pastoral "from friends who themselves received it from an employee of the military government."[55] Various translations of *One World* acquired a life of their own and became something of an underground sensation.

In April 1947, a rash of excerpts from *One World* appeared in secular newspapers across Germany. Extensive passages appeared in the 4 April edition of the *Aachener Nachrichten*. On 24 April, a brief excerpt appeared on the front page of the *Berliner Tagesspiegel*. The next day, the *Rhein-Ruhr Zeitung* and the *Kölnische Rundschau* did the same.[56] Muench, quite concerned about official U.S. reaction to his comments on the Allies, dispatched his assistant, Father Stanley Bertke, to political advisor Robert Murphy's office in Berlin "in order to explain to him under what circumstances the pastoral letter had been written." Bertke was to tell Murphy that Muench authored the pastoral letter in December 1945, before learning of his position as liaison representative. Further, added Muench, Allied policy toward Germany had improved a great deal since 1945, so much so that Muench believed his complaints in *One World* to now be outdated.[57] Muench did not, however, issue a public statement to this effect.

Two months later, on 13 June 1947, Muench noted in his diary that "Father John LaFarge of New York" paid him a visit in Kronberg.[58] LaFarge carried a copy of *One World,* translated into French, and asked Muench's permission to circulate it. Several months later, in a letter to Cardinal Spellman in New York, Muench claimed to have denied LaFarge permission.[59] Muench's diary dated LaFarge's visit 13 June but included no details. In a letter to Father Georg Meixner a week later,

Muench acknowledged that he and LaFarge discussed an article entitled "The Nazi Movement in Bavaria" (*Bayern und die Hitlerbewegung*), but it did not mention *One World*.[60] LaFarge later wrote Muench and, similarly, recalled that the two discussed the topic of Catholic Bavaria and Nazism.[61] Neither LaFarge nor Muench specifically mentioned *One World* in their letters to each other after the visit. But LaFarge's autobiography offers potential insight. On 12 June, one day before traveling to Kronberg, LaFarge visited the French priest Father Du Rivau in Offenburg. Du Rivau ran a German-French cultural center and its monthly magazine *Dokumente,* consisting of German articles translated into French.[62] It is possible that Du Rivau gave LaFarge a copy of *One World* translated into French. LaFarge probably brought this copy to Muench the next day.

After their June meeting, Muench wrote to LaFarge several times and expressed support for Germans who repudiated "collective" guilt.[63] LaFarge's own position on the matter of German guilt was not clear in either Muench's diary or in their subsequent correspondence. Whether it was the one possibly given to Muench by LaFarge is unclear, but a French translation of *One World* did eventually circulate in the French zone that summer. It was so widely disseminated that the military ordinary (bishop) to French chaplains in Germany, Bishop Picard de la Vacquerie, sent Muench a letter on the subject in early September.[64] Muench replied that he composed the pastoral letter in December 1945, and gave it to the printer "toward the end of January 1946." He released it to Fargo diocesan pastors "about the middle of February," while still in Rome with Stritch. Upon his return to the United States on 4 March, he "found" that his pastoral letter "had not only been circulated in [his] diocese but had also [been distributed] throughout the Catholic press of the United States."[65] Muench's reply to de la Vacquerie, dated 30 September 1947, is important, in that Muench would later misrepresent his receipt of the French (or any) translation of *One World*. He misled Sister Maura of the *Missionare* when telling her in June 1948 that he himself had "no" copies of illegally circulating translations, and that he "never received one, even though," he acknowledged, "the pastoral was distributed all across Germany."[66] Though Lauter did not appear to enclose a copy of the sixteen-page version circulating in Cologne in January, de la Vacquerie and others sent Muench a copy of the five-page French translation in the summer and fall of 1947.

In mid-September 1947, U.S. intelligence officials again reported that "a pastoral letter allegedly written by Bishop Aloisius Muench of

Fargo, U.S.A." was being circulated, this time in Schwabach, Bavaria. It differed from the Cologne version described by Lauter in that it was a "six-page" (not "sixteen-page") German translation. U.S. intelligence officials "doubted its authenticity" remarkably because it was "too well adapted to German psychology." The letter "severely criticize[ed] U.S. occupation policies in Germany[,] comparing [them] with brutalities committed by the Hitler organizations." Because the letter was not dated and contained press commentary from December 1945, intelligence officials correctly surmised that it was not of recent issue.[67]

By the end of August 1947, a Dutch translation of *One World* existed in Holland.[68] In *Landkreis* Offenburg (French zone), the *Stadtpfarrer* of St. Cyriakus church in Oberkirch mimeographed 500 copies of *One World,* or, to be more exact, a twelve-page extraction from it. He distributed it not only to his parish members, but also to "the most prominent personalities and families . . . in the Baden *Landtag* and *Gemeinde.*"[69] But Muench's biggest troubles began when the five-page French translation referred to by de la Vacquerie reached the French military governor in Germany, General Pierre Joseph Koenig. On 23 September 1947, Koenig wrote to his counterpart in the American zone, Lucius Clay, and included a reproduction of the five-page version. Koenig described it as signed by "Monsignor," versus the higher and correct rank of "Bishop," "addressed [with the date of] April 1946, to the Catholics of the diocese of Fargo at the time when he was quitting it." Koenig reported that it enjoyed wide circulation in the French zone, especially in Baden-Baden. Like OMGUS officer Riedl, Koenig traced the translation back to the *Familienblatt,* and also to "the English journal *Universe* of 17 January 1947."[70]

Nearly two weeks after Koenig wrote to Clay, Riedl contacted Muench to ask for clarification on *One World.* "We are frequently asked for an opinion in regard to it and to other emendations of it, and do not have the information necessary to give a factual answer."[71] But Riedl's concerns were eclipsed by anxiety on much higher levels. On 6 October, Muench flew to the United States with Clay in his private plane, none the wiser about General Koenig's letter to Clay.[72] Clay carried it in his personal pouch,[73] but had decided not to discuss Koenig's letter with Muench at this time.[74] Instead, he asked his political advisor, Robert Murphy, to conduct a quiet investigation of the affair in order to "get the facts."[75] In the first few days of October, Murphy contacted Cardinal Francis Spellman of New York to ask for an invitation to the upcoming Alfred E.

Smith Memorial Foundation dinner in New York City. Among other things, he hoped to discuss the Muench pastoral letter with Spellman.[76]

Spellman was one of five American archbishops who were elevated to the coveted rank of cardinal together with Stritch in February 1946. Spellman's fame was such that he was dubbed "the American pope" after Vatican Secretary of State Eugenio Pacelli's visit to Washington in 1936. Spellman accompanied Pacelli everywhere, including Pacelli's audiences with President Franklin D. Roosevelt. Spellman and Roosevelt developed a close relationship, and Spellman came to be regarded as "the" intermediary between Rome and Washington.[77] This explained Murphy's decision to contact Spellman about the *One World* matter. On 12 November, with Muench still in the United States, Spellman "had a short visit with Bishop Muench and showed him an information note" sent by Murphy.[78] Spellman appeared to Muench "overworked and quite nervous."[79] Spellman disclosed that "the French accused [Muench] of having written a letter to the German bishops in the French zone," but Spellman did not yet know more details.[80] Muench, apparently not yet wise to the Koenig-Clay exchange, immediately suspected that Spellman referred to the distribution of *One World* in the French zone. Muench, already alerted to its distribution by Bishop de la Vacquerie, was not taken by surprise.[81]

Clay spoke to Spellman about Muench and *One World* in mid-October.[82] Clay warned Spellman that he "would ask for [Muench's] recall." Spellman discouraged Clay from dismissing Muench, conjecturing that "maybe the letter [was] not authentic." To verify its authenticity, Spellman asked Clay to send him a copy of the translation included in Koenig's 23 September letter. Because Spellman had heard nothing further by 12 November, he assumed the matter was "settled." Murphy apparently relayed to Spellman that "Clay [was] a hot-head [and went] off half-cocked," and therefore Spellman should not be too worried.[83] But Spellman's assumption that the matter was settled was false. In a letter dated 24 October, Murphy again prompted a discussion of the matter with Spellman and enclosed the five-page French translation of *One World.*[84] Murphy's letter reached Spellman on 17 November.[85] Hoping to appease Murphy and Clay, Spellman asked Muench to write a formal explanation of *One World,* which Muench did, on that very day. In his explanation, Muench emphasized first and foremost that he wrote the letter in December 1945 and gave it to the printer in January 1946, prior to his leaving for the Stritch ceremony in February and therefore several months before he heard of his assignment in Germany.[86] As to the anti-Allied excerpts, Muench claimed they were torn from their context, and they were therefore "unfair." In his 17 November letter to Spellman, Muench shed no light on how *One World* might have appeared in Germany. He said only that "extensive excerpts . . . appeared in German translation without [his] authorization," though he acknowledged that "a request came to [him] from an (unnamed) publication in Bonn" to print it, which he claimed to have rejected.[87]

On 25 November, Spellman formally replied to Murphy's 24 October query, and he included a copy of Muench's two-page explanation.[88] Murphy "showed the enclosure to Clay" and thereafter assumed the matter to be "satisfactorily closed."[89] Though no documentation of this conversation between Clay and Murphy is available, it appears that Murphy intervened on Muench's behalf. One possible explanation for such an intervention might be their shared views on ethnic German expellees. As for Muench, he never showed misgivings about having written *One World*. "I regret only that merely excerpts [of *One World*] have appeared," Muench told Bishop de la Vacquerie.[90] He told CCVA member Mary Filser Lohr that he felt glad of the fact that his pastoral "brought much comfort to the German people," and had "gone through all Germany," mimeographed again and again by "people who wished to get it circulated." He was "naturally happy" that "so much good [was] done by means of it."[91] It gave him "great joy" that the letter provided consolation and encouragement to Germans.[92] In his diary, he privately mused he "would fight [his own] recall based on calumny" concerning his pastoral.[93]

American military government intelligence analysts in *Kreis* Schwabach believed that *One World's* "attacks on American policies in Germany provid[ed] welcome reading material for certain dissatisfied elements of the people." According to Schwabach military government officials, "quite a number of the [German] population" believed that the United States withheld material aid from Germany out of spite; that "German reconstruction and rehabilitation [were] being obstructed by dilatory policies on the part of the Allies," resulting in "many ready customers" for such a letter.[94] But citing American interpretations of *One World's* popularity is hardly necessary, as Germans spoke for themselves clearly enough. Cardinal Frings of Cologne summarized *One World's* effects on

German Catholics most succinctly in a conversation with Muench: "no bishop in the world is so welcome [here] as you."[95] A number of other German bishops wrote letters of praise about Muench to the pope.[96] The *Stadtpfarrer* of St. Cyriakus in Oberkirch called the pastoral letter "courageous," showing "how justifiable it was, that His Holiness Pope Pius XII named [His] Excellency Muench apostolic visitor to Germany." The parish of St. Cyriakus sent deepest thanks, but did not stop there, mimeographing and circulating five hundred copies of the pastoral letter.[97] Scores of letters to Muench from German Catholics indicate widespread knowledge of and support for *One World,* indicating also the rejection of notions of German guilt or responsibility for Nazi crimes. "Daily I express my deepest respect for Your Excellency's valiant and resolute pastoral letter, a copy of which came into my hands. It is an apostolic speech which cannot be ignored," Auxiliary Bishop Höcht of Regensburg wrote to Muench in 1946.[98] Many German Catholics interpreted *One World* as proof that they had done nothing wrong, even if they had an undeniable level of involvement with the Nazi party.

A case in point is that of architect August Syndikus of Bamberg. Syndikus was an active Catholic and member of the Catholic student confraternity, *Carolingia.* He married a Catholic and raised his three young sons to serve as communicants and altar boys. "There was no room for Hitler's picture in [his] home, but the crucifix and pictures of God's Saints occupied all the prominent places," his sister later said.[99] Syndikus was also a Nazi party member. Employed by the *Kultusministerium* in Munich since the early 1920s, Syndikus joined the party in 1933. His German-American sister, a Catholic nun living in Holy Cross, Indiana, after the war, described his decision this way: "when Hitler seized the government there was just one choice for public officials—lose their position for which they had prepared for by years of study, or become members of the National Socialist Party. My brother liked his work and because of pressure became a nominal member of the party."[100] The attitude of Sister Crescentia as a German American toward party membership in 1946, when the most heinous Nazi crimes were fully known, showed that she fully agreed with Muench's point in *One World:* she believed that only the "real war criminals" were responsible; the majority of Germans were not. She wrote Muench after reading *One World* in the *Saint Josefsblatt* of Saint Benedict, Oregon, in July 1946, both to praise *One World* and to ask for help in clearing her brother's name.[101] She viewed Muench as sympathetic to Germans, a proponent of their general innocence, and someone with connections who could help her brother.

More than anything else, *One World* was the document that established Muench's reputation among German Catholics early on. Franz Lauter of Munich, mentioned previously with regard to the distribution of *One World* in Cologne, urged Muench excitedly, "if this letter is authentic, [I] recommend it be spread further, for today it is important and cheering for us German Catholics to know [the message of] the pope and his representative."[102] Lauter's comment demonstrated his awareness of Muench's position as Pius XII's papal visitor. Lauter may also have been alluding to the pope's June 1945 radio address rejecting German "collective" guilt and praising Catholic anti-Nazi efforts.

"Just an hour ago I read your pastoral in the *Tagesspiegel,* wrote Sudeten expellee Franz Münnich, now of Ostlutter. "No one feels its truth like we *Flüchtlinge* (refugees) and *Ausgewiesenen* (ethnic German expellees)."[103] Master builder Franz Grübert residing in Furth-im-Wald, an ethnic German expellee from Silesia, elaborated more on what made it so cheering: it validated his belief that the majority of Germans now paid for the crimes of the few. "Again, the great masses, who had no influence on [Germany's] fate and yet were exposed to its promises and led astray by it, now suffer for it, and I am one of these."[104] Elisabeth Baumgart of Selingen, after thanking Muench for his *One World,* wrote indignantly, "admittedly, the Nazis plunged the world into this chaos. But, does that give others the right to use the same means employed by the Nazis? The Nazis were not the German people."[105] H. Mertens, an ethnic German Sudeten expellee now living in *Kreis* Hersfeld, claimed to have read an excerpt of *One World* in *Der Ruf* in September 1947. He too soundly rejected the idea of "collective" guilt. A convert to Catholicism in 1936, Mertens wrote, "We did not contribute to the many things for which Germans are today reproached. We refused to contribute, held high our faith and therefore are not guilty for the many things that have so besmirched the German name in the world today."[106]

A few took the lessons to be learned from Nazism to heart, such as Wilhelm Heinrich Ewald Freiherr von Freyberg. Ewald had been a successful textile merchant from the Bunzlauer area in Lower Silesia, and one of a small number of non-Catholics (Ewald was Protestant) who wrote to Muench. "I was against the Nazipest, and belonged to no party," explained Ewald. "I hated the so-called fraudulent nobility—i.e.

criminals [like Joachim von] Ribbentrop and the other so-called noble looters and robber barons who brought Germany to ruin," he wrote. Despite his hatred for the Nazis, Ewald collaborated with wartime forced labor policies. In Eichberg, Ewald was in charge of foreign forced labor in a textile factory, in this case French prisoners of war and Polish forced laborers. "I saw these foreigners (*Ausländer*) as my fellow men (*Mitmenschen*)," remembered Ewald. He claimed to have given "over thirty of them" extra clothing, despite the fact that he could have been severely fined for this by the Nazis. This potential discovery and punishment never came to pass. In February 1945, he and others in Eichberg were taken into captivity by the Russian army. Ironically, he became a forced laborer in Upper Silesia for several weeks.[107]

By 1947, Ewald, now living in the Spandau district of Berlin as an ethnic German expellee, experienced a crisis of conscience of a sort. Muench's pastoral, read by Ewald in the 25 April edition of the *Berlin Tagesspiegel*, prompted Ewald to write Muench with a personal request: to "save humanity." Like many who wrote to Muench, he described his hardships in detail, but unlike many, he reflected on the moral implications of Nazism, now evident to him. "I asked myself over and over again, what has humanity done, and is there a God who rules over justice and injustice? It is said that all injustice avenges itself on earth. National Socialism has been avenged, as I prophesied it would years ago." But Ewald's reflections were not fully objective, as he did not see himself as a collaborator, but only as a victim, when in reality he was both. "I asked myself, is this the way the innocent are treated? Are these not crimes against humanity? Were not such crimes judged at Nuremberg?"[108]

A strong sense of victimization was certainly not limited to ethnic German expellees. It also extended to so-called *Reich* Germans. Barbara Vincenz, teacher in a Koblenz *Volksschule*, obtained a copy of Muench's pastoral in February 1947. "Why is one German treated like the next? There are so many, who wanted nothing to do with Hitler. I was not in the party, but I am punished. Why don't people like myself get more to eat?"[109] Therese Wagner, a teacher in Munich, read an excerpt from *One World* in the *Isar Post* in March 1947. "On your extended trip through Germany [in winter 1946], you saw our distress and you know . . . that the majority of the German people were not susceptible to National Socialism, were against National Socialism."[110]

A deeply distressing response to *One World* came from Hedwig Rohmer, a teacher in a Munich public school. "We understand that other peoples shrink from our deeds, thinking we [are] all of bad character. It is deeply humiliating and depressing, though we did not know anything, most of us, of those cruel acts and places [revealed after the war's end]." Her sense of victimization bordered on paranoia. "There are real plans to kill millions and millions of Germans." "We all wish to give satisfaction to those countries suffering from us and to help those victims of the past time. But we presume that the idea is of killing us in a slow way instead of doing it with gas. Sometimes we think it more merciful to die like them in the KZ."[111]

Even after making a splash in 1947, the fame of *One World* and the reputation it imparted to its author continued to spread. In telling his friend Muench about a new booklet published by the Neuberg Abbey in September 1951, Vollmar noted that the last page referred to the word *Liebe* (translated as "charity") from the Holy Scripture, a noble tradition that Muench, too, stressed in his 1946 *One World*.[112] Vollmar called Muench's *One World* "a heroic act and a document of historical importance [written] in a time of hate" against Germans.[113] In December 1952, Dr. H. Hassenbach wrote Muench to request additional copies of *One World*, noting that "among the colleagues in his circles, there was a great interest for it."[114] Hassenbach did not specify which of the many circulated versions he wanted. In response, Howard Smith, Muench's secretary at the nunciature, wrote to the home diocese in Fargo requesting more copies of *One World*. "The archbishop occasionally receives requests for a copy of his 1946 pastoral *One World in Charity*, [and] we have only one copy here," wrote Smith. He went on to request that a dozen copies be sent to the nunciature in Germany, for distribution when the request arose.[115] Allied censorship ceased with the end of military occupation in 1949, so Muench's willingness to distribute *One World*, while now legal, showed lack of change in his openly pro-German position.

One ironic manifestation of Muench's reputation as a friend to Germans was the myth of his association with Adolf Eichmann. In 1961, the *Chicago Daily Tribune* and the New York *Daily News* reported that the defense lawyer to Adolf Eichmann, Dr. Robert Servatius, planned to approach Muench on behalf of his client. Servatius held the erroneous belief that Muench was the Vatican's nuncio to Germany during World War II, and that "Muench visited Eichmann several times during the war to help Jews escape Nazi persecution."[116] Servatius reportedly said that he hoped Muench "would testify, and [Muench's] evidence will show Eichmann is not the monster he is made out to be."[117]

The New York *Daily News* printed a correction several weeks later, acknowledging that Monsignor Cesare Orsenigo was papal nuncio from 1930 until his death in March 1946. A recheck by *Daily News* correspondent for Jerusalem, Joseph Fried, revealed that Servatius based his false statement on Eichmann's police interrogation. Purportedly asked about his church contacts, Eichmann said, "I can remember that the then permanent—what was the man who was executive of the Fulda Bishops Conference—the then Bishop Muench. I believe that later he was dean of the diplomatic corps in Bonn and I believe he is the same who a short time ago was appointed cardinal by the Pope." Eichmann claimed to have met Muench "twice a month in 1943."[118] In any case, Eichmann mistook Muench for either Orsenigo or for Cardinal Adolf Bertram, archbishop of Breslau and chair of the Fulda bishops' conference in 1943.

In the eyes of some of its German Catholic readers, *One World* put Muench on par with the likes of the famous anti-Nazi bishop von Galen and even with the Holy Father himself. Master builder Grübert linked it to speeches by von Galen. "Reading your words, my thoughts quickly go back to the now-famous preaching of Cardinal Count (*Graf*) Galen. He, too, was a brave confessor in a godless state."[119] Priest Franz Weimar drew a similar connection. "Yours were the most powerful lines written since the most holy bishop of Münster against the Nazis some years ago."[120] Priest Franz Schmal of Todtnauberg told Muench that *One World* embodied "the spirit of Pope Pius XII." "I cannot remember an Episcopal manifesting in such a high degree the very mentality of our Holy Father."[121]

When Muench retired from the nunciature in Bad Godesberg in December 1959 to join the College of Cardinals in Rome, he still remained famous for *One World.* In an article entitled "Friend and Champion of the Germans," the *Kirchliche Nachrichten Agentur* quoted the very same passage Hering had chosen two years earlier to capture the spirit of Muench.[122] *One World* was viewed as "bread for the hungry soul" by a great many German Catholics, as one Nuremberg Catholic, Barbara Muschweck, described it.[123] *One World* made him accessible in the eyes of German Catholics, to whom he even became a sort of "confessor." It greatly helped spread Muench's fame as a pro-German figure of German parentage, sympathetic to German Catholics, who held a great deal of power as the Vatican emissary to German Catholics.

3

Comfort and Consensus

*Muench and the German Catholic Hierarchy,
Clergy, and Laity*

In 1952, Bishop Michael Keller of Münster wrote Muench an agitated letter regarding a request from Carl Zietlow, employed in the Frankfurt office of the National Conference of Christians and Jews (NCCJ). Apparently Zietlow contacted Keller and other German bishops to request that they attend an upcoming NCCJ conference in Bremen. Zietlow also asked that Keller and other bishops promote the conference in Catholic newspapers. Feeling "pressured" by Zietlow's letter and unfamiliar with the New York–based NCCJ, Keller wrote to Muench for advice. Keller wished to know the reputation of the NCCJ among American bishops. "The whole affair strikes me as suspicious, in that it smacks of a growing inter-confessionalism. I cannot decide if I should participate," Keller told Muench.[1]

Muench asked an unidentified member of the Bad Godesberg household for advice. Muench passed on what he was told to Keller. "Bishop Keller can easily get out of going to the Bremen Conference by saying that a bishop does not usually take part in a conference in another bishop's diocese except by invitation from that bishop. As for the newspaper article he could graciously excuse himself on the [following] grounds: 1) being too busy to write a suitable article. 2) [Keller] would have to know more about the organization, [such as] who in Germany are the leading officers, etc. 3) As a matter of policy he does not write articles [unless] they have to do with ecclesiastical matters on which he believes clarification is needed."[2] Muench stressed that while American bishops did not disapprove of the NCCJ per se, they distanced themselves from it. "Some American bishops thought the activities of the NCCJ provoked anti-Semitism rather than mitigated it,"[3] wrote Muench. He also criticized the NCCJ for failing to improve relations between Catholics and Protestants. The recent appointment of a Protestant as U.S. ambassador to the Vatican, the stress on "humanism" as opposed to Christianity, and the fact that Zietlow was Protestant all pointed to the anti-Catholic bent of the NCCJ, added Muench.[4]

Muench advised Keller to simply refuse the NCCJ's invitation to the Bremen conference. Keller need not provide Zietlow with an explanation. If he felt compelled to provide a reason for his refusal, he should tell Zietlow that Catholics and Protestants in Germany already got on tolerably well, and, furthermore, the Catholic Church's position condemning anti-Semitism was already clear.[5] The stated goals of the NCCJ had already been met in Germany.[6] Keller's unwillingness to participate in the NCCJ-sponsored Bremen conference implied that he did not wish Catholicism to become "watered down" by other denominations. The incident also illustrated that mitigating anti-Semitism among German Catholics was not a high priority for either Muench or Keller, this despite the now-known horrors of the Holocaust and Muench's recognition in private letters that anti-Semitism was growing—not disappearing—in postwar Germany.[7]

Fate placed Aloisius Muench in Germany in the critical years 1946 to 1959. He might well have influenced the trend of denying German guilt and responsibility (individual and collective) toward a more truthful and inclusive direction, but he did not. Rather, if anything, he strengthened denial of guilt and responsibility. The importance of Pope Pius XII's June radio broadcast, the German bishops' Fulda pastoral letter, its numerous counterparts from individual prelates, and *One World* lay in the legitimacy they conferred on the argument that German Catholics needed no examination of conscience. Such pastoral letters were public statements that allowed already existing whispered notions and *Stammtisch* bravado about Catholic "resistance" or "victimization" to become more acceptable. German Catholics missed the historical moment for remembering all Catholic experiences under Nazism, which included not only victimization and resistance to anti-Catholic measures, but also indifference to and active participation in deadly anti-Semitism.

Archbishop Conrad Gröber of Freiburg-im-Breisgau publicly addressed the guilt issue in a pastoral letter dated 21 June 1945. Gröber told clergymen: "[You] must ask God to instill Christian thinking into the Allied powers [so as] not to let an entire people pay because certain criminals went overboard in their arrogance and madness."[8] In September 1945, Gröber issued another pastoral letter entirely devoted to the topic of "accusations against the German people." In it, he summarized what he understood to be the various charges against Germans, including that Germany was at fault for her current state of poverty due to the lost war, that Christian soldiers had not mutinied, and that German bishops had not opposed the errors of Nazism forcefully enough.

He included the charges that neither the honest and law-abiding bishops nor the Catholic laity condemned or prevented the monstrous crimes of the Nazis, and that German bishops should have protested against Nazism more strongly, more publicly, and without regard to their own safety. Had they risked their lives, things might have transpired differently. And he was aware of the accusation that the entire German people, including those who were strongly opposed to Nazism, had committed a criminal offense, because all Germans built the so-called community of blood (*Blutsgemeinschaft*) that brought war, eternal shame, and disgrace to Germany and the world. The final charge, wrote Gröber, was that German soldiers had been particularly brutal in their occupation policies. Gröber knew what critics were saying about "German" culpability for Nazi crimes, and he rejected them all.

Gröber mentioned Jews specifically in his discussion about the response of the Catholic episcopate to Nazism. The German bishops knew of the persecution and deportation of the Jews, he admitted. They knew, too, of the concentration camps, and protested against them. "But none of the bishops knew for sure (*beweiskräftig erfahren*) what the camps for Jews in the east were like. . . . The way thousands upon thousands [of Jews] were brutalized there, and of the mass graves on the edges of the camps, dug by the victims themselves."[9] Gröber's claim was a myth, albeit a popular one. In August 1942, Catholic SS Colonel Kurt Gerstein told Bishop Konrad Preysing of Berlin about the gassing of Jews in Lublin (Poland). Intelligence (*Abwehr*) officer Dr. Joseph Müller kept Cardinal Faulhaber (Munich) informed about atrocities in Poland.[10] Bishop Wilhelm Berning of Osnabrück knew about the Nazi plan to murder the Jews of Europe in February 1942. In the same month, Berlin Catholic Margarete Sommer told Berning of the massacre in Kovno (Lithuania). Berning wrote in his diary, "it appears likely that a plan exists to murder the Jews."[11]

Gröber and Muench personally discussed the persecution of Jews under Nazism, and the Church's reaction to it, on the occasion of Gröber's request that the National Catholic Welfare Conference aid in the work of Dr. Gertrud Luckner.[12] To his credit, Gröber continued to support Luckner's work after World War II ended. In November 1946, using Muench as a conduit, Gröber wrote the chair of NCWC–War Relief Services, Cardinal Samuel Stritch. In it, he praised himself, the other German bishops, and Luckner:

> During the Nazi regime, I used every opportunity to help. I supported the activities of Dr. Luckner on their behalf [by using] my name and my authority, without thought of possible unfavorable reactions as to my own person . . . if it is asserted in other countries that the Catholic Church failed the racially persecuted, we declare that this is not true. Unhappily, the measures taken by the Nazi regime were so drastic that what was done to aid Jews and [the] Jewish Christian could not always be made publicly known. But we did for them what lay within our powers. Commendatory letters from France and the United States are in my possession. In Dr. Luckner I have a person who knows these Jew-Christians well. Because of her interest in them she was sent to the concentration camp at Ravensburg [Ravensbrück]. Before her capture I sought to protect her and covered up her activities with the use of my name. She will be in a position to help the needy Jew Christians should gifts be placed at her disposal.[13]

Gröber took the position that he personally did what he could on behalf of Jewish converts to Catholicism. It is true that his concrete efforts eclipsed those of other German bishops save Preysing of Berlin. After his death in 1948, his support of Luckner's work proved not to be universal among his peers. Cardinal Frings of Cologne, who was "suspicious of the Freiburg circle's philo-Semitic efforts," blocked Luckner's plan to emphasize Christian-Jewish reconciliation at the 1950 annual *Katholikentag*.[14] Also in 1950, the Vatican issued a monitum (warning) regarding indifferentism. Phayer interprets this monitum as "clearly intended for the Freiburg activists," in that "the Vatican sent a team of investigators to check into Luckner's work."[15]

At Gröber's request, Muench forwarded the archbishop of Freiburg's petition to Stritch in Chicago, expressing support for Gröber. "Perhaps something could be done for converted Jews through papal relief, if the [the NCWC-WRS gave] the Holy Father a small sum of money for this purpose," said Muench. "The apologetical value of such a papal gift would be great, in view of the many deeds of charity of the Holy Father in the interest of Jews."[16] What Muench meant was that a gift would demonstrate to non-Catholics the beneficence he believed the Holy See practiced toward Jews. Muench in no way meant Pius XII needed to "apologize" to Jews (in Catholic theology, "apologetics" is the science of defending Catholic doctrine to so-called nonbelievers).

Stritch, no longer chair of War Relief Services, forwarded the request to the new leader, Archbishop John T. McNicholas of Cincinnati. McNicholas "sought the advice of the administrative board," and asked Bishop John Mark Gannon "to send $5,000 to [Muench's] chancellor in Fargo." McNicholas asked that Muench tell Gröber the $5,000 grant "was in response to [Gröber's] appeal . . . for *deserving* [emphasis mine], converted Jews."[17] When thanking Bishop Gannon for the $5,000 donation, Muench expressed primary concern for non-Jewish Germans. "While I already wrote Archbishop McNicholas to thank him for the appropriation of $5,000 for Archbishop Gröber's charity work in behalf of the Catholic Jews, I wish to add my own words of deep appreciation and gratitude. Each day brings new experiences in my work, than which none could be more interesting. But the distress continues to be very great, particularly among the 10 to 12 million refugees who have been expelled from their homes and driven into Germany. Their plight is miserable," he wrote.[18]

When Luckner sent a copy of each new *Freiburger Rundbrief* issue[19] to the papal visitor-regent, he replied in writing, that he read the *Rundbrief* "with great interest" and "had great confidence in the good it would do."[20] But he compromised the sincerity of his positive comments when Luckner requested that he make the *Rundbrief* available to parishes in the diocese of Fargo.[21] He refused, writing Luckner that the diocese of Fargo was a "diaspora" diocese that contained only a small number of Catholics (he cited the figure 75,000). "We have no special pastoral office (*Seelsorgsamt*), therefore I cannot fulfill your request that I pass on a copy of your *Rundbrief*,"[22] betraying his lack of interest in passing the *Rundbrief* (and its message about Christian-Jewish reconciliation) along to American Catholics. Further, when in 1952 Luckner appealed to Muench for funds to bolster the ailing periodical, Muench ordered his secretary to send Luckner a meager one hundred deutschmarks from the nunciature's charity account.[23]

Muench was not afraid to use Luckner as an example of Catholic efforts on behalf of Jews—never mind Luckner's uniqueness in this regard—when dealing with military government officials. In the May 1950 issue of the *Rundbrief*, Luckner described aiding Jews in her capacity as a *Caritas* employee. Muench requested that she send this issue to High Commissioner John J. McCloy, to his deputy Benjamin Buttenwieser, and to Ralph Nicholson and John Riddleberger, who worked at U.S. High Commission headquarters.[24] Muench knew the *Rundbrief* put a good face on Catholic "philo-Semitism," which in reality was confined to Luckner and her small circle. Muench misled commission officials, because most German Catholic prelates, clergymen, and laypersons did *not* support the *Rundbrief*, whose circulation never exceeded four thousand subscribers.[25]

When Luckner celebrated her sixtieth birthday, the *Rundbrief*, now preparing its forty-ninth issue, contacted those public figures deemed close to Luckner so that each might express their thoughts about her work. *Caritas* officer Dr. Karl Borgmann approached Muench, who cooperated. To his credit, he sent the following to Borgmann for publication in the September 1960 issue of the *Rundbrief:* "Dear *Frau Doktor!* I extend heartfelt wishes and blessings to you on the occasion of your birthday of 26 September 1960. I know of your commendable endeavors and your tireless works in a very specific branch of *Caritas*. May God sustain your remarkable enthusiasm for many days to come. With bishops' blessings, I am your humble servant in Christ, Alois Cardinal Muench."[26] Muench did not openly acknowledge Luckner's role as *Caritas* director for aiding Catholics who converted from Judaism, but his public praise of Luckner was still positive.

In addition to Gröber, a number of other individual German Catholic bishops commented on "collective" guilt. Joseph Frings of Cologne, named a cardinal by Pope Pius XII in December 1945, joyfully repeated the pope's consecration address in Rome: that only God could determine whether a whole people could be called "collectively guilty."[27] The cardinal disliked the American occupiers, telling Muench that "had Russia not been a communist country, he would have thrown in his lot with Russia against England and the United States."[28] In an August 1947 interview with Richard Akselrad, Frings repeated the classic arguments for Catholic bishops' silence about the Holocaust. "Public struggle" against the Nazis, argued Frings, would have "intensified" the "inhumanities" of the Hitler regime, and the Nazis would have "dropped all prudence towards the Church." He also picked up an argument popular among ethnic German expellees and some German Americans: "However revolting the injustice of the Hitler regime has been when it ordered the forced evacuation of peoples,[29] wrong will never become right, even if the same is done by the victors." He told Akselrad that at this critical juncture in German history, churchmen must stick together and emphasize the positive; it was no time for critical self-evaluation.[30]

In 1956, Frings pressed Muench to recommend that Pius XII grant West German State Secretary Hans Globke "papal honors."[31] Globke, a jurist, Rhineland Catholic, and former Center party member during the Weimar Republic, served in the Reich Interior Ministry when Nazism came to power in 1933. In 1935, Globke wrote interpretive commentary for the anti-Jewish Nuremberg Laws, thus playing a significant role in creating the legal principles that culminated in the Holocaust. After the war, he joined the Christian Democratic Union and continued his civil service career under Adenauer. Frings thought Globke should be honored for his contributions to Catholicism. Muench "suggested that an appropriate occasion be awaited" before the Holy See endorse such a move.[32] Upon conferring with officers in the Vatican secretariat of state, Muench concluded that Vatican honors for Globke might stir "reactions among non-Catholics." Muench knew that German "Socialists and some liberals" attacked Globke and thus felt papal honors to be politically unwise.[33] The nuncio did not appear to view Globke as a Catholic of morally questionable standing due to his activities during the Nazi period. Incidentally, when Muench retired from the nunciature in

December 1959 and reported to Rome, Globke gave Muench a parting gift: a Mercedes Benz limousine. It arrived in Rome in March 1960.[34]

Bishop Wilhelm Berning of Osnabrück likened the devastation in Germany to the destruction of Jerusalem (70 c.e.) in a 1947 pastoral letter that blasted the idea of collective guilt: "Are the entire German people responsible for the suffering that has come upon Germany? No. The entire German people are not guilty for the crimes against humanity, nor for the war crimes committed by a few."[35] Bishop Michael Buchberger of Regensburg commented indirectly on guilt when he bemoaned the fate of Germans interned in POW camps. He told Muench, "some of these SS men earned harsh punishment, but there are many internees who did not invite punishment upon themselves and became SS members automatically. Their lot reminds one of the notorious concentration camps," echoing the arguments of *One World*.

Buchberger made the erroneous assumption that faithful Catholics could not be Nazis. "One thousand men took part in Christmas mass, and more would have done so, but there was no more room. Nearly 400 took communion. These are not criminals!"[36] His sympathy for Germans also extended to Jews who, whether German or not, had converted to Catholicism. In 1948, Buchberger wrote Muench on behalf of a man named Widmansky, a Pole who had converted to Catholicism after the war. Widmansky "suffered greatly" due to his now-renounced Judaism, said Buchberger, describing him as "very worthy" of any help Muench could extend him. Buchberger wanted to facilitate Widmansky's emigration. Muench, responding in his typical way to any requests for help on behalf of Jews (in this case, one who had converted to Catholicism), told Buchberger the Vatican Migration Bureau in Geneva would likely be a dead end, this despite having referred hundreds of other Catholics to the bureau. Instead, he told Buchberger to contact the umbrella International Refugee Organization (successor to the UNRRA), which prepared Jewish (and other) displaced persons for emigration.[37] Muench's response indicated that he preferred Widmansky to rely on International Refugee Organization funds (aimed at Jews and other groups) rather than Vatican funds (aimed at Catholics).

The examples of Gröber, Frings, Berning, and Buchberger demonstrate the complex mixture of antipathy toward Nazism, concrete efforts or statements on behalf of former Jews who had converted to Catholicism, and denial of Catholic participation in what proved to be murderous anti-Semitism. Other German bishops were less conflicted. Bishop Albert Stohr of Mainz belittled Catholics like Eugen Kogon, who had been sent to Buchenwald for anti-Nazi activities. Kogon (1903–87), originally from Munich, was a Catholic journalist and political scientist who penned critical commentary on Nazi policy from the safety of Vienna until his arrest after the *Anschluss* in 1938. From 1939 to 1943, he survived hard labor in Buchenwald, and from 1943 until April 1945, he worked as a medical clerk in the Buchenwald "infirmary." Kogon survived by working with German Communists, who smuggled him out of Buchenwald on 12 April before the Gestapo could carry out plans to murder him. In 1946, Kogon wrote a report for Supreme Headquarters, Allied Expeditionary Forces that became the book entitled *Der SS Staat: Das System der deutschen Konzentrationslager.* This book was the first comprehensive description of the Nazi concentration camp system. In 1950, Kogon's book was translated into English as *The Theory and Practice of Hell: The German Concentration Camps and the System behind Them.*[38] Kogon was an important postwar Catholic for his contributions to the leftist and intellectual Catholic monthly *Frankfurter Hefte*, which he founded in 1946 with Walter Dirks. Kogon remained one of several regular *Hefte* contributors commenting critically on Nazism, racist ideology, and the murder of European Jewry.

Stohr dismissed Kogon and his *Hefte* publications. In the previously described 1947 interview, the bishop told Richard Akselrad that he "knew [Kogon] personally very well and valued him highly as a courageous and true Catholic." But, added Stohr, he "had the impression that [Kogon's *Hefte*] article [for July 1947] was the expression of a concentration camp psychosis, which had not remained without influence even on such a sharp and analytic mind as Dr. Kogon's." Stohr referred to Kogon's editorial, "Kirchliche Kundgebungen von politischer Bedeutung," which argued that German church leaders had failed to protest Nazism decisively and thus lost the moral authority to protest against present "human rights violations" such as the fate of ethnic Germans under the Potsdam accords.[39] Stohr repeated to Akselrad what became typical arguments absolving Germans for Holocaust guilt: A "numerically small group" committed "atrocities," not Germans at large. Germans did not speak up because they would lose their lives if they did so. "One cannot expect the German people as a whole to have acted like death-defying heroes, of whom there are only very few within any people," Stohr told Akselrad. Like Muench in *One World*, Stohr then mentioned Jews specifically, but to defend Germans: "one of the most flagrant violations of the law committed by National Socialism was the proclamation of collective guilt of the Jews. Only because of race, the Jewish people were exterminated down to the youngest child. This ideology, which seemed to have been buried with the defeat of National Socialism, is now dangerously revived through the thesis of the collective guilt of the German people. Without distinction each German is declared guilty and responsible only because he is German.[40]

In a 1947 pastoral letter, archbishop of Paderborn Lorenz Jäger affirmed, "we [Germans] reject collective guilt."[41] Jäger told Akselrad that public castigation of Nazism would only feed its appetite for atrocities. He recognized Nazism as a competitor for the German soul, suggesting less noble motives for silence on his and other bishops' parts. "Many members of our church who had been blinded and misled by deceitful propaganda would have been driven into the arms of National Socialism all the more by too sharp a language [on our part]."[42] Evidently, enough "blinded and misled" German Catholics existed to cause Jäger serious concern. Jäger essentially said the Church willingly sacrificed the interests of Nazism's victims (especially Jewish Germans) in order to win the perceived popularity contest between Catholics and Nazis.

As a group, German Catholic bishops took a stance against collective guilt and responsibility. Their public statements along these lines are clear. The opinions of German Catholic clerics and laypersons are more challenging to determine. Available sources indicate that by and large, they rejected guilt in emphatic fashion. OMGUS interviewer Morris Janowitz found "an almost universal tendency" among Germans "to lay responsibility upon the Nazi party or the SS."[43] Dr. Otto Hipp, a Catholic member of the postwar Christian Social Union (CSU) political party and prominent politician, wrote much the same to Cardinal Faulhaber: "the basic cause for all the burdens and strains are due to the criminal and irrational Hitler and the National Socialists."[44] Hipp did not acknowledge the millions of Germans who were members of the National Socialist party. At the time of Adolf Hitler's appointment as chancellor in January 1933, roughly 1 million Germans were members of the Nazi party. By 1935, this number rose to 2.5 million, and, by 1945, to 8.5 million.[45] A small clique led the well-intentioned German people into great misery, August Hardick of Kirchen wrote to Muench.[46] In an OMGUS survey conducted in April 1946, 94 percent of German respondents agreed that those guilty of "war crimes" should stand trial. Only 30 percent saw the "German people" as a guilty party meriting punishment. Five years later, only 4 percent of Germans surveyed nationwide endorsed the proposition that "every individual German bears a certain guilt for Germans' actions during the Third Reich and everybody should acknowledge this guilt."[47]

Catholics used a variety of arguments to combat accusations of guilt for Nazism. In late 1947, Muench had a conversation with Monsignor Schwickert about Germans and Nazism. The monsignor told Muench that "Nazi ideas were still in the German people." He called Hitler's followers "bankrupt people, mostly militarists, businessmen or psychopaths, who had no sense of guilt."[48] In Catholic confessional booths, such Germans revealed "no consciousness of wrong," said Schwickert. But those that had what he called "religious pride" remained immune to Nazism.[49] Schwickert's argument equating "religious pride" with rejection of Nazism is questionable. Due to traditional loyalties to the Catholic Center party prior to its dissolution in 1933, as a rule Catholic support for Nazism was weaker than Protestant in the years leading up to 1933.[50] But its weakness relative to Protestantism did not exclude the possibility of Catholic electoral support for Nazism. Oded Heilbronner has examined the expansion of national socialism in the predominantly Catholic Black Forest–Baar region of southern Baden. As early as 1930, the Nazis won above-average votes and significant support in a number of Catholic communities in the region, belying the long-held notion that Catholic electoral support for Nazism was nonexistent.[51] In his quantitative study of 1,581 men and women involved in Nazi genocide, Michael Mann concludes that among Holocaust perpetrators, a majority came from Catholic regions.[52] Aleksander Lasik's study of Auschwitz SS men and women showed Catholics as more likely to become perpetrators than were their Protestant counterparts. Information about religious persuasion was available for 9 percent (roughly 630) of the 7,000 SS personnel under study. Of these 630, a total of 237 (nearly 40%) proclaimed themselves to be Catholic.[53]

Franz Burger of Munich put forth five commonly held beliefs about who was accountable for Nazism. The first was that "the non-German world met the pre-1933 German regime halfway and thus, through erroneous politics, favored developments toward Hitler." This was a common argument that blamed the post World War I diplomacy and the Treaty of Versailles for the rise of Nazism. Second, Burger pointed to "the pre-1933 political parties erroneously carried on a policy leading to mass unemployment and ever greater, more widespread misery." This argument blamed the ruling Weimar political parties for acquiescing in the economic stipulations of the Treaty of Versailles and for causing rising taxes, unstable currency, and unemployment. Third, Burger noted, "the Austrian bishops, through solemn demonstration, likewise supported Hitler's *Anschluss*." "We submit that all the above-mentioned circles, including those who voted for the law authorizing Hitler as the sole power in Germany, are likewise of the chief criminal group," argued Burger in his fourth point. He referred here to the Enabling Law of March 1933, which abolished the democratic Weimar constitution and formed a quasi-legal base for a dictatorship. In his final point, Burger reminded Muench that Paul von Hindenburg called Hitler to power. "Therefore all those who voted for Hindenburg should be punished," he wrote.[54] While Burger's arguments had undeniable merit (these factors indeed contributed to the rise of Nazism), they cannot fully explain widespread German acquiescence and cooperation in the face of Nazism, including its anti-Jewish measures.[55]

Catholics who wrote to Muench also denied the validity of German guilt and responsibility by focusing on what they considered to be similarities between Nazism and post-1945 Allied occupation policies. One curate complained of "countless house searches, days-long interrogations, and the bitter taste of exile . . . the same as experienced under the Nazis."[56] Georg Kretschner of Baden-Baden told Muench, "today's world is outraged by those war criminals who committed bestial atrocities [and were] executed by hanging [at Nuremberg]. And yet, the same world remains silent when 200,000 German brothers and sisters in the occupied territory [of] Poland—annexed by the Polish State—are forced into slavery and separated from their families in Germany."[57] Expelled westward due to the Potsdam accords, Kretschner was originally from Breslau. As demonstrated by their reaction to *One World*, many ethnic Germans believed themselves to be as much victims as those who perished at the hands of the Nazis.

Germans accused American occupation officials of focusing on the "little fish" while the "great criminals" of Nazism escaped punishment. Munich politician Dr. Otto Hipp wrote in a letter to Cardinal Faulhaber, "the main criminals (*Hauptschuldige*) and their followers are increasingly forgotten . . . singular personalities and institutions [place] blame for widespread poverty and oppression on those who have not earned it."[58] Wilhelm Zimmermann of Karlsruhe expressed his opinion that "Little Nazis were hung while the Big Nazis were allowed to escape." Zimmermann waited three years before his *Spruchkammer* decision (classifying him as a *Mitläufer*) was handed down, meaning gainful employment was delayed for these three years.[59]

Some Catholics at least acknowledged the wrongful war but still eschewed collective guilt. Catholic canon and *Caritas* employee Felise Book of Borken told Muench that she realized Germans "lost the war because we were arrogant and wanted to occupy the entire world. But a great percentage of the German people are as humble as you yourself, and we must suffer all the consequences."[60] When Heinz Krämer of Rüsselheim wrote to Lucius Clay in Berlin, he admitted it was "true that this nation was abused by irresponsible subjects . . . Germany's own criminal government . . . to bring disaster to mankind." But Krämer continued, "this does not change the fact, however, that the Germans too had to suffer immensely, and faced heaviest mental depression. [And our] situation is not eased by the "hunger cure" lasting over two years now."[61] Josefa Reiter of Bad Tolz agreed. "No one loathes the crimes of our former *Führer* more than we Germans. But the picture of justice and humanity painted by the Allies has not materialized," said Reiter.[62]

Still others fell back on the argument that some Germans "just followed orders." Dr. Leisler Kiep of Kronberg, a former admiral in the German navy, disagreed with the conviction of thirteen I.G. Farben employees as "war criminals" by United States Military Court IV in Nuremberg (Case Six). Leisler Kiep, brother to Otto Karl Kiep and married to Eugenie (von Rath) Kiep, ran in the highest circles.[63] Leisler Kiep was on the board of directors at I.G. Farben.[64] After its liquidation in 1950, he was affiliated with one of its largest successor companies, Höchst.[65] Kiep's son married the daughter of Dr. Fritz Meer, a German chemist who was one of the thirteen men convicted at the 1948 I.G. Farben trial. Kiep wrote frequent correspondent Muench that he was "the last person in the world to condone the sins and crimes committed under the Nazi regime." But, wrote Kiep, "these industrialists only did what they were obliged to do, as did their colleagues in other countries, under the orders of their governments. . . .

This seems to me to be a question of clemency and that certainly pertains to the Church."[66]

A number of German Catholics told Muench that their own priests advised them to join the Nazi party. Bishop Heinrich Wienken of Meissen told Muench some priests "thought they might influence trends, protect livelihoods and families, or channel the Nazi movement into right acts."[67] August Unseld, *Ortsleiter* of Achsteffen was one example. In 1937, Unseld decided to resign as *Ortsleiter*. The local pastor, Father Strahl, visited Unseld in his home and begged him not to resign. Otherwise, worried Strahl, an "unjust and radical man could get [the position]."[68] Wienken claimed other priests "feared concentration camps, [were] natural leaders for [presumably anti-Nazi] political activity, or feared communism." Generally speaking, Wienken told Muench, Catholic priests knew that "speaking [up against the regime] was not desired."[69] Whether Wienken meant that speaking up was "not desired" by the Holy See, by his superiors in the German hierarchy, or by the Nazi regime itself is unclear.

German Catholics viewed Muench as a trustworthy figure and knew of his pro-German, anti-guilt, and anti-responsibility views; hence they opened up to him in a way that they would not to occupation officials or even, in some cases, their own friends and families. *One World* confirmed and articulated publicly what most writing to him already believed privately, and the pastoral letter's popularity indicates that its message was broadly accepted. German bishops' pastoral letters as well as personal letters to Muench from clerics and lay Catholics reflected intense discussion about guilt and responsibility and, in particular, collective guilt and collective responsibility on public and grassroots levels.[70] Bishop Muench was a vibrant part of this discussion and an important catalyst for it. The correspondence indicates that German Catholic public and private memory at all levels reflected a rejection of their role in Nazism's success. It also demonstrates the German Catholic perception that only a few Germans really believed in Nazi ideology and even fewer participated in Nazi so-called "excesses."

4

Granting Absolution

Muench and the Catholic Clemency Campaign

uring the first weeks of December 1948, Muench met with Vatican nuncio to the United States, Amleto Cicognani, in Washington, D.C., to discuss Germans indicted and convicted for war crimes by Allied courts in occupied Germany and now incarcerated in Landsberg and Spandau prisons. Monsignor Giovanni Battista Montini—undersecretary of state, future pope, one of Pope Pius XII's closest confidants[1]—had requested that Cicognani approach Washington officials on behalf of convicted German war criminals sentenced to imprisonment or death. Cicognani in turn requested a meeting with Muench, who was visiting the United States on furlough from his post as relief officer for the Vatican mission in Kronberg and liaison representative between American occupation officials and the German Catholic Church.

After a discussion with Cicognani on 6 December, Muench "wrote a memorandum on the Landsberg cases" for the nuncio, dated 7 December.[2] On 14 December, Cicognani submitted the following petition "at the urgent request of the Holy See": "The Holy See . . . presents . . . a plea for mercy on behalf of German nationals condemned to death as war criminals by the military tribunals in Germany. Without any violation of justice, it is hoped that [occupation authorities will] commute the existing death sentences into other penalties at least in those cases where there is even a slight doubt of guilt or where mitigating circumstances may be found. The Holy See is encouraged to present this plea in recalling that during the major trial before the International Military Tribunal at Nuremberg, the American prosecutor at no time asked for the death penalty."[3] It is unclear to what degree Muench himself was responsible for this wording. There is little wonder that Muench kept his own name off of Cicognani's petition. In his capacity as liaison representative between the American military government and the German Catholic Church between 1946 and 1949, he was not to intervene in matters beyond the "spiritual." In his capacity as Vatican head of the Kronberg mission, he was to facilitate relief for displaced persons and prisoners of war, not clemency for convicted war criminals.

The summer and early fall of 1949 marked the end of military occupation in the French, British, and American zones of Germany and marked also two important changes in Muench's status. First, the position of liaison representative between American occupation authorities and the German churches ceased to exist. Second, and in accordance with the Federal Republic's new status as a recognized but still not fully autonomous nation, Pope Pius XII named Muench apostolic regent to Germany in October 1949. In short, Muench ceased having any obligations to American authorities, while his Vatican duties became increasingly formalized.

In February 1950 Pope Pius XII instructed Muench to write a letter supporting clemency for convicted German war criminals to General Thomas Handy, who, as head of the U.S. Army European Command, had the final say with respect to clemency decisions. Now papal regent, Muench could openly speak as a representative of the pope. "In the spirit of centuries-old traditions, the Church seeks to have justice tempered with mercy, and in accord with the time-honored prerogative of the Church to intercede for even the worst of criminals, Pope Pius XII respectfully requests that clemency be shown if and to whatever extent the circumstances may so warrant."[4] The Vatican involved itself in clemency efforts for convicted German war criminals, most especially Catholic ones, and Muench played a critical role in these efforts.

Significant grassroots support for the Church's clemency campaign existed among the broader German Catholic public. Let us take the example of support for SS-Obergruppenführer Oswald Pohl. Born in Duisburg, Pohl joined the Nazi party in 1926 and the SS in 1929. He became chief of administration at SS headquarters in February 1934, responsible for the armed SS units and the concentration camps. In June 1939, he also was made ministerial director in the Reich Interior Ministry. In this capacity, he focused his energies on cooperating with German industry to build SS economic enterprises.[5] In December 1942, his endeavors were merged into the Economic and Administrative Main Office of the SS (*Wirtschafts- und Verwaltungshauptamt*),[6] responsible for recruiting concentration camp inmates for forced labor units, and also responsible for selling Jewish possessions—jewelry, gold fillings, hair, and clothing—to provide funds to Nazi Germany. On 3 November 1947, in the "U.S. versus Oswald Pohl et al." (Nuremberg successor trial case four), Pohl was sentenced to death.

Emil Vogt of Sannerz informed American officials "he was personally acquainted with Pohl, and considered the accused a just and steadfast man, helpful and good, and not guilty of the crimes charged against him." Georg Hechler of Reichenbach-in-der-Odenwald met Oswald Pohl in 1943. Hechler argued that Pohl "treated concentration camp prisoners from Dachau and Ravensbrück now working on a Bavarian farm with kind consideration." Hechler thus "concluded that Pohl was a humane and just person, not a criminal." Herr von Brincken of Ruppersdorf "explained that Pohl was not responsible for atrocities committed against concentration camp prisoners. Further, it was inhuman to carry out death sentences three years after the sentence had been passed."[7] These are but three examples among hundreds concerning Pohl specifically. During his three-year confinement, Pohl converted to Catholicism. This conversion did not prevent his execution by hanging on 8 June 1951.[8]

Endeavors on behalf of Pohl fit into a pattern of enormous popular support for clemency for convicted German war criminals.[9] Catholic clemency efforts can be traced back to an address sharply attacking the International Military Tribunal at Nuremberg published by Bishop Clemens August Graf von Galen in early 1946. *Rechtsbewusstsein und Rechtsunsicherheit* (roughly translated as "legal certainty and uncertainty"), published in Rome in March 1946, called the International Military Tribunal and its successor trials in Nuremberg "show trials" that were "not about justice, but about the defamation of the German people." Von Galen even claimed that accused war criminals endured

conditions worse than those suffered by inmates of former Nazi concentration camps in the east.[10]

Rechtsbewusstsein und Rechtsunsicherheit marked the beginning of
a long and relatively successful campaign by German bishops (both
Catholic and Protestant)[11] to free imprisoned criminals and have death
sentences commuted to incarceration.[12] The Catholic clemency campaign played out on all levels, receiving support from Rome, the German
bishops, German priests and nuns, and lay Catholics. Telling is the support a group of Berlin nuns showed to SS-Gruppenführer Dr. Karl
Brandt, who became Hitler's attending physician in 1934. In 1942, Hitler
appointed him general commissar for sanitation and health, with control
over all military and civilian medical institutions.

Brandt was instrumental in the very first instance of murder in what
would become the euthanasia program. In 1938, the Knauer family
appealed to Hitler through his private chancellery (*Kanzlei des Führers,*
KdF), headed by Philipp Bouhler, regarding their severely handicapped
infant. Apparently the child was born with "a leg and part of an arm
missing," and was also possibly blind.[13] Hitler instructed Brandt to
"visit the Knauer infant, consult with Leipzig physicians, and kill the
child if his diagnosis agreed with the conditions outlined in the
[Knauer's] appeal." Brandt "consulted with the attending physicians,
confirmed the diagnosis, and authorized euthanasia; the baby was
killed." After this act, Hitler authorized Brandt and Bouhler to institute
a program "of killing children suffering from physical or mental
defects."[14] An army court tried Brandt in Nuremberg successor trial case
one, "the U.S. versus Karl Brandt et al.," the so-called Doctors' Trial.
Indicted and convicted for "carrying out cruel medical experiments . . .
on concentration camp inmates, prisoners of war," and others unable to
defend themselves, and for his role in the Nazi euthanasia program,
Brandt was executed at Landsberg prison on 2 June 1948.[15]

Several mother superiors and priests praised Brandt when solicited
by his attorney, German jurist Dr. Robert Servatius of Cologne.[16] Sister
Peregrina Recknagel, mother superior to the nuns of the Franciscus
Hospital in Berlin-Berchtesgaden, described Brandt as "gentle in his
behavior." Brandt, one of three head doctors at the hospital, had "an
excellent understanding with the sisters," claimed Sister Recknagel.[17] On
8 December 1946, Servatius wrote to Sister Potamiena, superior general
of the Sisters of Charity of Saint Vincent de Paul, an order of nuns who

ran a surgical hospital in Munich. Sister Potamiena had passed away, so Sister M. Castella Blöckl, the new superior general, replied to Servatius's letter. "I know, however, that she could refer to Dr. Brandt as throughout a high-minded person in his behavior towards herself and towards the sisters. He even mentioned that he would put in a decisive word so that the nuns could stay in the hospitals in Munich. In this regard there exsisted actually great danger . . . I myself do not know Herr Brandt nor had I never to do with him."[18]

Sister M. Sebalda, mother superior of the Franciscan Nursing Sisters of the district hospital in Berchtesgaden, "saw a picture of Herr Professor Dr. med. Karl Brandt in the local paper (the *Südostkurier*) and read an article regarding his imminent condemnation in Nuremberg." She told her fellow nuns, "if I could be of help to this man, I should do so gladly, for we are very much obliged to him." She referred to the fact that "we sisters were always of the opinion that this man thoughtlessly got himself into a trap from which he could not free himself. . . . Whether Herr Professor Brandt was otherwise politically active I do not know, but do not believe so."[19] Servatius got several other similar supportive responses from priests and nuns who worked with Brandt at various clinics and hospitals.[20]

A brief background on war crimes trials in the first decade after the war and the nearly simultaneous campaign for clemency is instructive for an understanding of Muench's role in this complex arena. Joint Chiefs of Staff (JCS) Directive 1023/10 (July 1945) authorized the commanders-in-chief of the Allied occupation forces to establish military courts to conduct war crimes trials.[21] The U.S. Army tried 1,672 defendants in 489 proceedings conducted before U.S. Army courts between summer 1945 and 31 December 1947.[22] Initially, the trials took place in Darmstadt, Ludwigsburg, and the Munich suburb of Dachau (the site of the first Nazi concentration camp). In October 1946, these separate jurisdictions were eliminated and the Army's war crimes operations combined at Dachau (thus earning their nickname, the "Dachau Trials").[23] Responsibility to prosecute war criminals was assigned to the deputy judge advocate for war crimes in the European theater. Ultimately, the Dachau Trials resulted in 1,416 convictions and 426 death sentences (of which 268 were executed).[24]

In addition to (and separate from) the series of Army trials was the International Military Tribunal (IMT) in Nuremberg, created in August

1945 and consisting of the United States, Great Britain, France, and the Soviet Union. The IMT indicted twenty-four of the highest-ranking Third Reich leaders still alive, and ultimately tried twenty-two of the twenty-four select political leaders, *Schutzstaffel* (SS) officers,[25] policemen, judges, medical doctors, industrialists, economists, and *Wehrmacht* (army) officers. The IMT charges against these defendants included crimes against peace, war crimes, crimes against humanity, and membership in criminal organizations.

Originally, the Allies intended to conduct further trials through the IMT, but this did not come to pass. Allied Control Council Law Number Ten (dated 20 December 1945) authorized zonal officials to establish "appropriate courts" for passing judgment on war criminals within each of the four occupation zones (American, British, French, and Soviet). In the American zone, the military government conducted twelve further trials in the city of Nuremberg. These trials took place between December 1946 and April 1949 and indicted a total of 185 persons, of whom 177 were actually tried.[26] Taken together, Americans tried a total of 1,871 war criminals in the Dachau Trials, the IMT (in cooperation with the Allies), and the successor trials also held in Nuremberg.

Then came a series of amnesties, which correlated directly to the growing U.S. conflict with the Soviet Union. The Cold War soon eclipsed memory of German atrocities. Since the Dachau Trials were under the jurisdiction of the U.S. Army, and hence the commander of U.S. forces in Europe retained control over these cases, between late 1945 and early 1951 clemency petitions and requests for review in the U.S. Army trials were directed to modification and parole boards under the War Crimes Branch and Theater Judge Advocate Division. The U.S. Army commander in Germany had final say in all such cases.[27]

Growing criticism of the Dachau Trial program, manifested in the Senate subcommittee chaired by Homer Ferguson (R-Michigan), instigated Army Secretary Kenneth C. Royall to name a three-person commission in July 1948. Named for Judge Gordon Simpson, the commission was to investigate and review the 139 death sentences still in force against Dachau defendants. The commission submitted its final report to the secretary of the Army on 14 September 1948.[28] At the recommendation of the Simpson Commission, General Thomas Handy established the War Crimes Modification Board on 28 November 1949. It reviewed 512 individual cases between November 1949 and October 1951, recommending sentence reductions in 370 (72%), including 150 to time served. General Handy and his successor, General Manton S. Eddy, approved two-thirds of these recommendations. Pretrial confinement was counted as time served, further reducing the sentences of many prisoners.[29]

The WCMB handled only the U.S. Army trials.[30] In March 1950, American zone High Commissioner John J. McCloy created the Advisory Board on Clemency for War Criminals to process those clemency petitions from the International Military Tribunal and the Nuremberg successor trials. The "Peck Panel" consisted of presiding justice of the New York State Appeals Court, David Peck; chairman of the New York Board of Parole, Frederick A. Moran; and legal advisor to the U.S. Department of State, Brigadier General Conrad E. Snow. Examining the cases of all 104 Nuremberg successor trial defendants still in Landsberg prison at the time, the Peck Panel began to conduct hearings in Munich on 11 July 1950.[31] Giving McCloy its report on the 104 defendants in late August 1950, the Peck Panel functioned as both a clemency board and an appeals court with the power to change previous juridical decisions. It recommended sentence reductions in 83 percent of the reviewed cases (77 of 93), and urged McCloy to commute seven of the remaining fifteen death sentences.[32]

On 31 January 1951, in a publication titled *Landsberg: A Documentary Report*, McCloy announced his final decision regarding clemency for prisoners sentenced at the twelve successor trials. McCloy affirmed five (of fifteen) pending death sentences, allowing those of Oswald Pohl and *Einsatzgruppen* officers Blobel, Braune, Naumann, and Ohlendorf to stand. It should be noted that he modified the punishment of the remaining defendants in the SS Economic and Administrative Main Office and *Einsatzgruppen* cases.[33] He reduced the sentences of seventy-nine inmates, and allowed for the immediate release of thirty-two prisoners.[34] Frank M. Buscher's examination of the McCloy papers shows that McCloy modified the sentences of all Krupp trial defendants to time served. Further, McCloy granted clemency to all those convicted in the ministries (*U.S. v. von Weizsäcker et al.*), Medical (*U.S. v. Brandt et al.*), Milch (*U.S. v. Milch*), and Race and Settlement Main Office (*U.S. v. Greifelt et al.*) cases. McCloy refused to reduce five sentences in the High Command (*U.S. v. von Leeb et al.*) and Hostages (*U.S. v. List et al.*) cases.

Following the 31 January 1951 sentence commutations, the U.S. war crimes program underwent massive change, due largely to political considerations. The Korean War, the intensifying Cold War, and the decision to secure the Federal Republic as part of the West's defense forces meant ending Allied war crimes programs as quickly as possible.[35] By August 1952, 338 prisoners who had been convicted in one of the Nuremberg successor trials or Dachau trials remained in Landsberg prison, a fortress in the Upper Bavarian city of Landsberg-am-Lech that American authorities also used as an execution site.[36] On 31 August 1953, U.S. High Commissioner James B. Conant and USAREUR Commander General Charles L. Bolte established the Interim Mixed Parole and Clemency Board, consisting of three Americans and two Germans, to handle future clemency cases. The British and French created their own zonal commissions. Unlike previous commissions, the board could grant clemency or parole, but did not have the right to "question the validity of the verdict and punishment." Its decisions did not have to be unanimous to be considered binding to U.S. officials. Both the prisoners and their attorneys could apply for a review. During the board's first year of operation, it released 60 percent of the Landsberg prisoners, reducing the population from 288 to 112.

On 15 June 1955, after the Federal Republic joined the North Atlantic Treaty Organization and gained full sovereignty (May 1955), the Interim Board was made permanent.[37] The Mixed Parole and Clemency Board accepted applications not only from prisoners and their attorneys, but also from the West German and Allied governments. It functioned from 11 August 1955 until 9 May 1958, staffed by three Germans, an American, a Frenchman, and an Englishman. In May 1958, the last four Landsberg prisoners were freed.[38]

In the privacy of his diary, Muench defined war criminals as persons participating in medical experiments or other brutal acts carried out at concentration camps, or those who became involved in "deportation of people for slave labor." But all other sentences given to those who didn't fit into these categories were "questionable."[39] During a private meeting with McCloy in November 1950, Muench discussed the fact that "some were up to their elbows in blood." He thought the press should "give facts to the public [to] answer sentimental objections." The SS cases were especially bad, Muench noted. The bottom line came to this: "some [were] gangster types [while] others deserved clemency."[40] These words showed his differentiation between those accused war criminals who personally carried out killing and those who passed along orders for killing.

Whatever his feelings might have been about such men, Muench was willing to consider cases of accused war criminals who initiated killing themselves and to transmit clemency documentation on their behalf to high-ranking American authorities. A case in point is that of Hans Eisele. Eisele was born in Donauschingen (Baden) on 13 March 1912. A Catholic, Eisele joined the NSDAP in May 1933 and the SS in November 1933. He was twenty-one years old at the time.[41] He later became a physician, and during the war, he worked (as a camp physician) in four concentration camps: Mauthausen (1940), Buchenwald (1941–42), Natzweiler (1942), and Dachau.[42] (Eisele acknowledged serving as camp physician in Buchenwald, Natzweiler, and Dachau.)[43] A report compiled by former Buchenwald inmates for U.S. Army intelligence indicated that Eisele was one of the "worst" camp doctors."[44]

According to former inmates, Eisele conducted experimental vivisection (surgery on living human beings for purposes of scientific research) on Dutch Jews transported to Buchenwald in February 1941. During the summer of 1941, he murdered almost 300 tuberculosis patients by injections of evipan sodium (either intravenously or directly into the heart) in order to reduce the number of patients in his infirmary.[45] The U.S. Army's Judge Advocate Division tried Eisele in the Buchenwald camp guard trial (one of the Dachau trials), found him guilty, and sentenced him to be hanged on 28 June 1948.

At least twenty-six Germans (family members, Catholics who had known Eisele in his youth, and Catholic concentration camp inmates whom Eisele helped) wrote to the War Crimes Modification board on his behalf. Among them were Heinrich Auer, director of the *Caritas* central library in Freiburg; Dr. Michael Höck, director of the Freising priests' seminar; Corbinian Hofmeister, abbot of Metten; Herr Carls, director of *Caritas* in Wuppertal; and Father Wessel of Weimar. All were former Buchenwald inmates.[46] Iconic figures like Protestant Pastor Martin Niemöller and Catholic Auxiliary Bishop Johannes Neuhäusler, also former Buchenwald prisoners, reported that Eisele treated them well. Other Germans appealed directly to Muench for help, including Elisabeth Bronberger of Munich. On 28 November 1947, she visited the Kronberg mission to plead on behalf of Eisele. She brought with her documentation that she believed would "convince" Muench of Eisele's "innocence" (*Unschuld*).[47] Three days earlier, on 25 November, she had written to a Colonel Dwinell at U.S. Army headquarters in Frankfurt, to whom she had apparently pleaded Eisele's case in the past. "I take the liberty, dear sir, to enclose a picture of [Eisele's] three children."[48] Acting in his capacity as liaison representative to the army (violating his role, which was to remain neutral), Muench provided information and documentation about the Eisele case to the Army's War Crimes Modification Board. In early June 1948, upon the urging of Heinrich Auer, Muench directly approached General Lucius Clay and requested the stay of Eisele's execution. Clay complied. A year later, the War Crimes Modification Board reduced Eisele's sentence to life imprisonment, then to ten years, and later remitted it completely on 19 February 1952. Eisele died a free man in 1967.[49]

Muench was approached in many other individual clemency cases. For example, auxiliary bishop of Munich Johannes Neuhäusler, the most active of all German Catholic prelates in his efforts to commute the sentences of German war criminals, enlisted—and received—Muench's help. Neuhäusler led the efforts of the Church Committee for Prisoners' Aid (*Komitee für kirchliche Gefangenenhilfe,* hereafter KKGH), whose mandate it was to assist Landsberg war criminals. He retained German jurist Dr. Rudolf Aschenauer to advocate on their behalf.[50] A young and ambitious lawyer from Munich, Aschenauer was a former Nazi party member, a devout Catholic, and Neuhäusler's close friend. He helped establish the KKGH, which was financed by Protestant and Catholic churches. Aschenauer and Georg Fröschmann acted as its principal attorneys. They officially began their work in May 1949, offering their services to Landsberg clients free of charge (all legal expenses were covered by the KKGH). At the behest of Neuhäusler, Aschenauer represented at least 102 Catholic war criminals convicted in a "Dachau" case.[51]

In a letter to five U.S. congressmen in March 1948, Neuhäusler stated his position on clemency in writing: "I had the impression that, generally speaking, the Nuremberg proceedings were justified, as they concerned those persons chiefly responsible. But there was great anxiety about the Dachau [trials], above all because some former concentration camp inmates appeared as 'professional witnesses,' housed, fed, clothed and so on for more than a year in the Dachau internment camp. In return they made statements at various trials that were strictly rejected by the defendants. But these were given credence and thus many death sentences resulted, the legality of which is very much questioned."[52] Neuhäusler alleged that no fewer than fifty-eight "professional witnesses" testified for the prosecution in the various Dachau trials against

concentration camp guards. Neuhäusler attached biographies of fourteen of these witnesses, who were variously alleged to be communists,
socialists, Jews, homosexuals, criminals, or some combination thereof,
and all of whom he called dishonest and untrustworthy.[53]

In November 1948, Muench described to Neuhäusler a recent conversation with an unnamed German priest: "in good Catholic circles,
voices critiquing the Catholic bishops for intervention on behalf of vul-
gar and cruel criminals are loud," the priest told Muench. Disturbed,
Muench wrote to Neuhäusler: "Have such comments gotten through
to you?" He then vented his own feelings on the matter. "Whatever
the many voices might be saying, one voice must be heard. That is the
voice of justice, so that the people's sense of justice is not dragged into
the grave with the executed [men] of Landsberg." This comment implies that Muench did not relay the priest's story about "critiquing
Catholics" to warn or reprimand Neuhäusler, but to ascertain the ve-
racity of rumored "voices critiquing Catholic bishops." Muench finished the exchange by thanking Neuhäusler for his "endeavors on behalf
of suffering people who approached [the auxiliary bishop] day and
night."[54]

In a letter dated 23 April 1949, Muench "confidentially" (*vertrau-
lich*) recommended that Neuhäusler "immediately" forward new material on "events in Landsberg" to "Senator Joseph McCarthy, Senate Office,
Washington, D.C." "Perhaps you could give him a short report concerning the happenings regarding the wreaths and crosses in the cemetery.
Senator McCarthy is a good Catholic and an outspoken opponent
regarding what happened in the course of the Landsberg trials," Muench
wrote.[55]

Earlier, Muench wrote to Father James Nellen recommending that
American GI Edward Siewert turn to Senator McCarthy for help getting
his German bride, Anneliese Schmidt, clearance for emigration to the
United States. "Mr. Siewert might have [his pastor] Monsignor Clark
write Senator McCarthy with the request that he use his influence at the
State Department to change the drastic regulations affecting a good
Catholic woman who because of circumstances had to join the Nazi
Party."[56] Even by mid-1954, when Senator McCarthy's practices had
attracted wide censure, Muench wrote to his sister Terry, "The
McCarthy affair has been causing quite a stir. There is no question that
he has done a lot of good in ferreting out the commies, the pinks, and
leftists, and intellectuals do not like it."[57]

Cardinal Josef Frings of Cologne, the other leading figure in the Catholic crusade on behalf of German war criminals, turned to Muench for help on behalf of one General Field Marshal List. In September 1947, he wrote to Muench regarding the so-called Hostage Trial, or Nuremberg trial (Case Seven), *U.S. v. Field Marshall Wilhelm List et al.* Defendants were charged with "the commission of war crimes and crimes against humanity . . . includ[ing] murder, ill-treatment, and deportation to slave labor of prisoners of war and other members of the armed forces of nations at war with Germany, and of civilian populations of territories occupied by the German armed forces, plunder of public and private property, wanton destruction of cities, towns and villages, and other atrocities against civilian populations."[58] General Field Marshal Wilhelm Siegmund Walter List was deeply involved in Third Reich military campaigns. He led the Fourteenth Army during the campaign against Poland (1939–40); the Twelfth Army in the west (1941) as well as during the campaign against and occupation of Greece, and Army Group A on the eastern front (1942).[59]

As Supreme Commander Southeast,[60] it was necessary for his signature to be on execution orders in that arena, including "the murder of hundreds of thousands of persons from the civilian populations" of Greece, Yugoslavia, and Albania.[61] To cite one example, in mid-September 1941, List received and implemented the following order from the Wehrmacht High Command: "In order to stop these [Communist] intrigues at their inception, severest measures are to be applied immediately at their first appearance. . . . One must keep in mind that a human life practically counts for naught in the affected countries and a deterring effect can only be achieved by unusual severity. In such a case, the death penalty for 50 to 100 Communists must in general be deemed appropriate as retaliation for the life of a German soldier. The manner of execution must increase the deterrent effect."[62] Cardinal Frings described List in the following manner: "General Field Marshall List [is] 68 years old, a Protestant, and a man who broke with the "Führer" and left military service in 1942. He was found guilty of signing one order to shoot hostages in October 1941. It is unclear whether or not the order was carried out. Eight days later, surgeons removed the general's appendix. He himself does not remember signing the order and made no note of it in his diaries. We have reason to hope that a postponement of the verdict will bring a milder sentence. Right now, List is threatened with execution by the rope. Would it be possible for Your

Excellency to take some kind of action? You best hurry, for the jury has already been addressed."[63]

The prosecution counsel called List a soldier who "was making himself a party to the 'cultural' work of the Third Reich."[64] From mid-October 1941 until 7 July 1942, List took leave for medical reasons. In July 1942, List returned to active duty and took command of Army Group A in Russia, participating in the Caucasus offensive. He was removed from his post in September 1942 due to his open remarks on the overextension of Wehrmacht forces.[65] Originally sentenced to life in prison, List was released from Landsberg on 24 December 1952 on grounds of ill health. He died at the age of 92 in 1971. The Muench correspondence does not provide us with evidence of whether Muench was partially responsible for List's early release. Frings continued his efforts on behalf of Landsberg inmates in 1950, asking General Thomas T. Handy to "establish a clemency board [for the Dachau trials] like the one [High Commissioner Clay] created for the Nuremberg trials." Frings cited the reason for his request as the "many" petitions sent to the German episcopate from dependents of the accused.[66] In May 1951, Frings again requested that Landsberg death sentences be revoked, on the grounds that the men sentenced to execution "already suffered much from the anticipatory pangs of death."[67]

A consistent theme present in German Catholic bishops' discussions about war criminals was the loose definition of what constituted "criminal" activity. The case of SS-Oberführer (and Catholic) Viktor Brack provides a poignant example of some bishops' arbitrary definitions of who was a criminal. Brack became SS liaison to Philipp Bouhler, head of the Chancellery of the Führer, in 1936. As deputy to Bouhler, Brack helped run the Nazi euthanasia program (Office T4 in the Reich Chancellery) as well as later helped to establish the extermination camps in Poland via this Berlin office. On 20 August 1947, an army tribunal in Nuremberg sentenced Brack to death for these crimes. On 3 September 1947, Brack's lawyer, Dr. Georg Fröschmann, filed a petition requesting that his client's sentence be reduced to imprisonment. Little more than two weeks later, on 19 September, Bishop Heinrich Wienken petitioned American Military Governor Lucius Clay on Bracks' behalf. In his capacity as commissar of the Fulda Bishops' Conference, Wienken had this to say about Brack:

In 1940, Cardinal Adolf Bertram of Breslau, acting in the name
of the Fulda Bishops' Conference, presented the Reich Chancellery with a petition objecting to euthanasia. Dr. [Herbert] Linden,
representative of the Reich Ministry of Interior, invited me to discuss this petition with him, as I was the Commissar of the German Catholic bishops. Viktor Brack took part in this discussion in
his capacity as representative of Philipp Bouhler, head of the
Chancellery of the Führer. During the lengthy discussion that followed, [Linden and Brack] tried to change the Church's stance on
euthanasia by arguing its justifiability and importance. A second
discussion that was much like the first one followed, and the Church
refused to alter her position. These two discussions allowed me to
understand Brack's position on euthanasia. *I am convinced that
Brack's position is not based on a base or criminal cast of mind*
[emphasis mine]. Brack studied the subject in some detail and—
falsely—came to be convinced that euthanasia is ethical and just. His
studies, combined with the influence of Nazi ideology, led him to
forget God's law "thou shalt not kill."[68]

Wienken's petition went on to note that Brack received his orders from
Bouhler and Hitler, a fact that he hoped might help to mitigate Brack's
sentence. Finally, argued Wienken, Brack was a good husband and father
to six children, aged two to twelve. All were baptized Catholics. It
would be a shame for these well-raised Catholic children to be without
a father, argued Wienken. He included an affidavit from Brack's local
priest confirming the good behavior and piety of the Brack family, as
well as a charming picture of the Brack children.[69] Clay rejected the
arguments of Fröschmann and Wienken and declined to support the
3 September clemency petition.

On 24 September 1947, Brack's wife, Thea, wrote a desperate letter
to Muench, asking him to support a planned appeal to the U.S. Supreme
Court. "Whatever his failings, [my husband] did not have bad intentions."[70] Several months later, she wrote to Bishop Wienken: "reliable
sources tell me that several bishops with fundamental misgivings about
the continued enforcement of the death penalty . . . turn to Bishop
Muench, the apostolic vicar for Germany."[71] Muench's response to Thea
Brack remains unclear, but her letter showed that Catholics believed
they could count on Muench to pass on their petitions to American

authorities, and to press their case using what they perceived to be his personal influence. In fact, he did not always intervene.

Muench displayed caution in becoming involved with war crimes cases if Germans asked for Vatican intercession. Muench wished to protect the reputation of the Vatican and in such cases acted with caution. Illustrative was his reaction to Frau Berta Krupp von Bohlen und Halbach's request that the pope intervene in the case of her son, Alfried Krupp. On 31 July 1948, Nuremberg successor trial (Case Ten) sentenced Alfried to twelve years' imprisonment for his role as chairman of Krupp in producing armaments.[72] The trial implicated the industrialists involved in armaments production, crimes against humanity (via employment of alien workers and prisoners of war), and the plundering of economic assets from occupied countries.[73] In November 1948, Vatican Undersecretary of State Montini told Muench of Berta Krupp's request. Muench turned to U.S. political advisor Robert Murphy. "I have been asked . . . to bring the [Krupp] petition to the attention of General Clay. Personally, I have my doubts whether it would be wise to take this course. May I kindly have your advice as to what might be the best course to pursue? I know that we want to be fair even with the guilty and the condemned, and yet also give assurance to the world that we want to give justice its proper due."[74] In his reply, Murphy told Muench that the pope should defer his intervention in the Krupp case, as it was already under review for revision.[75] History would have it that the pope's intervention was not necessary. High Commissioner McCloy granted amnesty to Alfried Krupp on 31 May 1951. He reassumed his directorship of the Krupp firm in 1953 with the agreement that his company would not produce arms.[76]

Muench's decision not to support clemency appeals for SS-Gruppenführer Otto Ohlendorf, and his advice to Vatican officials to steer clear of the Ohlendorf campaign as well, is a second case in point. Ohlendorf was chief of *Einsatzgruppe* (Mobile Killing Squad) D, responsible for the murder of some 90,000 civilians, mostly Jews, on the Eastern Front. On 10 April 1948, Ohlendorf was sentenced to death in Nuremberg successor trial (Case Nine), *U.S. v. Otto Ohlendorf et al.*[77] One of Ohlendorf's champions was Princess Helene Elisabeth von Isenburg of Munich. Called "Mother Elizabeth" by the Landsberg prisoners, she was active in the Association for Truth and Justice (*Bund für Wahrheit und Gerechtigkeit*), understood by occupation officials to be an organization of so-called former Nazis.[78] In December 1950, she wrote to Muench that she avoided this particular case until receiving word from Ohlendorf himself. "As I got to know him, I was shocked to discover the false picture created by propaganda in this case." The princess determined that the U.S. Army did Ohlendorf "a great injustice." She sent her opinions to McCloy, his wife, Aschenauer, and Muench.[79] Muench replied to Isenburg in a letter dated 12 December 1950. He wrote her that "some among the condemned are heavily burdened. We must also reckon with another argument evident among the German people, namely, the accusation that yesterday the Small Nazis were heavily punished, while today the Big Nazis run free." Inferring from his letter that Muench might agree to help Ohlendorf, the princess showed Muench's response to Rudolf Aschenauer of the KKGH, who in turn wrote the papal regent himself, quoting the above passage from Muench's letter to the princess. On the basis of these words, Aschenauer pleaded the case to Muench: "I approach you concerning Otto Ohlendorf, whose public image has been falsified. I would be indebted to you if you could help . . . truth and enlightenment [win out] in the case."[80]

Ohlendorf had other clerical defenders who wrote to Muench for help. In January 1951, the exiled Sudeten German Augustinian priest Paulus Sladek wrote to Muench: "it strikes me that Ohlendorf is not guilty to such an extent that he deserves the death penalty. To my knowledge, Ohlendorf is one of very few clean characters in the corrupt National Socialist hierarchy, and earned the enmity of Himmler and Heydrich by fighting against injustice and violence. It is important to consider that Ohlendorf supported retention of Jewish legal status during the Third Reich. Ohlendorf was ordered to command an *Einsatzgruppe* in the Ukraine so that those in Berlin could be rid of him and burden his conscience. In the Ukraine, Ohlendorf tried to reduce the effects of the ghastly *Führerbefehl.* I enclose [Aschenauer's essay] describing Ohlendorf's endeavors in this regard."[81] Father Sladek continued with a petition that Muench pass his letter defending Ohlendorf to McCloy. "I hear that advocates of the Morganthau directives sit in [McCloy's] anteroom and make sure that no favorable evidence concerning Ohlendorf reaches the high commissioner." Sladek's phrase "advocates of the Morgenthau directives" was likely a code for Jews. Sladek hurried on to say that he "registered such rumors, but took no position on them." McCloy should certainly consider the mitigating circumstances of Ohlendorf's stint in the Ukraine, thought Sladek. Sladek had other worries, too. Further executions of the Landsberg criminals "could have dangerous psychological consequences for the German people, especially in nationalistic circles," he warned Muench. In considering clemency for the Landsberg criminals, Father Sladek believed "purely humanitarian motives should not be the decisive factor in this matter. The question of law and justice should be the single consideration." Sladek must have had a peculiar understanding of what he called "law and justice."[82] He apparently did not worry about the psychological consequences of clemency for the few surviving family members of—in Ohlendorf's case—90,000 murdered civilians.

Ten days after writing this letter to Muench, Father Sladek visited Ohlendorf in prison. The two men conversed for four hours. That day, Sladek sent McCloy the following telegram: "Repeated pastoral conversations with Ohlendorf in Landsberg [prison] lead me to the conviction that Ohlendorf is unjustly shown as the one mainly responsible for the mass murder of many thousands. He was involved by way of [enacting] military orders. One can cast serious doubts as to whether [Ohlendorf's case involves] personal guilt meriting execution." Along the lines of the popular "Germans just followed orders" argument, Sladek went on to challenge McCloy to prove "in what ways Ohlendorf was really active" in the murder process itself, and, further, to prove that Ohlendorf acted on his own initiative. For Sladek, organizing the act of murder did not merit guilt, only initiating the act of murder.

Sladek also begged McCloy to consider that Ohlendorf softened Hitler's order instituting the mass killings (or so Aschenauer claimed). "The personality of Ohlendorf, together with his remarks, have made a deep impression on me," Sladek told Muench. "It strikes me as crucial that accusations made against Ohlendorf hold true for thousands of soldiers and officers, who, against their personal will, were embroiled in Hitler's orders to conduct mass murder," meaning those soldiers who actually performed the killing. In a backhanded manner, Sladek here acknowledged a crucial point—that Hitler could only achieve the murder of at least six million European Jews with the active cooperation of thousands of Germans. In the abstract, Sladek could grasp this: "One cannot understand why such soldiers and officers do not have to answer for themselves, or [why they] do not face the death penalty." But when faced with the concrete, Sladek abandoned the idea of German "soldiers and officers answering for themselves." "So Ohlendorf is judged as a symbol for these horrible crimes. He does not symbolize personal guilt."[83] Sladek argued that Ohlendorf did not kill anyone himself, but passed on orders to kill given to him from his own superiors, a fact that alleviated his "guilt."

Muench declined to respond personally to Sladek's letter of 19 January. On 23 January 1951, Muench's secretary Robert Deubel informed Sladek that the papal regent "regretted to say he could do nothing more for the Landsberg prisoners, though, up to this point, [Muench] never shied away from trying to help them."[84] On 31 January 1951, McCloy issued his far-reaching commutation for Landsberg prisoners, a measure that Muench surely heard about prior to its passage via his connections to prominent military personnel. But, Ohlendorf was one of four Landsberg criminals excluded from the January 1951 clemency decision. He was executed on 7 June. Father Sladek continued on as spiritual director of the Ackermann Gemeinde Arbeitskreis der Sudetendeutschen, the Munich-based society for (mostly Catholic) Sudeten expellees,[85] and, with the Kirchliche Hilfsstelle,[86] would go on to establish a Catholic newspaper, *Der Volksbote*.[87]

The explanation for Muench's reluctance in the Ohlendorf case lies in his letter to Montini, dated 24 February 1951. Muench wrote it only weeks after hearing arguments on behalf of Ohlendorf in letters from Princess Helene (7 December 1950), Aschenauer (23 December 1950), and Sladek (10 and 19 January 1951). In it, Muench noted that "various parties" had approached him to "intervene on behalf of those Landsberg [prisoners] condemned to death." Specifically, Muench cited Princess Helene and two (unnamed) "functionaries from the [West German] Ministry of Justice." None had presented arguments that were "truly new or convincing." Muench acknowledged earlier efforts by the Holy See on behalf of the condemned men, but thought that the Holy See should now disengage. "It doesn't strike me, then, to be able to make new efforts given the *numerous interventions* [emphasis mine] made earlier to Mr. McCloy and General Handy, and it goes without saying that this was done years earlier with Generals Clay and Huebner."[88]

Muench went on to write about the danger to the Vatican's reputation should it become associated with right-wing groups like the *Bund für Wahrheit und Gerechtigkeit*: "The action promoted by the *Bund* . . . is not a very clear undertaking . . . Princess von Isenberg and other activists . . . certainly have good intentions, but there is reason to believe that they, unconsciously, are none other than the instruments of certain

political circles (Nazi) that aim to take advantage of the Landsberg con-
victs for their own political, nationalistic ends. For this reason I have
not dared to advise, in my above-mentioned communication an intervention by the Holy See, *especially as it would inevitably be publicized* [em-
phasis mine] . . . The Holy See . . . must keep in mind that it could be
interpreted as help for the nationalist movements that mentioned
above. The entire affair is more political than juridical."[89] In this letter,
Muench's priorities were absolutely clear: safeguarding the good reputation of the Holy See in what he called a new international climate,
and avoiding the image of the Vatican as a pawn for Nazi circles, was
paramount.

Nor did Muench wholly ignore the ethical implications of crimes
committed by German war criminals. Privately, he expressed misgivings not evident in his letter to Undersecretary Montini. The mixed
nature of Muench's personal views on the war criminals issue is evident in a 1952 letter to his sister Terry: "the problem of amnesty for
war criminals is not an easy one. Unfortunately the German public,
generally speaking, does not know much about the deeds for which
these people are now in prison. [An American officer named]
Donnelly brought me his file [on war criminals], a big heap of papers,
which carry the record of their wrong-doings. In most cases the
record is really shocking. Yet Mr. Donnelly wants to do what is right.
He is especially anxious to commute sentences or grant pardons in
cases where the punishment was too severe or where clemency is justified because of age or ill health. To me, it is clear, however, that a
general amnesty cannot be granted, nor will the Germans who know
the facts want such a thing."[90] Muench's honest letter to his sister
betrayed the misgivings that lay beneath Muench's notions that so-
called Thirty-Niners lay behind convictions of Germans who were
not truly "criminal." While he certainly believed this, Muench could
not completely dismiss German complicity. Therefore, he did not
believe a "general amnesty" for all war criminals to be allowable. But,
he appeared to use the same mental mechanism employed by many
German Catholics writing to him, namely, the notion that those who
performed killing with their own hands might be considered culpable,
but those who passed along orders for killing (e.g., high-ranking officers and industrialists) were somehow less culpable and perhaps not
culpable at all.

5

The Longest Hatred

In 1950, Monsignor Paul Tanner sent Muench an unflattering National Catholic Welfare Conference (NCWC) report on Jewish affairs in Germany. Muench's response to Tanner was this: "It is unfortunate that the report speaks only of the resentment and profound disappointment of Jews that their friends and neighbors were indifferent to their plight during the Hitler period, but says not a single word in commendation of Christians who risked their lives to help Jews in distress . . . Many, like the writer of this [NCWC] report, seem to close their eyes to deeds that inevitably cause reactions in the direction of anti-Semitism. We regret this, and so do sensible Jews to whom I have spoken about this, but apparently little can be done to change insides and attitudes."[1] Muench's regard for Jews who had converted to Catholicism also had its limits. For instance, he still referred to their "Jewishness" when commenting favorably on their "Catholic" deeds. In one example, he described Italian merchant Arico Aseoli of Milan as a "Catholic Jew" as opposed to a "Catholic."[2] During a luncheon at the Swiss Consulate, Muench met a "Mr. Merton," the Swiss vice-consul, whom he described in his diary as "interesting" and as "a Jew-Christian married to a Christian." Merton had what Muench deemed a "sensible attitude": Merton told

Muench, "Jews brought many ills upon themselves [by making] race a religion."[3]

Within weeks of his arrival at Kronberg (28 July 1946), Muench tried to ease interzonal travel restrictions on German Catholic bishops and clergy. He noted in his diary that American occupation authorities gave him difficulties. Muench interpreted the problem to be the "Jews in control [of the] Public Safety [division]." These Jews, wrote Muench, "knew the suffering of their people—taking retribution."[4] It is impossible to determine the actual percentage of German-Jewish émigrés later employed (as American citizens) by the American occupation. We do know that there existed what Rebecca Boehling calls the "Other Germany" School. She describes it as "a school of thought, located primarily in academic and émigré circles, promoting the cause of democratic structural change to be implemented by anti-Fascist Germans" who survived the Third Reich in Germany or in exile. This group supported "stringent denazification and demilitarization." Boehling describes these émigrés as having fled Germany "for political reasons," namely, their "leftist leanings." Likely, at least some Jewish Germans belonged to this émigré group. Prior to the war's end, these émigrés played a role in "information gathering," especially for the Research and Analysis Branch of the Office of Strategic Services (OSS) and later in the Information Control Division.[5] This trend continued in the later occupation years. But these émigrés had no direct access to government policy-making, and, further, held "subordinate, advisory positions."[6]

In September 1946, Muench described an encounter with an American army officer he met when taking a train to Berlin: "New York Jew—Claims department [was] in compartment with me. . . . Spoke English with a thick German accent. . . . Migrated to New York in 1936. These men do not know our history[,] traditions[;] have no spirit of fair play. Use European methods in occupation. Are hurting American interests. Have no qualifications for work except that they speak German."[7] In 1949, when mediating a conflict between Auxiliary Bishop Johannes Neuhäusler (Munich) and military government officials supervising the concentration-turned-internment camp Dachau,[8] Muench noted his impression of a Colonel Weisberg, an American soldier who was Jewish. According to Muench, Weisberg was "suave but hardly friendly to German Catholics—Morganthau complex,"[9] a reference to Jewish-American Henry J. Morganthau Jr., secretary of the treasury under the Roosevelt

Administration and the man most strongly associated with the collective guilt thesis.[10]

Muench described Nuremberg Deputy Chief Counsel for War Crimes Robert M. Kempner as "a Berlin lawyer" who "fled" to the United States and became an American citizen.[11] Kempner was but "a vindictive refugee," accused Muench.[12] Kempner had a few choice words of his own for Muench. In November 1949, Muench sent Kempner a copy of the article "Kampf gegen die Kirche" (*Der Monat*, vol. 10).[13] Presumably, Muench did so to push his point about Catholic resistance and victimization. Kempner responded by noting that the Catholic charitable organization *Hilfswerk,* which provided relief to displaced persons in Stuttgart, "has done a lot of harm by their propaganda for certain war criminals who were connected with the mass slaughter of Jews instead of using all their influence for the refugees."[14]

When Muench heard that editor Hans Habe might assume the editorship of the *Muenchner Illustrierte Zeitung,* he wrote to Father (Major) Thomas Corcoran, Chaplain Division, to warn him. "Hans Habe is described as a leftist who . . . has shown a lack of understanding for Christian ideals. . . . He may be one of the recent Americans who . . . wants to come to Germany for easy pickings."[15] Muench believed the "Thirty-Niners" in the Religious Affairs Division hindered efforts for allocation of newsprint to Catholic publications. Muench recorded in his diary: "the émigrés (Thirty-Niners)—Urman, Schechter, Fleischer, Langerfeld—blocked the Church whenever possible."[16] In 1947, Muench told his secretary, Howard Smith, that denazification was an "ugly mess," the fault of "German émigrés, now naturalized Americans and back in Germany," who were, "the worst enemies of a better, peaceful Germany."[17]

In December 1952, the state of Hesse indicted Frankfurt banker Franz Cueppers for conducting illegal foreign exchange. The state accused him of participating in a scheme with French customs officials in which French "kingpins" imported illegally traded, American-made camouflage netting (for military use) from Germany at a cut-rate price. German banks in Baden-Baden sold the netting to the French at the (cheaper) rate charged to German firms instead of at the agreed-upon foreign exchange rate. Banks like Cueppers's profited from the resulting commissions. The case dragged on until 1957, when a jury convicted Cueppers and sentenced him to a fine of 20,000 *deutschmarks* or eighty days in jail.[18] Muench called Cueppers a "victim of Jewish lawyers in Hesse."[19]

In 1953, Muench told friend Osco Cole that the American policy of "good will toward Germans" was "unfortunately still encumbered by many of the ideas that [were] carried into Germany by the type that you and I learned to know; men here to carry out a policy of revenge."[20] As late as 1956, Muench even described the West German Federal Supreme Court as controlled by "secularists, Jews and Socialists" who "sought to destroy" the 1933 Concordat, which remained valid under the Federal Republic.[21] Ironically, in reality, the West German Supreme Court staff included former Nazi party members. "The blame for what happened at Nuremberg lies chiefly with the Morgenthou crowd who succeeded in packing key positions of the prosecution staff with 'recent Americans'— the so-called Thirty-niners," Muench wrote to Father Peter Leo Johnson of St. Francis Seminary in Milwaukee.[22]

In 1957, Muench received a letter from German Catholic and former Nazi prison guard Joseph Hering. Hering complained to Muench about his treatment under American occupiers. In his response, Muench told him that "in truth, many former Germans were among the Americans who came to Germany after the collapse. These former Germans fled to America during the Hitler era and were permitted to apply for American citizenship after five years of residence. These German-Americans appeared in American uniform after the end of the war, and due to their language skills, obtained positions among the occupation officials. To my great dismay, these people overstepped their bounds. But this does not justify [your] incrimination of the American nation as a whole."[23]

Muench was far from alone in his anti-Jewish sentiments. Such views resonated with many Germans and Americans in his Catholic and Army circles. Anti-Semitism—which Robert Wistrich has called "the longest hatred"—was considered acceptable by many Americans before, during, and after World War II.[24] In March 1938, for example, the majority of Americans believed that German Jews were either partially or wholly at fault for Nazi attacks against them,[25] and about 80 percent opposed increasing U.S. immigration quotas for German and Austrian political refugees. In 1944, Jews were listed "least desirable" as immigrants, in the same group as German and Japanese Axis enemies.[26] In postwar Germany, new strains of anti-Semitism appeared alongside older forms. The post-Holocaust issues of guilt, restitution, and reparations, as well as the reality of Israel (in 1948),[27] created what Werner Bergmann and Rainer Erb call a form of "secondary" anti-Semitism. In postwar surveys, Germans made it clear that above all, they wished the

"annoying" debate about the past, the guilt associated with it, and demands for reparations to end.[28]

United Nations Relief and Rehabilitation Agency (UNRRA) statistics for September 1945 showed that of approximately 1.5 million
"uprooted" European citizens remaining in Germany, Austria, or Italy,
roughly 50,000 (3.6%) were Jewish. These 50,000 Jews who had survived
the Holocaust came from all parts of Europe.[29] Yet, some Germans still
perceived Jews as excessively influential. In 1946, Muench arrived to aid
a German population of which, according to American military government surveys in the American zone, 39 percent of the total population
was either intensely (18%) or moderately (21%) anti-Semitic.[30] In 1945,
the advisor on Jewish Affairs (Rabbi) Phillip S. Bernstein, who worked
for General McNarney in USFET (United States Forces, European
Theater), reported to his superior:

> The reasons assigned for the emergence of the new anti-Semitism in
> Germany fall into several distinct categories. Most of the Germans
> suggested that economic plight of the German people is the princi-
> pal cause. Jews serve as a convenient scapegoat that can be held
> responsible for the plight of the average German. In addition, there
> is the popular belief that American Jewry is shaping the occupation
> policy in Germany, and that to avenge the deaths of the millions of
> their co-religionists, the Jews are deliberately standing in the way of
> Germany's recovery.[31] Another group of Germans and indigenous
> Jews consider the Jewish DPs as a provocative element in the German
> scene. . . . Stemming as they do from east European Jewry, they are
> the type with whom the German is either not familiar or whom he
> has traditionally resented. The Jewish DPs are believed to be the hub
> of the black market. Some German workers . . . have swelled the
> ranks of anti-Semites because they were dispossessed to make room
> for the Jewish DPs. The Germans are uneasy by the presence . . . of
> people to whom they owe a colossal debt, and relieve themselves
> of their guilt by proving to the world that the Jews deserved their
> fate under the Nazi regime. The DP representatives are unanimous
> in their belief that the interaction between the American troops and
> the German civilian population conditions (promotes) rising anti-
> Semitism. The Jewish DPs recall the sympathetic attitude of the
> American troops that liberated them, and invariably contrast them
> with the type of men they now encounter among occupation troops.

The Germans in turn discard their veneer as soon as they feel secure that the American troops are either indifferent to or are in accord with their anti-Semitic views. Finally, there is a group that offers the simple explanation that anti-Semitism is now deeply rooted in the German culture as a result of the unchallenged indoctrination of the Hitler regime.[32]

In this remarkable report, Rabbi Bernstein hinted at the disturbingly symbiotic relationship between German and American anti-Semitism.

From the U.S. Congress to U.S. Army offices to Catholic relief agencies in Muench's bailiwick, many perceived Jewish displaced persons negatively. In heavily war-damaged Germany, coping with an influx of expellees, refugees, and displaced persons—a small minority of whom were Jewish—proved overwhelming. Jewish displaced persons in particular were often scapegoats for problems associated with overcrowding and displaced populations. In 1946, the displaced persons population in Germany and Austria, Jewish and otherwise, began to increase significantly. Eastern European states, with the consent of the Allied Control Council under the terms of the Potsdam Agreement, forcibly expelled roughly twelve million ethnic German citizens (*Volksdeutsche*) to Germany. Roughly 8 million ethnic Germans came to the Western zones of Germany, most to the American zone.

The Jewish displaced persons population increased from 50,000 to 145,000 in 1946 alone. By the summer of 1947, about 182,000 Jewish displaced persons lived in Germany, 80 percent of them from Poland. The remainder came from Hungary, Czechoslovakia, Russia, and Romania. This group of Jewish refugees, Eastern European nationals who had sought refuge from the Nazis in the Soviet Union in 1939, had escaped death in the Holocaust, but many returned to their homes only to encounter rampant anti-Semitism. Thus they sought refuge once again in the western zones of occupied Germany. Even at its peak in 1947, the Jewish displaced persons population never exceeded more than 10–20 percent of all "uprooted" Europeans who came to be called "displaced persons."[33]

Most displaced persons were sent to the British and American zones of Germany. In the British zone of occupied Germany, 9,000 (of 12,000 total) Jewish displaced persons lived in the Hohne-Belsen camp.[34] The American zone contained several camps of approximately 5,000 inhabitants each to accommodate the total American zone Jewish displaced persons population of 150,000 (this number fluctuated). These included Jewish displaced persons camps in Landsberg, Feldafing, and Föhrenwald (Bavaria) as well as mixed camps in Pocking and Leipheim (Bavaria), Frankfurt-Zeilsheim, Wetzlar, and Eschwege (Hesse). About one-fourth of Jewish displaced persons did not live in camps but in cities. Munich, for example, had up to 7,000 Jewish displaced persons. A little more than 1,000 Jewish displaced persons lived in the French zone.[35]

In the American zone, 80–90 percent of displaced persons were Christian (predominantly Catholic), and 10–20 percent were Jewish. The numbers of Jewish displaced persons in Europe peaked in 1947 and rapidly declined thereafter. By October 1948, fewer than 85,000 Jewish displaced persons remained in Europe, most of the rest having emigrated to the new state of Israel (formed 15 May 1948).[36] Between 1946 and 1953, a total of 140,000 "Holocaust survivors" emigrated to the United States.[37] As of 1952, only 12,000 Jewish displaced persons remained in Germany, only a tiny percentage of which were of German nationality prior to the war. In 1959, the Jewish community in the Federal Republic (mostly of East European origins) numbered a mere 23,000.[38]

In 1947, Otto Kling of Munich wrote a lengthy letter to Cardinal Michael Faulhaber of Munich on the dangers Jews supposedly still presented in Germany, using the views of Muench as justification. Kling penned the following anti-Semitic diatribe, quoted in part in the Introduction but worth quoting here in its entirety due to its particular viciousness:

> Your Eminence! When you read the Holy Scripture, you will find a passage in which Christ says to the Jews, "you have always been murderers of peoples." . . . Bolshevism is the intellectual property of the Jews. The author of *The Communist Manifesto* and *Das Kapital* is the Jew Karl Marx. [He] did not write this epistle to "free the proletariat from their chains," but instead to put a guide for attaining power into the hands of his racial brethren. . . . The American generals, [Lucius] Clay and [Walter] Muller, are Jews! . . . [They] arrived at their goal due to the moral and spiritual depravity of church and state! They will cause a Third World War—just as they caused the first two—when they hold both capitalism and communism in their

hands. . . . [They] consider no means too reprehensible to attain this goal. Lies, intrigue, murder, and manslaughter are milestones on their way! A few weeks before the war's end, the merciful President Roosevelt allegedly died of a 'stroke'—you will recall the Talmud saying "the Gentile is like the sacrificial animal—you must murder the most noble among him.". . . His successor, Harry *Salomon* Truman, was the business partner of the Jew Jacobson in his hometown in Missouri for more than twenty years. The likelihood that we are dealing with a Jew or baptized Jew who sprinkles sand in the eyes of the Holy Father [Pius XII] is very great. Cardinal [Bishop] Muench, who is currently in Germany, can best attest to this, as you can see in this letter and the enclosed articles.[39]

Stereotypes of Jews as morally lax, natural criminals and black marketers, leftist agitators, and communists appeared and reappeared in letters to Muench from German Catholics. Karl Lüssenhop of Wiesbaden provides another example. Lüssenhop, born in Frankfurt am Main during World War I in 1915, was a self-described convinced and idealistic Nazi who worshipped the Führer. Active in the Hitler Youth, Lüssenhop was a civil servant (a train operator and city administrator). At the onset of war in 1939, he became a *Wehrmacht* office clerk. Lüssenhop was an unapologetic anti-Semite:

The Jew played a leading role in Marxism. Often in history, especially in Russia and Poland (and also in the German case) the Jew served as scapegoat. [Jews] provided a focus for all that is evil and foreign. And this was often purely instinctive, an inherited attitude. [My] strong anti-Semitism was a combination of my bad personal experiences with Jews . . . and purely instinctive moments. Finally, I felt religious [anti-Judaism]. I simply rejected the Jews. . . . I did not know that all Jews were consigned to concentration camps. I agree with the Nazi policy of segregating them from other camp inmates. . . . My opinion that Jews are racially inferior cannot be changed. But this does not mean I thought Jews should be eradicated. I thought they should be resettled in the East. . . . There, they could live in their own state, reservation, protectorate, or what have you. Jews are people too and deserve to live. Due to their minority status, Jews should have welcomed efforts to establish a state for them. The fact that Jews did not welcome these efforts proved to me that Jews could

only live as parasites, from trade and from goods produced by
Aryans. They did not want it any other way, nor did they want to
be engaged in creative enterprises. But no one has the right to kill
someone out of simple dislike.[40]

Bishop Muench did not appear to support the views of such overtly
ideologically convinced Nazis. Initially asking that his secretary send
a brief and polite note of acknowledgment, Muench ceased correspond-
ing with Lüssenhop, who he considered mentally unstable.

Even if Muench did not respond positively to such extreme letters
(which on the whole he did not), he failed to support improved
Christian-Jewish relations when given opportunity to do so. In 1948,
Carl Zietlow, a Minnesota native and a Protestant pastor, heard he was
to go to occupied Germany to form local chapters of the National
Conference of Christians and Jews (NCCJ). He wrote to Muench, who
at that time functioned as liaison representative and as Vatican relief officer, requesting a meeting. Zietlow was hopeful that Muench could help.
As he had when asked for advice by Bishop Michael Keller of Münster,
Muench discouraged the efforts of the newly founded International
Council for Christians and Jews (ICCJ) to form local branches in
German cities. He told Zietlow that it would be "difficult to establish
local Council branches in Germany due to the *Una Sancta* movement,"
which already met the need for Catholic-Protestant dialogue. "New
organizations sprouted up like dandelions in a warm June sun" in over-
burdened Germany, said Muench. Therefore, the ICCJ would not be
successful there.[41] Muench's skepticism may or may not have been
linked to his lack of concern for Christian-Jewish reconciliation efforts.
Years later, he doubted the feasibility of transplanting the Catholic
organization Knights of Columbus to Germany, for exactly the same
reasons he cited in his letter to Zietlow in 1948.[42]

Muench openly lied in his response to Zietlow, whose efforts on
behalf of Christian-Jewish dialogue were badly needed. Muench denied
any residual anti-Semitism in Germany, implying that no need for the
ICCJ existed in Germany at that time. "Regarding anti-Semitism I can
talk only from hearsay, and very little at that. I myself have found very
little of it, possibly because my contacts have been largely with people
who are not anti-Semitic."[43] In a different letter, Muench told long-time
friend Bishop William T. Mulloy, "it seems that many fear the [Stratton]
bill would open the doors of the U.S. to displaced Jews, and for this

reason a good many in the States are opposed to the bill. Anti-Semitism has grown to an alarming extent among American personnel."[44]

When U.S. military government officials requisitioned the Catholic seminary in Dieburg to provide housing for Jewish displaced persons, Muench worked in tandem with Bishop Albert Stohr of Mainz to restore the Dieburg seminary to German seminarians. Bishop Stohr told Religious Affairs officer Captain Kenny that so-called *Ostjuden* "severely damaged" the Dieburg building, adding that German civilians in Dieburg were "very bitter" at having their homes requisitioned "for the Jews." He asked that Kenny make repair materials available to restore the seminary, including new bedding, desks, and chairs. Otherwise, said Bishop Stohr, the "liberation of the Jews would become a psychological burden for civilians." The bishop told Kenny he also heard complaints from Germans in the town of Lampertheim: "The civilian population is on the edge of despair. The Jews sit in beautiful and spacious homes (sources assure me that a single Jew lives in a three-room home), while seven or eight expelled Germans live in one room, married couples and children together. One can imagine the negative effect on morality. One could easily see that under these circumstances, a new anti-Semitism grows, anti-Semitism perhaps even stronger than that of National Socialism."[45] Bishop Stohr suggested that *Ostjuden* be evacuated from private homes in Lampertheim and placed instead in larger buildings, such as schools or soldiers' barracks. "This has the advantage," he argued, "that Germans thrown out of their homes would no longer have to watch [them] rob and sell off their entire household, which Jews are doing in a shameless manner."[46]

In June 1947, the Catholic sisters of Cloister Bad Wörishofen asked Muench for help in ridding their two cloisters-turned-infirmaries, Josefsheim and Kneippianum, of displaced persons. The sisters implied that most of the displaced persons there were Jewish. Sister Reifsmeier told Muench, "I can assure you all the sisters carried out their duty of Christian love for their neighbor (*christlicher Nächstenliebe*), despite suspicion and mistrust. It is heroic for the sisters to dutifully remain at their posts. . . . The sisters must remove the crucifixes from each room because the current patients do not like them. . . . It is easy to see that the routines of our Order are greatly disrupted.[47] Muench responded by writing to General Clarence R. Huebner, commander in chief of European Ground Forces, to alert him to the sisters' situation. "I deeply appreciate your interest in taking this matter personally in hand."[48]

Initially, Huebner did not offer Muench his help. On 11 July, Huebner told him that it was "not considered advisable that the property in question be released at the present time because of the unavailability of a suitable alternative location." Further, added Huebner, an army investigation revealed that 242 tubercular children of all faiths received treatment at Josefsheim and Kneippianum.[49] Huebner suspected the sisters of shading the truth, telling Muench's German secretary, Robert Deubel that "untrue allegations [were] made by some Bad Wörisfhofen people about the real situation there."[50]

Several of the Catholic nuns laid bare their anti-Semitic feelings in letters to Muench. Sister Reifsmeier implied that only Jewish patients inhabited the former cloister. According to the army, this was not the case; only *some* patients were Jewish. Sister Fernanda Weip was more direct. She contacted Dr. Phillip Auerbach,[51] Bavarian state commissioner for restitution, to demand the removal of displaced persons from Josefsheim and Kneippianum. She told Muench, "[Auerbach] personally pleaded to the military government in Munich for our rights as order nurses, and will have his Jews moved from our houses."[52] When, in August, Jewish displaced persons still remained at Kneippianum, she complained bitterly to Muench: "German personnel who have worked with our order nurses for years are being replaced by DPs. These boys, aged between fourteen and eighteen, have no upbringing whatsoever. The sisters must defend themselves against physical abuse and stealing, and often without success."[53]

On 3 October 1947, all patients were moved to the Hotel Kreuzer in Bad Wörishofen. The sisters were ecstatic and thanked Muench profusely for his intervention.[54] At some point between July and October, General Huebner must have reversed his earlier position or felt the situation had changed, and intervened after all. For in late October, Muench wrote to him in order to thank Huebner for his "prompt and energetic intervention in the Bad Wörishofen case." Without Huebner's aid, said Muench, the sisters' houses "would not have been released."[55] But the saga was not yet over. Though the displaced persons were removed from the two cloisters, they remained in Bad Wörishofen living in requisitioned homes and hotels.

In 1948, the mayor of Bad Wörishofen, named Stöckle, wrote to his diocesan bishop, Dr. Ferdinand Dirichs of Limburg, for help in ridding Bad Wörishofen of these (in his view) troublesome and physically unwell displaced persons. Bishop Dirichs approached Muench forthwith asking for his intervention.[56] This time, Muench refused, claiming his duties were of a "religious" nature only.[57] One can only speculate as to the reason for Muench's refusal. During the summer of 1947, he remained in good standing with Military Governor Clay and political advisor Murphy. But with the distribution of his pro-German and anti-Allied *One World* pastoral letter in October–November 1947, Muench's reputation (with Clay at least) was tarnished. Perhaps this made him more cautious when approached by Bishop Dirichs.

A particularly controversial Jewish displaced persons camp was located in Zeilsheim, an industrial suburb of Frankfurt am Main that housed thousands of IG Farben workers during the Third Reich. After the war, the Hoechst Factory replaced IG Farben facilities in Zeilsheim. In 1945, the American army ordered approximately 1,300 working-class Germans out of their homes (without their furniture) to make room for the Jewish displaced persons camp.[58] For army officers, the requisitioning of some three hundred German homes for Jewish displaced persons was a "hot problem" that "no one wanted to touch."[59]

Occupation officials knew a "Jewish DP smuggling ring" operated out of Frankfurt-Zeilsheim. They discovered its existence after arresting Polish-Jewish displaced persons, Martin Amsterdam and Markus Goldberg, who were illegally crossing the American zone border with the help of German national Otto Krecht. Their Opel vehicle contained 2,216,000 Reichsmarks. Distressed army officials alleged that several members of the Zeilsheim ring had Communist sympathies.[60] Jewish displaced persons in Zeilsheim disturbed Germans as well. Father Rupp of Zeilsheim wrote to Bishop Dirichs of Limburg to describe alleged goings-on in the "Jewish quarter" (*Judenviertel*): "Nearly 5,000 Jews have been put into their own camp. They have their own so-called 'police.' The German police referred an official report regarding the production of false German money to the Americans, who ignored it for the last four months. Then, after renewed urging from the German police, the Americans conducted a raid. But they did not find anything. The black market activity in Zeilsheim—in the Jewish quarter—is notorious," Father Rupp told Dirichs and, subsequently, Muench.[61] In a separate letter, Rupp told Muench that prejudice against the Jewish displaced persons stemmed not only from their "Jewishness" but also from their "Russian" way of thinking.[62]

Six days later, Muench received a petition from a Catholic priest named Father Brim, also signed by sixteen Zeilsheim Catholics. In great detail—indeed, on a street-by-street basis, it described the requisitioning of Zeilsheim homes for "Polish Jews." It also described in detail the living conditions of now-displaced Germans. It should be noted that according to one contemporary American Jewish chaplain and several residents, overcrowding in the Jewish camp was also atrocious.[63] The petition included political arguments. Begging Muench for help, these sixteen Zeilsheim Catholics told Muench of rumors that more homes would soon be requisitioned for Jews. They warned of the negative political effects any new confiscation would have:

> The Communist Party places itself in the middle of these critical days by holding a meeting in Zeilsheim . . . to give the impression that only they endeavor to ease the situation in Zeilsheim. [The Communists] successfully strengthen this impression. After repeated evacuations, fear and resignation have set in among those Germans affected. They have become mistrusting and inclined toward radicalism. This showed itself in recent elections, when voices in favor of Christian Democracy declined, and opposition to the Christian Democratic Party (CDU) grew. Stoppage to these requisitionings must be achieved. This is the only way to stem the tide of radicalism and avoid the moral pitfalls of so many persons living in unnaturally close proximity. We Zeilsheim Catholics beg you for help.[64]

Muench had already attempted to intervene, even before receiving this petition, by writing to General Joseph T. McNarney to describe the "problematic" situation.[65] When roughly one-third of Zeilsheim's homes still remained occupied by Jewish displaced persons in April 1948, Rupp wrote to Muench again, this time to report the dire consequences that befell Germans forced to live among Jewish displaced persons. Zeilsheim was now world-famous for its black market, said Father Rupp. "Some of our good farming community (*Bauernschaft*) have mixed themselves up in such activities," lamented Rupp, implying the common anti-Semitic stereotype that Jews "corrupted" Germans. "Our working-class Germans turn to Jews, who have lots of cash, to earn a little on the side. Even children participate, and thereby lose the correct understanding of money's true value." Rupp also implied that Jewish males were sexual predators who took advantage of innocent German girls, a staple anti-Semitic argument. "Many good families have fallen to the ways of Mammon. Over one hundred young German girls live among Jews, in primitive conditions. Pregnancies outside of marriage result from this. To date, four or five civil marriages have taken place between German girls and Jews."[66]

In the fall of 1948, the U.S. Army dismantled the Zeilsheim camp.[67] Rupp reported that even the departure of the Jewish displaced persons was disastrous. In a long letter, he described the manner in which "Ukrainian-, Lithuanian-, and Polish-Jewish DPs" packed furniture, bedding, and china belonging to "simple German workers who had to count every penny" as they evacuated the Zeilsheim camp.[68] Muench's secretary, Robert Deubel, informed him "some of the German families did not want to go back to their homes, because in some instances they received better accommodations in the meantime."[69]

An assessment of the attitudes of Muench's American Catholic colleagues, many of them of German origin, is hardly more flattering. Father L. A. Fritsch of Chicago called the German people the "defenders of the white race, the protectors of Christendom and the saviors of today's civilization." America fought on the "wrong side" of World War II, thought Father Fritsch."[70] In his diary, Muench noted that Dr. Goetz, professor at Catholic University and later Georgetown University (both in Washington, D.C.), thought "Jews predominated as policymakers" and were "influential" in pushing the "German collective guilt" thesis at home.[71]

Father James Nellen, instrumental in helping Muench ship relief foodstuffs to Germany from the United States, told Muench he suspected their supplier, the New York City–based Old World Shipping Service, consisted of "a bunch of Jews" who could avoid shipping charges by shipping to an APO (army depot) number. "Instead of selling their products at the regular price, they charge much more but keep under the price of goods and postage from outside of New York."[72] In reply, Muench told Nellen "we shall not want you to send any more [coffee] from this firm."[73]

According to a notation in Muench's diary, a Bishop O'Brien complained to Muench, "Jews were buying up property in the U.S. and raising rents."[74] Monsignor Walter Fasnacht labeled Jews "black marketers" and subscribed to physical stereotypes about Jews as well. In 1950, Fasnacht's superior Stritch asked that his rectory take in a German student from Munich named Eugene Vetter. Vetter, who majored in psychology and sociology, had a scholarship at DePaul University in Chicago and needed affordable room and board. Suspicious because Vetter's host was the Chicago-based Christian Jewish Association, Fasnacht told Muench that Vetter "assures me, in spite of a rather prominent nose, that he is a very good Catholic. At present the young man is traveling all over the country at government expense. I tested him out a little by suggesting that he might be able to do good work among the Jewish contingent because from my own personal observation I felt that they were doing harm to themselves by some of the methods they were using. Particularly in Munich where they have a wide-open black market against which U.S. officials seem powerless to proceed." He did not take Vetter in, but sent him instead to Kolping House, a German-American-run Catholic charity in Chicago.[75]

Other American Catholic prelates displayed a disturbing blindness toward their own Catholic ranks with regard to anti-Semitism. An example was the response of Cardinal Samuel Stritch of Chicago to the Kielce pogrom in Catholic Poland. On 4 July 1946, in Kielce, townspeople massacred at least forty-one Jews. A Polish boy who falsely claimed to have been kidnapped by Jews incited the pogrom. Rabbi Philip Bernstein, USFET advisor on Jewish affairs, held a private audience with Pope Pius XII in September 1946 and urged the pope to condemn the Kielce massacre. The pope, while willing to call the massacre "dreadful," blamed it on the influence of Russian nationalism and communism in Poland (as opposed to Catholic anti-Semitism).[76]

The Primate of the Catholic Church in Poland, Cardinal August Hlond, described Kielce as a tragedy that he sincerely regretted, but denied that its cause was racial. Instead, he claimed it was "a reaction against Jewish bureaucrats serving the Communist regime's attempts to restructure Polish life."[77] When Jewish organizations criticized Hlond's statement, Cardinal Stritch was outraged at their criticism. He told the papal nuncio to the United States, Amleto Cicognani,

All over Europe in the dark days, bishops stood out in defense of the rights of the Jews and offered them refuge and protection. The whole world knows what our Holy Father did for them. Here in the United States, time and again we have defended their rights. Even when we have protested any discrimination by our government in the way of closing the camps of displaced persons and keeping the Jewish camps in the American zone of occupation in Germany open. And we have always said that we have no thought of doing anything to prevent the Jews from getting proper treatment and relief. Our whole thought is that there should not be unfair discriminations. Now some of these people simply, when something comes up that at first sight isn't clear, will not interpret it in the background of all that the Church has done for the Jews in our times. . . . It is true that not knowing all the facts in the Polish situation, the first accounts of the statement of the Cardinal were a bit surprising. But the facts have been made known, and every fair mind knows now that the Cardinal was not in any way anti-Semitic. Look at what the Polish priests and the Polish Catholics did in sympathy for the Jew during the Nazi occupation of Poland. When anyone dares to write to express his indignation regarding the present policy of the Catholic Church towards the Jew, he simply isn't looking at the facts. The present policy of the Catholic Church towards the Jew is the policy that is dictated by morals. . . . I don't think this letter [of American Jew Seymour Siegel, of Chicago, to Pope Pius XII in Rome] ought to receive any attention at all.[78]

A telling example of antipathy toward Jewish displaced persons on the part of members of Congress involved Muench's acquaintance, Senator William Langer of North Dakota, a Republican who held a key position on the Senate Judiciary Committee. This committee was the crucial source of legislation defining and governing both immigration and control over displaced persons. Langer's was the swing vote over an otherwise evenly divided committee of thirteen, with six "restrictionists" and six "liberals."[79] Langer's ancestry was German. He began his political career in central and southwestern North Dakota, heavily populated by German-Russian immigrants. According to two Washington reporters, Robert S. Allen and William V. Shannon, Langer's pro-German proclivities had "strong Nazi and anti-Semitic overtones" during the early 1940s. One Senate Judiciary Committee staff member called Langer "almost pro-Nazi."[80] Muench and Langer had a sort of gentlemen's agreement to help each other in causes that interested them. When Muench left Fargo, North Dakota, for Germany in late summer 1946, Langer told Muench that the senator "might like to write [the bishop] confidentially, in line with his duties as senator, in regard to some matters concerning the common people of Europe." Langer's letter was "meant to assure [Muench] that anything [Muench] wrote would be kept in the strictest confidence."[81] Muench turned to Langer for help on a number of occasions, and also shared his prejudices openly with the North Dakota senator. On one occasion, Muench wrote Langer, "I enclose a memorandum, which I must ask you to use without connecting my name to it. . . . Former emigrants, now naturalized Americans back in Germany, are hurting our American interests more than Americans back home realize. . . . Former concentration camp inmates, who were such for reasons of crime and not for anti-Nazism, have been among our worst enemies."[82]

During the fall of 1946, Langer and Muench shared an interest in the welfare of approximately 1,500 Catholic German-Russians now in displaced persons camps. In 1944, retreating German troops sent approximately 240,000 Russians of ethnic German stock from the North Caucasus Mountains, the Crimea, and the Ukraine to the German Reich. Most were "resettled" in Saxony and Thuringia. When Russian troops overran Saxony and Thuringia in 1945, the majority of these German-Russians were taken to Siberia. About 1,500 Catholic German-Russians remained in occupied Germany after the war.[83] Muench told Father Aberle of Dickinson, North Dakota, that "the Jews enjoyed the special status of political refugees. Why not the German-Russians?"[84] In November 1946, he wrote to Langer to suggest that German-Russians be granted the status of stateless political refugees, making their status "similar to the Jews."[85]

Muench's references to supposed "special status" for Jews concerned the Truman Directive, issued on 22 December 1945. This allowed for preferential immigration policy for displaced persons within the existing quota system (which would not be revised until June 1948). The quota for all of Eastern Europe amounted to only 13,000. The quota for German immigrants was double that number, at 26,000. But, of these German immigrants, Nazi victims (i.e., German Jews, German political persecutees, etc.) were given precedence. As of 30 June 1947, 22,950 visas to the United States were issued under the Truman Directive. "Jews" received 15,478, "Catholics" received 3,424, "Protestants" received 2,968, and 1,080 visas went to "other" denominations.[86]

Muench enlarged his efforts to encompass not only German-Russians, but any and all Germans who were not of Jewish descent or of leftist political background. German Jews were able to emigrate, Muench told Langer. Other Germans, complained Muench, could not,

because unlike German Jews, they could not show persecution by
Hitler, survival of a concentration camp, or loss of "position, etc."
Muench found this wrong-headed in that he believed "many were excel-
lent people, never were Hitlerites, in fact to the contrary, though [they
were] not persecuted."[87] In an interview with President Truman in 1949,
Muench dismissed critics who recalled the collaboration of ethnic
Germans who lived outside Germany, especially in Eastern Europe.
"These good people really fought our battle against Communism long
before we did," Muench told Truman. Muench believed German-
Russians should not be judged too harshly because they "linked arms
with one devil, Hitler, whom they did not know [!], to destroy another
devil, Stalin, whom they knew."[88]

Muench's comments might have influenced Truman and surely
influenced Langer. The senator from North Dakota was an important
actor in the passage of Public Law 774, known as the Displaced Persons
Act of 1948. Passed in the second session of the Eightieth Congress on
2 June 1948, the Displaced Persons Act increased the total number of displaced persons to be admitted to the United States to 205,000 per year.[89]
Qualified displaced persons had to be in Germany, Austria, or Italy by
22 December 1945. Fifty percent of the visas were to be reserved for
agricultural workers, and 50 percent of immigrating displaced persons
were to come from Estonia, Latvia, and Lithuania, nations annexed by
the Soviet Union after the war.[90]

The bill was disastrous for Jewish displaced persons, who at their
peak constituted about 10 to 20 percent of the displaced persons population but were perceived as a much larger group by anti-Semitic imagi-
nations in the United States and occupied Germany. The Displaced
Persons Act of 1948 benefited Catholic displaced persons and (largely
Catholic) ethnic German *Volksdeutsche;* for after 1946, most Jewish displaced persons were Polish nationals who arrived in the American zone
only that year and were thus excluded under the act. Few Jewish displaced persons came from Estonia, Latvia, or Lithuania (few members of
these Jewish communities survived) and few were agricultural workers.
President Truman, who reluctantly signed the bill, recognized that it
"excluded Jewish displaced persons." A number of congressmen acknowledged and reviled its anti-Jewish nature.[91]

Langer introduced Section Twelve of the Displaced Persons Act of
1948 (dubbed the "Langer amendment") that gave preference to ethnic
Germans. He wrote U.S. political advisor to Germany Robert Murphy

to remind him of the specifics contained in Section Twelve. Of the 205,000 total displaced persons population approved for emigration to the United States annually, 27,000 German and Austrian candidates were eligible, of whom half, or 13,500, were to be exclusively *Volksdeutsche,* that is to say, persons of ethnic German origin born in Poland, Czechoslovakia, Hungary, Rumania, or Yugoslavia residing in Germany and Austria as of 1 July 1948.[92] In short, the Langer Amendment excluded German Jews and Austrian Jews from half of all emigration slots available to them. It also stipulated a much larger window for arrival in the U.S. zone (July 1948 versus December 1945) *for Volksdeutsche only.* William Haber, Clay's advisor on Jewish affairs, called it "the most anti-Semitic bill in U.S. history."[93] On 16 June 1950, Truman signed the second Displaced Persons Bill, increasing the total number of displaced persons to be granted entry to 415,744 and removed restrictions applying largely to Jewish displaced persons.[94]

Langer and Muench agreed that ethnic Germans suffered disproportionately among displaced persons. Muench told Monsignor Luigi Ligutti that he thought them "as much victims of the war as the Jews, and in many cases much more so."[95] Langer thought Jewish displaced persons "had relatives in New York to help them."[96] Murphy also unfairly compared Jewish displaced persons with ethnic Germans affected by the Potsdam Agreement. In October 1945, Murphy sent a memorandum to H. Freeman Matthews, director of the State Department's European Affairs office. In it, he compared the fate of ethnic German expellees under Allied victory to that of Jews under Nazism. "Knowledge that they are the victims of a harsh political decision carried out with the utmost ruthlessness and disregard for the humanities does not cushion the effect . . . of viewing innocent children, women and old people. The mind reverts to the other recent mass deportations that horrified the world and brought upon the Nazis the odium that they so deserved. . . . Now the situation is reversed. . . . It would be most unfortunate were the record to indicate that we are particeps to methods we have often condemned in other instances." He was more explicit in another section of the memorandum, noting that in "viewing the distress and despair of these wretches, in smelling the odor of their filthy condition, the mind reverts instantly to Dachau and Buchenwald."[97] Murphy knew his sentiments constituted political dynamite. Murphy told Matthews that criticizing Allied policy on the ethnic German expellees "exposed one to the charge of softness on the Germans."[98] Muench and

Murphy probably discussed their similar views on ethnic German expellees as they did their views of "alien Americans," a code-phrase for leftist or Jewish émigrés.

In a speech before the U.S. Senate delivered on 25 August 1949, Langer defended the rights of ethnic Germans affected by the Potsdam Agreement of 1945 and praised the efforts of Senator Pat McCarren of Nevada. McCarren led an attack on the "too lenient" Displaced Persons Commission's tendency to interpret the Displaced Persons Act of 1948 in favor of Jewish displaced persons when possible. Langer "commended" McCarren, who he said was "threatened by powerful cliques . . . powerful groups who would set themselves up in the place of the Congress of the United States in determining the immigration policy of this nation."[99] It took little imagination to gather that Langer referred to Jewish groups unhappy with the discriminatory Displaced Persons Act of 1948.

Many U.S. army officers held anti-Semitic views as well. Only recently has this come to the attention of scholars by way of Joseph Bendersky's excellent study.[100] Lucius Clay and Robert Murphy demonstrated tolerance for remarks against Jewish émigrés working in occupied Germany, reflecting a general dislike for those with left-wing political inclinations (Jewish or not) and for the supposedly "Jewish" qualities often associated with left-wing political movements. On 7 April 1947, Clay issued a secret directive to purge émigrés from service in the military government. General Frank L. Keating, deputy military governor to Clay, wrote that Clay "decided we shall not employ anyone or renew any contracts of anyone who has been naturalized since 1933." Keating instructed that this directive should be kept confidential. Though the penciled word "recalled" (by whose authority is unclear) was found on the original directive, a wave of dismissals followed.[101]

The aborted directive was not so confidential that Muench did not hear of it. After a conversation with two American colonels, Muench noted in his diary that Clay tried to bar employment of "German Americans . . . Thirty-Niners." Clay wanted only those who had attained citizenship prior to 1933, but was overruled by the State Department, the colonels told Muench. Unlike the War Department, the State Department bowed to the pressure of public opinion, the army men noted. They did not further specify the source of "public pressure,"[102] but this may have been a veiled reference to so-called Jewish influences in the media and government. Other incidents marked Clay's frustration with "émigrés" as well. Clay looked down upon General Robert A. McClure, supposedly telling Muench that McClure had "no backbone" and was "in the hands of émigrés." McClure supported personnel working for him "whether they were right or wrong," and his underlings, presumably meaning his émigré underlings, "took advantage of this."[103]

General Walter Mueller, a Catholic, served as director of military government for Bavaria (1947), deputy chief of staff in the U.S. Army-European Command, and, in 1954, was the sole American representative on the Allied High Commission Interim Mixed Parole and Clemency Board, seated in Bonn. In 1947 in his diary, Muench recorded that General Mueller told him "Jews used the press against our actions [and] caused us trouble."[104] In 1952, the general told Muench that "Thirty-Niners were in control of denazification."[105] In 1954, Muench told his secretary Howard Smith that Mueller had warned him, "if we would commute sentences too generously or give war criminals their freedom, the Jews in the United States, specifically in New York, would raise a big furor."[106] Army men were afraid of "pressure groups [like] those in New York, [meaning] Jews after the General Patton case," Mueller apparently told Muench.[107]

In early 1947, Muench's distant cousin Colonel William G. Brey, a Catholic, apparently told Muench that his fellow army officers were "very critical of émigré, naturalized German-Americans, especially Jews." Brey added that an "investigation" into the matter would, in his opinion, "help occupation forces."[108] A general named Walsh, stationed in Berlin, purportedly told Muench that a "Morganthau atmosphere" permeated the twelve Nuremberg successor trials.[109] Major Lawrence H. Brown, stationed in Dillenburg (Hesse), apparently also made comments to Muench that were "critical of Jews." In civilian life, Brown was a professor of sociology at Creighton University.[110]

Highly educated army intelligence officer and Catholic Zsolt Aradi (himself a former Hungarian national) told Muench, "Jews in the Counterintelligence Corps [hereafter CIC] strictly enforced denazification."[111] Aradi also said that he believed Jews in the CIC caused him difficulties and prevented his promotion.[112] In August 1946, Muench had lunch with Theobald Dengler, Catholic chief of the Religious Affairs Berlin (sector) office, and a "Captain Thompson." According to the bishop's diary, the three men discussed, among other things, "Jews in the CIC and Public Safety divisions."[113]

The CIC had a poor reputation among army and state department officials.[114] Political officer Parker Buhrman, stationed in Munich, told his superior Robert Murphy in Berlin that the "CIC arrests all over Bavaria has gained [the U.S. occupation forces] the reputation of being arbitrary, unjust, and whimsical." Buhrman initially assumed these problems were due to "personnel that were too young and inexperienced in dealing with occupation conditions."[115] Further inquiries by Buhrman changed his mind as to the explanation for CIC "irregularities." Buhrman told Murphy, "it appears that a great many of the agents of the CIC are men or women who acquired their citizenship in recent years, or very recently as a result of service in the American armed forces." He added, "many of them do not speak English well and do not have an American educational background or any conception of common law procedure and justice. They are pursuing methods of interrogation here which are sometimes unfavorably compared with those of the Gestapo and which are a grave reflection upon our national character. [This] constantly bring[s] into disrepute and question the entire American system of justice."[116] Murphy had heard such words many times, often from Muench. Ironically, Buhrman found out that the particular incident he investigated did not involve the CIC, but the Information Control Division (ICD).[117] Buhrman's mistake typified the manner in which émigrés working in the occupation forces—some of whom were Jewish, leftist, or both—served as scapegoats for complaints.

Acts potentially indicating anti-Semitism among the German population, such as desecration of Jewish cemeteries (most common in *Länder* with large populations of Jewish displaced persons), were a source of disagreement among army officers. Some called the desecration of Jewish graves in Bavaria and Hesse (American zone) "pranks"; others deemed such acts worthy of serious attention. In June 1948, the *Land* military governor for OMGUS-Bavaria met with representatives from the Intelligence Branch, the CIC, the DP branch, Public Safety, and other divisions. International Council of Christians and Jews (ICCJ) representative Carl Zietlow made a presentation to the group that included snapshots of desecrated Jewish graves in the *Unterfranken* (Lower Franconia) region of Bavaria. Zietlow's report called the incidents "the work of individuals, in some cases probably boys at play." Or, said Zietlow's report, "the [headstone] foundations were in bad disrepair and could easily have been turned over by the wind." He doubted the desecration was part of an "organized effort," but nonetheless recommended that the cemetery incidents "had more than passing significance." In a 28 May meeting with Muench, Zietlow repeated his assessment that "wind" or boys at play were probably responsible. As to anti-Semitism in Bavaria, Zietlow told Muench that Germans believed "Jews to be in control in the U.S." and these Jews "deliberately starved" Germans.[118]

Upon hearing from Zietlow, CIC officer (Captain) Heckler cited 108 reported cases in the area around Landsberg from January to June 1948.[119] A large cemetery in Munich remained untouched, observed Heckler, who suspected that desecration took place "near camps, where feeling [ran] high at times." But Public Welfare and DP officer Gosser played down the problem by hinting that Dr. Philipp Auerbach, state commissioner for political and racial persecutees for Bavaria and a Jew himself, exaggerated in his complaints concerning the grave desecration. Auerbach, complained Gosser, was not to be trusted. "His complaints do not mean much until they are verified. There are more of his complaints which one cannot verify than those on which it can be said he is right." Public safety officer (Lieutenant) Hugunin seemed to concur, noting, "Auerbach's reports differed considerably from those of the German police."[120] Despite the criticism levied at him by army officials and large segments of German society, Auerbach was forthright in both his criticism and defense of Jews.[121]

Other army officers present at the meeting did not agree with Gosser. Intelligence officer Moeller scoffed at Gosser and Zietlow's explanation, retorting that "it was difficult to believe that children should be playing in three or four different locations at the same time in Jewish cemeteries." Nor was it "reasonable that the wind would turn up tombstones in three or four different places at the same time," said Moeller. The graves affected were "completely wrecked," certainly indicating more than the "pranks of children."[122]

Anti-Semitic stereotypes flourished among Americans and Germans, and certainly in the Catholic and military circles of Muench's acquaintance, between 1946 and 1959. "The Jew," especially the Jewish displaced person, was imagined to be a Christ-killer and abusive of Christians; capable of disguising his Jewishness to control key positions in the

American Army and even the White House; responsible for a merciless capitalism and radical communism; capable of dishonesty, intrigue, and even murder; careless with "German" property; responsible for "psychologically burdening" Germans; overfed and overhoused; sexually predatory in nature; without shame or modesty; politically unreliable; physically abusive; a smuggler; "Russianized" in his way of thinking; rich; and greedy. Aloisius Muench—whose Church honored him with the privileged positions of priest, monsignor, bishop, archbishop, Vatican visitor, regent, and nuncio, and cardinal—contributed to this list "recent American, Thirty-Niner, or émigré," with "no sense of American justice and fair play."

Conclusion:

The Holocaust and Catholic Conscience

As liaison representative to the U.S. occupation forces and as Vatican emissary to Germany, Cardinal Aloisius Muench was very much a part of ongoing and active discussions about the Nazi past in postwar Germany. His papers are especially fruitful when one looks at Catholic participation in this discussion. The sentiments of Catholics writing to the cardinal in general and certainly the sentiments of Muench in particular reflected a selective process of remembrance, with emphasis on victimization or heroism. Discussions about the Nazi past were often couched in religious terms, and, as letters to (and by) Muench demonstrate, some contained anti-Jewish overtones. The unique nature of the Muench collection allows for a rare glimpse into candid German commentary about Nazism, the Holocaust, and surviving Jews.

Were it not for Muench's pastoral letter, *One World,* these tens of thousands of letters might never have come into existence at all. *One World* established the cardinal as a trustworthy figure of German descent who "understood" German "victimization." Muench held the philo-German and anti-Jewish notions that animated *One World* before he knew of his assignment to Germany as Vatican apostolic visitor. He expressed no regret over its defensively pro-German (postwar) message or its widespread illegal dissemination; he merely expressed concern at defamation of his character or possible damage to his standing with the Army brass. For their part, many German Catholics who wrote to Muench viewed *One World* as, to quote one respondent, "bread for the hungry soul," for it validated the already popular notion that Germans were by and large victims.

It is clear also that the cardinal and the Germanophile Pope Pius XII held each other in mutual high regard. This seems also to have been true for German bishops in contact with Muench, who liked him, and, in some cases, treated him like family. They issued their own pastoral letters rejecting "collective" guilt and responsibility, so the message contained in *One World* was welcome (but not new) news to them. Nor was it a case of "top down" insistence on German Catholic "victimhood"; letters to Muench from common laity indicate a high degree of popular support for notions of victimization and resistance.

If *One World* introduced Muench as a champion for German Catholics, surely his active participation in the Catholic clemency campaign confirmed it. He received hundreds of unsolicited letters—such was the strength of his reputation—from German Catholics trying to commute the sentences of war criminals who were proven participants in the *Einsatzgruppen* campaigns, the concentration and extermination camp systems, the confiscation of Jewish assets, medical experiments, and more. In some cases, he offered his help, petitioning Army brass and clemency boards on behalf of these convicted criminals. He was far from alone in such efforts. He was part of a vast campaign that played out in both the Catholic and Protestant churches, among the German population, and among some U.S. government officials on both sides of the Atlantic. Only when he feared damage to his or the Vatican's reputation did he refuse to intervene. Some letters indicate that he worried over the bloodier killing performed by war criminals like Otto Ohlendorf, but such thoughts did not guide all of his actions.

Evidence suggests that Cardinal Muench's openly partisan, philo-German position provided psychological comfort to many German Catholics. The appeal of his message even reached some Germans who were Protestant or who opted to be outside the reach of organized religion at all. The wide popularity of *One World* earned Muench a platform from which he might have encouraged a real reckoning with the years 1933 to 1945. Instead, Muench concerned himself with those whose self-congratulatory or self-pitying labeling of themselves as "victims" or "resistors" was often questionable. He bemoaned the fate of ethnic German expellees and other refugee groups across Europe, sometimes at great length. Muench excluded Jewish Holocaust survivors, Jewish refugees, and Soviet prisoners of war in his litany of victims. These exceptions were unsurprising given Muench's anti-Jewish and equally strong anti-communist tendencies.

That Muench concerned himself with Catholics or even Christians at large would be far more palatable were this the whole story, as one might believe from reading Colman Barry's biography of the cardinal. But an honest look at the sources indicates that Aloisius Muench was not merely indifferent to Jews and concerned foremost with his co-religionists. He viewed Jews as harmful in a number of very specific ways. He viewed German Jews now in America as "alien" or "recent" Americans, unfamiliar with "American" standards of fairness and incapable of true loyalty to the United States. He believed them to be "in control" of American policy-making in Germany. He feared them as "avengers" who wished to harm "victimized" Germans. He believed Jews to be excessively involved in leftist activities, and Muench feared communism deeply. Cardinal Muench entertained without protest letters from German Catholics (including clergy) calling Jews sexual predators, thieves, and anarchists. He supported Germans (again including clerics) in their efforts to retain Jewish property gained by way of "Aryanization" during the Nazi period. In some cases, he helped to defend German Catholics convicted of murder. In none of this was he alone. He had support for these notions in his American (clerical, hierarchical, and military) as well as German circles.

Coupled with his activism in combating notions of "collective" German guilt and, worse, collective German responsibility for Nazi crimes and the Holocaust, Cardinal Muench's anti-Semitism was damaging to the Church and faith he sought to defend. Any assessment of his overall legacy as a prelate and as a servant of the Church should take into account not only his positive deeds on behalf of his co-religionists but his blatant and unapologetic anti-Semitism. Cardinal Muench is an important figure in any study of German "selective memory" of the Nazi past and in the Catholic Church's failure during this period to confront its own complicity in Nazism's anti-Jewish ideology. He exemplified both of these phenomena. So long as the cardinal remained prudent about maintaining his (and sometimes their) agendas without attracting undue attention or bad publicity to himself or his Church, his superiors granted him the Church's highest honors and titles.

Appendix A

Pope Pius XII and the Holocaust:
A Historiographical Essay

The wartime record of Pope Pius XII is fraught with ambiguity. Until the early 1960s, little major public criticism of Pius XII's wartime behavior emerged. This changed in 1963 with Rolf Hochhuth's play, *Der Stellvertreter* (The Deputy),[1] representing the first major attack on Pius XII's alleged inaction during the Holocaust. Saul Friedländer followed with the first significant scholarly criticism of the pope in *Pie XII et le IIIᵉ Reich.*[2] Critics' voices were loud enough that Pope Paul VI (1963–78), who served as papal undersecretary of state to ordinary affairs during World War II, granted four Jesuit scholars permission to research the Vatican's still-unorganized holdings for the wartime period. The result was the eleven-volume series *Actes et Documents du Saint Siège relatifs à la seconde guerre mondiale.*[3]

Recent or resurrected select works with the stated aim of defending Pius XII include: David Alvarez and *Actes* editor Robert A. Graham, S.J., *Nothing Sacred: Nazi Espionage Against the Vatican, 1939–1945;* *Actes* editor Pierre Blet, S.J., *Pius XII and the Second World War: According to the Archives of the Vatican;* Robert A. Graham, S.J., "How to Manufacture a Legend"; Pinchas Lapide, *The Last Three Popes and the Jews: Pope Pius XII Did Not Remain Silent;* Margherita Marchione,

Pope Pius XII: Architect for Peace; and Ronald Rychlak, *Hitler, the War, and the Pope.*[4]

Studies focusing more on the shortcomings of the papacy of Pius XII include: James Carroll, *Constantine's Sword: The Church and the Jews,* a beautifully written philosophical-historical work aimed at Church policy toward Judaism since the crucifixion; John Cornwell, *Hitler's Pope: The Secret History of Pius XII,* which makes a number of insupportable claims (e.g., documentation of open hostility toward Jews on Pius's part) but remains valuable for its focus on his early career, dedicated to centralizing authority in Rome by way of the new Code of Canon Law; Heinz Hürten, *Pius XII und die Juden;* Uki Goni, *The Real Odessa: Smuggling the Nazis to Peron's Argentina;* Robert Katz, *The Battle for Rome: The Germans, the Allies, the Partisans, and the Pope, Summer 1943–June 1944;* David Kertzer, *The Popes Against the Jews: The Vatican's Role in the Rise of Modern Antisemitism,* an astounding study that dismantles the strict characterization of so-called religious anti-Judaism as separate from and less dangerous than modern anti-Semitism (political, economic, racial, etc.) by bringing to bear clear evidence of the Holy See's involvement in forced conversions and blood libel charges as well as anti-Semitic political movements and anti-Jewish economic and racial rhetoric; Ernst Klee, *Persilscheine und falsche Pässe: Wie die Kirchen den Nazis halfen,* which documents the involvement of the German Churches in the postwar clemency campaign; John F. Morley, *Vatican Diplomacy and the Jews During the Holocaust, 1939–1943,* one of the first critical studies of the Holy See by a Roman Catholic priest; Michael Phayer, *The Catholic Church and the Holocaust, 1930–1965,* which brings out Pius's fear of communism and his desire to protect the institutional Church, even at the cost of Jewish lives; Carol Rittner and John K. Roth, eds., *Pope Pius XII and the Holocaust,* a rich book with contributions by Doris L. Bergen, James J. Doyle, Eugene J. Fisher, ·Eva Fleischner, Albert Friedlander, Gershon Greenberg, Michael R. Marrus, Sergio I. Minerbi, John F. Morley, John T. Pawlikowski, Carol Rittner, John K. Roth, Richard L. Rubenstein, and Susan Zuccotti; and Zuccotti, *Under His Very Windows: The Vatican and the Holocaust in Italy,* a very important and meticulous study that debunks the myth of a "written order" by Pope Pius to save Italian Jews from deportation.[5]

In his recent book *Pius XII and the Holocaust: Understanding the Controversy,* José M. Sánchez synthesizes the controversies surrounding

Pius's pontificate. The pope, writes Sánchez, faced a "cruel" choice: he could preserve the institutional Roman Catholic Church or he could act as Vicar of Christ. "Given the circumstances he could not be both."[6] Preserving the institutional Church meant meeting its material needs and demands, namely, protecting Catholic clergy, schools, buildings, and property so that priests could administer the all-crucial sacraments—which, in Catholic theology, provide the grace needed for salvation. But the pope had another duty: as Bishop of Rome, he was to act as Vicar of Christ, meaning, to "take the place of Christ in this world" and to make all persons aware of their obligation to "love God and one's neighbor as oneself." Pius, argues Sánchez, could not reconcile his conflicting duties, at least to the satisfaction of those "critics that would come to judge his wartime role."[7] "Cruel" or not, Pius and German Catholics lived at a time in history that indeed forced them to choose between state and faith. That he and so many members of the Church chose the former testifies to the ultimate and wrenching failure—and futility—of the Roman Catholic faith as they understood it.

Sánchez calls "untenable" or "lacking in substance" the following claims: that Pius was an anti-Semite and "uninterested" in the fate of European Jewry (an argument rejected by nearly all scholars of the subject, with the exceptions of John Cornwell in *Hitler's Pope* and Daniel Jonah Goldhagen in *A Moral Reckoning: The Role of the Catholic Church in the Holocaust and its Unfulfilled Duty of Repair*);[8] that he desisted from making a strong protest naming Jews specifically due to his fear for the physical security of Rome and the Vatican; that his fear of Soviet communism meant he saw Nazi Germany as a bulwark against Soviet expansion (Phayer disagrees, as does Peter C. Kent in *The Lonely Cold War of Pope Pius XII: The Roman Catholic Church and the Division of Europe, 1943–1950*);[9] and that his admiration for German cultural tradition affected his relationship to the Nazi government. Of "some substance," writes Sánchez, are claims that he feared open protest might result in abrogation of the German Concordat and jeopardize German Catholics; that his personality and diplomatic training cultivated "caution" in his dealings with the Nazi regime; that he avoided forthright denunciation so as to temper a "crisis of conscience" for German Catholics forced to choose between state and faith; that he wished to maintain the Holy See's neutrality so as to be available for mediation; and, "the strongest argument for Pius's response," that he did not want to "make things worse."[10]

Despite a valiant effort at impartiality and at times forthright criticism of Pius (such as in the case of Croatia), Sánchez falls reluctantly into the camp of the pope's so-called defenders. It is telling that Sánchez finds it "difficult to deny" that *L'Osservatore Romano* "had the full support of the Pope, who was, after all, the sovereign of the Vatican state and by law [its] publisher" when he cites the 3 December 1943 edition of *L'Osservatore Romano,* which called the deportation of Italian Jewry "unreasonable, unchristian, and inhuman."[11] Sánchez's view of the newspaper as a papal pulpit is sure to dissatisfy critics of David Kertzer, whose *Popes Against the Jews* demonstrates—by way of anti-Jewish text in *L'Osservatore Romano*—rampant anti-Semitism in the nineteenth-century Holy See.[12]

The assertion that the pope "never saw Germany, under Nazism, as a bulwark of Western Christianity against the advance of Bolshevism from the Soviet Union" is not credible, as we know from Kent.[13] Sánchez repeats the oft-cited canon that "almost 5,000" Roman Jews sought shelter in the Vatican and its buildings in October 1943. Yet Zuccotti finds Vatican officials "deeply divided" on the presence of Jews in Vatican properties. On 11 December 1943, Monsignor Roberto Ronca, rector of the Pontificio Seminario Romano Maggiore, wrote to Pius apologizing for "displeasing" the pope for accepting too many "refugees."[14]

In my view, several key factors in Pope Pius's background—pointed out in the works of Cornwell, Kertzer, and Richard Rubenstein,[15] among others—are of note. As a prelate, canon (Church) lawyer, nuncio, secretary of state, and finally as pope, he understood his mission to be the strengthening and defense of the Church against Russian "bolshevism," liberalism, and other forms of modernity. As pope, he understood himself to be the "Vicar of Christ" on earth. He believed the Roman Catholic Church to be the "one true Church" and humanity's sole medium of redemption. His grandfather, Marcantonio Pacelli, was a lay canon lawyer for Pope Pius IX ("Pio Nono"), who began office with temporal power over the Italian Papal States including Rome, Bologna, Parma, and Modena, but ended his papacy a self-proclaimed prisoner within the walls of the Vatican. "Pio Nono" regarded the French Revolution and its byproduct, the civic emancipation of Jewry, to be a "dangerous political legacy" and was committed to its undoing, as reflected in his order in 1850 to return Rome's Jews to the squalid Roman ghetto. The Inquisition was alive and well until 1870 (the year marking the end of papal sovereignty). The Roman Catholic Church actively supported Europe's anti-Semitic movements from the time of the French Revolution until the end of World War II. Although the Church proclaimed to reject "crude" Nazi racism, it saw Christian Europe as "under a multifaceted religious, military, political, and cultural threat" in which "Jews . . . play[ed] a hostile role."[16]

During Nazi domination of Europe, the Holy See regarded the disenfranchisement of Jews as a "positive step forward." It did not object to the anti-Jewish legislation of 3 October 1940, *Statut des Juifs,* imposed in Vichy France, or for that matter to Nazi legislation barring Jews from civil service, certain professions, or even revoking their citizenship, as long as such measures were characterized as religious—as opposed to racial—discrimination, and as long as anti-Jewish measures were carried forth with "Christian love and charity."[17]

Murder was the final and extreme end to the long series of discriminations enacted across Europe (not limited to Germany) in this period. Michael Phayer's research indicates that Pius first learned directly of the mass murder of European Jewry in May 1942, via a letter from Italian priest Pirro Scavizzi. It is likely he had already heard this news indirectly, given that his secretary of state, Luigi Maglione, was told in March 1942 that 80,000 Slovakian Jews faced deportation, which, as stated an earlier report (February 1942) to Maglione from Chargé d'Affaires Giuseppe Burzio, meant certain death.[18] In February 1942, Nazi leaders demanded that the Slovak government, under the directorship of Roman Catholic Monsignor Joseph Tiso, supply Jewish workers for German factories in Poland. Nuncios in both Bratislava and Budapest protested. On 13 March, Archbishop Angelo Rotta (Budapest) passed on to the pope an appeal from the World Jewish Congress asking him to persuade Tiso to cancel the deportation of Slovakian Jews. The response came from Maglione, who wrote a note of protest to the Slovak government. The Holy See's protest was ignored.[19]

This incident itself encapsulates the problem of assessing Pius's actions and inactions in the face of the Holocaust. John Pawlikowski interprets this instance as a clear example of attempted intervention by Pius, via Maglione. Michael Marrus considers this same instance a failure on the part of the Holy See. Marrus cites the pope's close associate Domenico Tardini as saying, "it is a great misfortune that the president of Slovakia [Tiso] is a priest. Everyone knows that the Holy See cannot bring Hitler to heel. But who will understand that we cannot even control a priest?"[20] It is worth noting as a postscript that on 26 April 1942, the Slovak parliament passed authorization for deportations of Slovakian Jewry. Not one Catholic priest who was a parliamentary representative voted against this measure. Also worth noting is that the General Presbytery of the Lutheran Bishops in Slovakia, under the leadership of Vladimir Cobdra and Dr. Samuel Stefan Osusky, issued a pastoral letter condemning the excesses accompanying the deportation of Slovakian Jewry.[21]

Maglione received other reports about the murder of European Jewry. On 3 October 1942, the Polish embassy at the Vatican sent two reports to him describing German atrocities against the Jews in Poland. The reports spoke of mass killing of Jews by asphyxiation, mass deportations from the ghettos of Vilna (Lithuania) and Warsaw (Poland), and camps where Jews were "gathered and killed."[22] Many reports followed in the next years, and the pope made the decision to desist from any public condemnation, verbal or written, specifically referring to Nazi mass murder of European Jewry. On 16 October 1943, German occupying troops rounded up and deported 1,022 Roman Jews near the Vatican, and the pope uttered no protest. In the previous week, on 9 October, he received German ambassador to the Holy See, Ernst von Weizsäcker, who told him about the impending deportations. In Weizsäcker's recollection, Pius, upon hearing this disturbing news, told the ambassador, "if one must make the deportation of the Jews, it is good to do it quickly."[23] If in fact he did say this or something like it, it fits an interpretation of a pope not willing to speak out for Jews and who, given his upbringing in a highly anti-Semitic Church, may even have seen their removal from Christian society as necessary—but hoped for "Christian" justice and charity in the unpleasant process.

The March 1998 document "We Remember: A Reflection on the Shoah," issued by the Holy See's Commission for Religious Relations with the Jews, asserts, and Sánchez repeats, that Pope Pius "did personally or through his representatives . . . save hundreds of thousands of Jewish lives." Cited as evidence in "We Remember" are the 7 September 1945 verbal statement of Italian Hebrew Commission representative Dr. Joseph Nathan; the 21 September 1945 statement of secretary general of the World Jewish Congress, A. Leo Kubowitzki; the 29 November 1945 words of approximately eighty Jewish survivors during a meeting with the pope; and, finally, praise from president of Israel Golda Meir upon Pius's death in 1958.[24] We learn, however, from Zuccotti's work, that

"Joseph" Nathan was in fact Guiseppe Nathan, president of the nation-wide Union of Italian Jewish Communities. A. Leo Kubowitzki, or Aryeh L. Kubovy, as he was later known, lived in New York during the war, meaning he had no first-hand knowledge of events in Rome. When examined carefully, "none of the four cases is convincing."[25]

In conclusion, since the February 2003 opening of select materials from the Vatican archives for the years 1922–39, cases of misuse of historical documentation to defend the role of Pope Pius XII and the Vatican have arisen. I will look at one such example in detail here, involving a letter written by Pius when, as Eugenio Pacelli, he was nuncio to Bavaria. It is addressed to Undersecretary of State Pietro Gasparri and dated 14 November 1923. This document was the subject of Antonio Gaspari's article, "New Letter Shows Pius XII Opposed Hitler," which appeared in the 4 March 2005 issue of *Inside the Vatican News.* Translated from the Italian in Gaspari's article, Pacelli's letter reads as follows:

> The facts about the nationalist uprising, which in recent days has disturbed the city of Munich (see dispatches No. 443, 444 and 445), are already known to your most reverend eminence from the Italian press; I therefore do not need to repeat them in this respectful report. Still, upon one point, which I alluded to already in dispatch No. 444, I believe it opportune to communicate to Your Eminence some further details, that is, regarding the demonstrations of an anti-Catholic character which accompanied the uprising itself, but which have not surprised those who have followed the publications of the papers of the right-wing radicals, like the *Volkischer Beobachter* (Folkish Observer) and *Heimatland* (Homeland). This character was revealed above all in the systematic attacks on the Catholic clergy with which the followers of Hitler and Ludendorff, especially in street speeches, stirred up the population, thus exposing the ecclesiastics to insults and abuse. The attacks were especially focused on this learned and zealous Cardinal Archbishop Michael Faulhaber, who, in a sermon he gave in the Duomo on the 4th of this month and in a letter of his to the Chancellor of the Reich Gustav Stresemann published by the Wolff Agency on the 7th, had denounced the persecutions against the Jews. To this was added the unfounded and absurd rumor in the city, probably spread intentionally, that accused the cardinal of having changed von Kahr's mind, who, as is known, while at the beginning in the *Bürger-*

braukeller (beer hall) had apparently, to avoid violence, adhered to the Hitler-Ludendorff coup d'etat, later came out against it. Thus it was that, during the confusing events of last Saturday, a numerous group of demonstrators gathered in front of the front door of the bishop's residence, shouting "Down with the Cardinal!" ("Nieder mit dem Kardinal!"). His Eminence was by good fortune absent from Munich, having left that day to consecrate a new church in a town near Müldorf; but, when he returned in his car the following evening, he was greeted by a similar hostile demonstration. These anti-Catholic sentiments also manifested themselves in chaotic student gatherings, the day before yesterday, in the University, which were attended by people who did not attend the university (and were not even from Bavaria) obliging the Rector in the end to close the university until further notice. Also in the university, object recently of repeated acts of the charitable solicitude and generosity of the Holy Father on behalf of the students, there were denunciations of the Pope, of the Archbishop, of the Catholic Church, of the clergy, of von Kahr, who, even though he is a Protestant, was characterized by one of the orators as an honorary member of the Society of Jesus (*Ehrenmitglied der Jesuiten*).[26]

According to Gaspari's article, Pacellis' above letter "denounces the National Socialist movement as an anti-Catholic threat" and "at the same time notes that the cardinal of Munich had already condemned acts of persecution against Bavaria's Jews." Indeed, the letter does both. Gaspari goes on to argue that "this letter is previously unpublished proof that Pacelli was in opposition to Nazism, seen both as anti-Catholic and as anti-Semitic, already in 1923—ten years before Hitler came to power, and sixteen years before Pacelli was elected Pope Pius XII. The letter thus is important evidence against the charge of Cornwell and others that Pius XII was in some way sympathetic to the Nazi regime."

Gaspari's treatment of the letter is misleading. First, no serious scholar claims that Pius was sympathetic to the National Socialist movement. Further, for decades, scholars have produced evidence of the Holy See's concern about Nazi anti-Catholic policy. Scholars have also long produced evidence that although the pope did not agree with all tenets of Nazi ideology, he was willing to negotiate with Nazi Germany as a legitimate state for what he perceived as the higher purpose of protecting German Catholics, e.g., the Concordat of 1933. Also, if one looks carefully at the wording of the letter, we have no evidence of Pacelli opposing Nazi anti-Semitism specifically. He merely recounts the negative right-wing reaction to Cardinal Faulhaber's sermon. He does not take a position on the sermon himself.

Let us look more closely at Faulhaber's comments, key to the argument Gaspari makes about so-called objections to anti-Semitism. The following is an excerpt from a letter written by Cardinal Faulhaber, addressed to Reich Chancellor Gustav Stresemann, dated 6 November 1923: "How else shall we dismantle the hate that condemns with blind rage our Israelite fellow citizens or other ethnic groups lock, stock, and barrel, without proof of guilt from individual to individual; how else shall we defend ourselves against Civil War that would instigate unforeseeable fresh devastation and ensure self-inflicted impoverishment of our poor People?" Cardinal Faulhaber refers to "Israelite fellow citizens" specifically in this single sentence only; in all, the letter is four paragraphs long and focuses on moral problems among Germans during the Weimar period broadly. For example, "Without intruding on purely political processes and [without] wishing to take a position on all the political questions of the day, I may still give Your Excellency [Stresemann] my assurance that the Church feels it to be her moral duty to work energetically toward the moral rebirth of the [German] people—in particular, to dismantle the obsession to criticize; to [teach] them duty of public spirit; to dismantle self-seeking and the cultivation of a of sense of victimization."[27] Cardinal Faulhaber's single sentence referring to "Israelite fellow citizens" does imply sympathy and empathy for Jewish Germans. This is positive, of course, but not new.

Now, to the sermon itself, referred to in Pacelli's 14 November 1923 letter as "a sermon he [Faulhaber] gave in the duomo on the 4th of this month [November]." The text of the "sermon [given on] All Souls Day by Herr Cardinal [Michael von Faulhaber] in the Cathedral, 1923, concerning the theme: The Afflicted (Suffering?) Church and the German Job" (*Die Leidende Kirche und der deutsche Job*), appeared in the *Bayerische Kurier*, dated 6 November 1923. The sermon consists of five paragraphs. It is three double-spaced pages long. In the last paragraph, Faulhaber says, "Hate directed against Jews and Catholics, against farmers and Bavarians will not cure any wounds." This is the only place in the sermon that mentions Jews specifically. The fact that Faulhaber draws from the Old Testament is significant, but is also something we have known about Faulhaber for some time: he publicly disagreed with

Nazism's call to purge the Bible of all Jewish references and disagreed with right-wing theologians who tried to dismiss the Old Testament as "Jewish." Faulhaber believed the Old Testament had lessons and relevance for modern Christians. For example, in his sermon he says, "every German Job could model himself after the biblical Job, who, as long as he still had some to give, shared his bread with the orphan and clothed the cold with the wool of his sheep."[28]

Pacelli's letter to Gasparri of 14 November 1923 is factually correct. Pacelli's comment on the attacks is historically accurate. Faulhaber did refer to Jews specifically (once) in his sermon. Faulhaber also referred to them specifically (again, once) in his letter to Reich Chancellor Gustav Stresemann. We still learn nothing about Pacelli and his views, however, except that he remarked at length on the anti-Catholic bent of the Nazis and other right-wing groups, and was aware that Faulhaber made reference to Catholics but also Jews specifically as well as to other groups. Pacelli's own opinions about Faulhaber's empathetic remarks are not reflected.

New studies, such as those by Peter Godman and Gerhard Besier, assessing the newly released documentation for 1922–39 have recently appeared, and more studies and insights are likely to follow.[29] For now, however, the Aloisius Muench papers do confirm the following points. Pacelli was inordinately interested in affairs in Germany and was indeed a "stout Germanophile," probably evidenced best by his insistence that he and Muench speak in German during their audiences. There is no evidence of either crude anti-Semitism on Pius's part or positive identification with Nazi ideology as such in the Muench papers. There is strong evidence that Pius was most concerned about the German Catholic institutional Church, episcopate, and lay population in Germany in the postwar period, at the expense of any sensitivity or positive actions toward European Jewry. There is also strong evidence that the pope and Muench shared the same unfortunate blind spot about German Catholic complicity in Nazism, and, worse, about the anti-Semitic ideologies (in different manifestations) common to both the Roman Catholic Church and the Nazi state. It was this painful lack of self-awareness concerning the Church's own anti-Jewish stereotypes that is most significant of all.

Appendix B

Muench's Function as Liaison Representative to OMGUS, 1946–1949

Functions

1. General Statement:
"The permanent representatives from each of the three major faiths in the United States should provide assistance to their respective German churches in meeting needs arising in the field of clerical functions. The liaison representatives should assist the German churches in every possible way with the heavy tasks now confronting them, particularly with reference to the problems of spiritual and moral education and reconstruction. In helping develop the spiritual life of the church the American representatives would serve, therefore, primarily as liaison in the area of spiritual reconstruction between the churches of Germany and religious resources in the United States. They should not serve as special pleaders to Military Government for the German churches. Their liaison functions with Military Government would primarily be to provide information to Military Government as to developments in the area of spiritual life and reconstruction of the German churches; to assist in making available to the German churches whatever information or service pertaining to clerical functions of the churches which Military Government might possess.

2. On the basis of the preceding general statement the U.S. religious liaison representative will perform the following functions: serve as liaison representatives between the churches of their respective faiths in Germany and in the United States in the field of purely religious, clerical functions of the churches; serve as liaison between Military Government and German churches: by providing information to Military Government as to developments in the area of spiritual life and reconstruction of German churches; and, by assisting in making available to the German churches whatever information or service pertaining to clerical functions of the churches which Military Government might possess; confer with German church leaders relative to problems relating to the field of clerical functions of the German churches; assist German church leaders in finding ways and means of developing spiritual resources of the church; assist in the development of a peaceful and democratic Germany.

3. The liaison representative shall not: become spiritual pleaders to Military Government for the churches of Germany; assume responsibilities in the functional fields of operation now directed and supervised by Religious Affairs officers of Military Government. These representatives shall not be attached to the Office of Military Government. They are representatives of their respective faiths in the United States and are functionally responsible to the United States agencies that pay their salaries. They shall not operate within the framework of nor under the functional direction of Military Government.

Military Government shall grant them billet and mess privileges as are commonly attached thereto. They shall be provided the necessary travel privileges on the rail, air, and motor facilities of Military Government, provided such transportation requests are reasonable. Office space, equipment, and other administrative facilities shall be provided. Liaison relations with Military Government pertaining to functional phases of religious affairs shall be directed to the Chief of the Religious Affairs Section.

4. Liaison between Military Government and the German Churches
An additional avenue of contact between Military Government and the German churches has been created through the recent appointment of the three permanent liaison representatives described in the

preceding section. While these representatives serve primarily as connecting links between the churches of the United States and Germany, they are nevertheless expected also to provide valuable assistance to Military Government officers through mutual discussion of experiences."[1]

Appendix C

One World in Charity, Full English Text (Fargo, 1946)

Lenten Pastoral of 1946, by his Excellency the most Reverend Aloisius J. Muench, D.D., bishop of Fargo, to our venerable brethren of the clergy and to our beloved religious and faithful of the laity [in] health and benediction.

Dearly Beloved in Christ:

For the first time in the history of Christian nations, powerful governments are making the exercise of Christian charity impossible through official regulations. We are practically told that it is wrong to love our enemy and to do good to those who have done us evil. Christian charity is not permitted to play the role of the good Samaritan. Food rations to the enemy are measured out according to a "disease and unrest" formula, carefully determined by calories, and not in accordance with weights and measures of Christian charity. Horrible stories of starvation, disease, and death are still coming to us from European and Asiatic lands. The savagery that the war excited in the hearts of men is incredible. Once more is verified the saying of the ancients: "Homo homini lupus—Man is a wolf to his fellow man." We can no longer be silent. If we Christians do not raise our voices in behalf of mercy, compassion, and charity, will the pagans in our midst do so? In these hate-laden times we must dare to be brave, and fearlessly voice our convictions, lest fear become "the parent of cruelty." No longer can we allow ourselves to be afraid of our virtues. Kindness and generosity must step forward boldly and claim their right to be heard, indeed claim their right, in the name of the charity of Christ, to do their deeds of mercy toward everyone in need, be he friend or foe. In a pointed and pithy phrase Mr. Churchill told England's citizens some months ago that they must put aside the "craven fear of being great." That admonition needs also to be addressed to us.

If our statesmen have shrunk to pygmy size because of their cowardice to proclaim the rights of Christian mercy, then let us, though in humble positions of citizenry, rise to the full stature of Christ and with Him proclaim the Lord's great law of love. Fear must not make us traitors to this law. The architects who are blue-printing the structure of peace have issued no specifications for charity for the One World which they want to build. Charity is not so much as mentioned in any of their statements on future peace.

It would seem that they have closed and tightly sealed their books of history. Surely, they are not consulted, or else they would see that peace has never yet been built on foundations of hatred and revenge. Charity has been civilization's most successful builder. With thoughts that breathe and words that flame we must proclaim our faith in the power of charity. Nations long to create One World. By Christ's all-powerful law of love, the goal can be achieved—One World in Charity.

An Eye for an Eye

Reading reports on barbaric cruelties committed before and during the recent World War II our hearts bleed with pain. No age records similar brutalities. The atrocities described in the history of wars and conquests of the Greeks and Romans, or in the history of the invasions of pillaging and murdering hordes of Huns and Goths, or in the history of the terrible Genghis Khan pale into insignificance alongside the horrible events of our age.

We shall not wonder at all, when historians will have had access to the entire record of the black and bloody happenings of these times, that they will call our age This Barbaric Age. Truly, the lights of human civilization have been extinguished. To our shame we shall have to own that we were destined to live in the darkest of all dark ages. There has been a complete blackout of all that is decent and human. The torture chambers and dungeons of medieval days, at their worst, reveal nothing comparable to the cruelties practiced by humans on humans in our day. Let no one venture even as much as to mention again the Inquisition or Bartholomew's Night. Maidanek, Belsen, Buchenwald, Lidice, Hiroshima and Nagasaki will cry out to their victims to arise and tell their story of horrible bestialities. The bombing of civilians in unfortified cities, the holocausts in them of defenseless men, women and children, flame-throwing and jellied gas—these and other cruel methods of total warfare create horror in the human mind at their mere mention. Then came the end of the war, but not the end of further atrocities—looting and pillaging, starvation and death by deliberate calculation, forced migration of millions from their homes and lands, indignities against womanhood and even against the choicest lambs of God, the violation of sanctuaries and temples, and other outrages of godlessness.

Men who were created a little less than the angels lowered themselves by their ferocious deeds below the level of the beasts of the jungle. To them apply the words of the prophet: "They are cruel, and will have no mercy."[1] Because of their cruelty, mankind bleeds today from a thousand wounds. War is brutal, and makes men brutal. World War I produced its foul and ugly crop of vicious gangsters. We remember only too well the criminal and horrifying episodes of gangsterdom in our land. With no regard for either life or property, they held nothing sacred. In Europe and Asia gangsters of a new type, pitiless and savage, rose to positions of power. They boasted of their totalitarian power; with reason, for they controlled not only a strong secret police but also military might of unheard of proportions. These black-hearted and cold-blooded gangster overlords set up concentration camps, the real horrors of which came to light only after the war, exterminated millions of persons because of theories of race inferiority, and dragged into labor slavery men whose countries they overran with lightning invasions. Nor was youth spared. Children as young as ten years of age were kidnapped into slavery, and babies, born on trains carrying women destined for exile, were thrown from the windows. Were it not supported by facts, such barbarism is unbelievable. The armies of occupation of Hitler and Stalin ushered in a reign of terror in Poland, Finland, the Baltic States, and the countries of southeastern Europe. The brutish things that took place the year that Soviet troops occupied Lithuania, when Hitler and Stalin were still collaborators in crime, are graphically described by the Lithuanian Bishops: "This evil year of terror will ever be marked with shame in history. Thousands of Lithuanians were literally slaughtered, put into jail, or banished to far regions of the Soviet Union. Within the mere space of three days, June 14–17, 1941, nearly 40,000 persons were deported, irrespective of age, calling or health. Children and old people, women and men, were crammed into cattle-cars without food or water. Large numbers died in the railroad stations before the trains even moved. Nothing more was ever heard of those who were deported." The lot of hundreds of thousands of Poles was just as tragic when Stalin's armies overran Poland in 1939 and occupied it until Hitler attacked Russia in June 1941. Wives were separated from their husbands, and children from their parents. Healthy men were taken off into the slavery of labor camps, and old men, women and children were forced onto roads, strewn with the bodies of not hundreds but of thousands of their countrymen. The dispersal of Polish refugees is one of the most horrifying episodes in the historical annals of nations. Today they are found in the British Isles, Italy, Egypt, Syria, Palestine, India, Kenya, Uganda, Tanganyika, Northern and Southern Rhodesia, the Union of South Africa, and in South American countries. What terrible things befell civilian populations through bombing from Warsaw to Rotterdam, from Coventry, London, Cologne, Berlin and Dresden to Hiroshima and Nagasaki, need not be told. All this is still fresh in the minds of men. The war was a total war, and total, too, in its atrocities. Brutalities hidden behind a veil of secrecy continue. Hundreds of thousands are still separated from wife and children, forced work in mines and factories under conditions of slavery not much different from that practiced by the Romans in the case of conquered peoples. Are we not making ourselves partners in the crimes of Hitler by now doing the very thing we once condemned and fought against? The hypocrisy is colossal. The fact that this forced labor goes now under the name of human reparations does not alter the fact that it is nothing less than labor slavery. We are wretched hypocrites if we do not denounce as a crime what we were quick to denounce when done by the enemy. The law of justice has no double yardstick for measuring misdeeds of friend and foe. Worse than labor slavery are the mass expulsions of approximately 20,000 persons—Poles, Hungarians, nationals of the Baltic States, Germans of Old Austria, and Prussia. Driven from family homesteads, in some instances several hundred years old, these miserable, uprooted people, homeless, famished, and desperate, suffered and died as few people before in all history. Secret and military police ordered them out, in numerous cases, on only a few hours notice, permitting them to carry no more than some sixty to seventy pounds of baggage, with food only enough to take them to the frontier. Money was limited to a ridiculously low sum; all other property was confiscated. History describes the atrocious outrages committed against the Acadians when they were expelled from their homeland, but never has anything so tragic happened on so colossal a scale as in these forced migrations.

The tongue grows mute in trying to describe the agony of these doomed people. The very ink in the pen freezes to ice as it moves to tell this story of horror. What dreadful misery! The sight of it caused a newspaper columnist, known for his humane sentiments, to write: "very soon, if the American news photographers do an honest job, as there is every reason to believe they will, the American people will see movies of starving German men, women, and children, which will rival in horror the pictures of Buchenwald concentration camps, where Germans tortured Germans. But these will be pictures of torture inflicted by reason of an Allied policy of indifference, or misguided revenge, or plain blundering."[2] A great deal of the misery is due, of course, to the chaotic conditions that arose out of a war as total in its destruction as World War II. Those responsible for the outbreak of the war and those who carried it on in an inhumane way can not escape condemnation for their heinous guilt. What is terrible beyond all words, however, is this that by a cold, calculated policy of revenge, suffering and death are brought upon millions of people, for the most part persons who are not responsible either for the outbreak of the war or its horrors. What responsibility, for instance, can be placed on little children, or on children born since the end of the war? What justification can be made for a war on helpless people, particularly the aged, women, and children? Why must they suffer bitterly and die wretched deaths just because some policy-makers in top-levels have revived the Mosaic idea of an eye for an eye, and a tooth for a tooth?[3] We reject this policy of vengeance because Christ in His Sermon on the Mount rejected it,[4] because He taught us to look upon our fellowmen, friend or foe, as our brethren, to love all men, even our enemies, to do good to those who hate us, and to pray for those who persecute us. We take our teaching from Christ, and most certainly we will never, never take it from the hate-mongers in our midst, other Hitlers in disguise who like him would make of a whole nation a "crawling Belsen," as one newspaper correspondent put it. In this matter we are with Christ, and being on His side we know that we are right. Men have talked and written much of building One World. It will never be built by those who hate, and hating take their inspiration from the hard teaching of an eye for an eye and a tooth for a tooth. It will have to be built by those who believe in Christ's law of love. They shall be the builders of One World in Charity.

Intervention of Mercy

As Christians we have no choice but to accept Christ's law of mercy. We can not follow the law of tooth and claw. This is the law of the beast in the jungle. We are not beasts. In body we are like animal, but in soul we are like to God. We were created in his image. We are His children. Being His children we must imitate Him in all our human deeds.

Such imitation is directly commanded by Christ. "Be merciful as your Father in heaven is merciful."[5] In a large number of places the Holy Scriptures praise the infinite mercy of God. Our God is "a God of compassion and mercy,"[6] writes the Psalmist. Again he tells us that the Lord is "plenteous in mercy."[7] With Him "there is merciful forgiveness."[8] We beg God not to withhold His "tender mercies,"[9] but rather to let His tender mercies come to us,[10] for "the Lord is good to all, and merciful toward all His works."[11] In view of the great mercy of our Father in heaven we fail in our duty as His children if we do not strive to be merciful to all, friend or foe. Indeed, is He not merciful to us poor sinners? Again and again we offend Him by sin, and again and again we go to Him to beg His mercy. Pleading for His mercy and receiving it, are we any better than the merciless servant of the parable of our Lord if we do not show mercy toward our fellowmen?[12] The lower they have fallen, the more must we be anxious to show them mercy, so that by means of it we may raise them up to a better life. We expect God to make a "soft" peace with us. How, then, can we make a "hard" peace with our fellowmen? True, this is not the way of a harsh, cruel world. But then as Christians we do not follow the way of the world. We follow the way of Christ. Christ's way is the sure road to peace. We deeply deplore the fact that claims of mercy receive scant recognition in the postwar remaking of the war-torn world. When have we heard any statesman of the great powers, who are assuming the responsibility of shaping the future peace among nations, raise his voice in behalf of mercy for the fallen foe? Hatreds have gone so deep that statesmen fear using Christian words in their official proclamations. They seek to appear tough before all the world. If there is even only a semblance of compassion in their utterances, they hasten to say at once that they are not seeking to coddle the enemy, or that they are not trying to make a soft peace. Genuine peace should be neither hard nor soft. It should be just and charitable. Such a peace will be a fair and generous peace, and will have lasting value.

In some quarters it is not popular to make a plea for mercy. We make it nevertheless, and make it in the consciousness that Christ commands us to be merciful. It may be difficult to put aside the pagan within us with his hard and cruel law of an eye for an eye and a tooth for a tooth, and to put on Christ with His law of mercy, kindness, and love, but we have no option. We have to be either for or against Christ. In making a plea for mercy for the conquered we do not mean to set aside the claims of justice with regard to proven war criminals. Nor do we mean to say that the conquered people should receive priorities over the distressed, starving people in liberated countries. We give our full assent to the policy expressed by Secretary of State, James F. Byrnes, in his statement of December 11, 1945, defining official policies for German. "In terms of world supply of food shipments from the United States, liberated areas must enjoy a higher priority than Germany throughout this first postwar winter." Every right-thinking person can see the reasonableness of such a policy. But as Christians and as Americans we raise our voice in indignation against an official inhumanity, which does not permit the United Nations Relief and Rehabilitation Administration (UNRRA) to ship relief supplies either to Germany or to Japan, and besides does not even allow private relief agencies to send and distribute food, clothing, and medicines to war-stricken people living a pitiable life in the ruins of their bombed-out cities. We condemn these inhumane and cruel regulations of the War Relief Control Board. Having condemned the atrocities of the Nazis, how can we sit by and not condemn atrocities perpetrated under official directives? We make our own the question of the editorial writer: "For, if we hold the individual German responsible for not investigating Belsen and doing something about it, will we not one day be judged for our present apathy?"[13] We sat in severe judgment of the vile atrocities that were committed by Nazi gangsters. Shall we not sit

in judgment now of the atrocities being committed in the name of retributive justice, which in actual fact, however, is not justice but plain
revenge. Let us give heed to the words of the Divine Judge of Nations:
"As you have judged, so will you be judged by the same rule; award
shall be made as you have made award, in the same measure."[14] The
conclusion of all this is that we must vigorously demand the intervention of mercy in international affairs. We cannot profess to have given
up isolationism in international politics, finance, and trade, and then
turn about to become the rankest isolationists in matters of simple
human decency. If we did not fight for a human world, for what did we
really fight? Can we obtain the intervention of mercy? We can if with
determination and persistence we force our religious and moral convictions on postwar policy-makers. "The average American can compel
such action by keeping track of his government's shortcomings and
writing letters to Congress. To neglect this duty is in a sense to 'pass by
on the other side.'"[15] But possibly there is not enough food to go
around? "Fortunately, this is not true. Agricultural and nutrition ex-
perts are in agreement that there are sufficient stocks of wheat in the
United States to avert starvation for every man, woman, and child now
alive in Europe. There are additional supplies of all kinds in Canada,
Argentina, and in other countries of the Western Hemisphere."[16] We
condemn, too, a conspiracy of silence on the part of a large influential
segment of our press for not making known to the American people the
real plight of the European people. Our people are generous; they
would respond with full hands to give even of what they need themselves to help stricken people. Most certainly, they would not do less
than the people of Great Britain who, even at the expense of their meager rations, have organized aid for their former foes. Were the American
people given a picture of the suffering and misery of these people, they
would force their Government to do what the Government of
Denmark has done. Despite the memories of hardships under Nazi
occupation, sending food and clothing at public expense to more than
200,000 civilians who had fled from Eastern Germany in order to escape
the onrush of the Red armies at the close of the war. We applaud the
Christian courage of the American Friends Service Committee. They
say: "With great humility, we Quakers undertake to speak for the
crushed and silent masses in Germany. We believe that millions of
Americans share our conviction that they must be fed insofar as it is
within our power. This is no humanitarian impulse merely. We speak

under a compelling sense of the power of love to heal our wounded universe. For, in this world of ours there are certain moral laws which operate irresistibly whether we acknowledge them or not. If we Americans want a rightly ordered world, we must put in operation the methods that will build it. The feeding of starving children is a sure step toward peace. We must try to see their human faces and feel for them in their agony. We must realize clearly that starvation produces abnormality in character, and that almost more important than food is the touch of a kindly human spirit with its creative power of hope and faith and courage." God's "mercies are many."[17] Our mercies also must be many. The war is over. We must not continue it against the common people, for they in the end are the real sufferers and not the wealthy or those who have access to black markets. An American soldier would loathe to make war on helpless people, and thank God he does not do so. He finds ways and means to circumvent heartless directives of heartless swivel-chair administrators in far-off official Washington. We want to build One World in Charity. Charity has the noblest of all programs of intervention. Charity is world-wide in its scope; knows neither walls nor frontiers; is not race conscious; asks not who is friend or foe; is color-blind, inquiring not what is the tint of the skin of a person in need. Under its sway all men are brothers under the fatherhood of God and in the brotherhood of Christ. Men want to build one world in peace. It can be done, but it must be done in charity—One World in Charity.

Bread on the Waters

The intervention of mercy must be carried out by strong ideals of charity. Unless inspired by motives of charity, mercy cannot remain vigorous in action. Certainly, mercy can not be based entirely on grounds of self-interest or gain. With sinking hearts, Christians learned from the official statement of the Department of State on the Policy of the United States on Reparations and Aid to Germany. "The present standard of supply in Germany, so far as the United States is concerned, is still governed by the 'disease and unrest' formula." In other words, if starving people through disease become a menace to our men in the armies of occupation, and if through unrest they become a threat to peace, supplies will be given to them, otherwise not. We repudiate such a heartless policy. It can not be productive of good. It forgets the blessings promised those who are merciful: "Blessed are the merciful, for they shall receive mercy." A policy of mercy motivated by charity contains within it the promise of a good peace. It builds up good will, without which there can be no enduring peace. A humane policy of mercy will give proof to conquered peoples that we are determined to redeem the pledge given Christmas, 1944, by the late President Roosevelt: "This country has no desire to crush or exterminate the German people." Mindful of this pledge we can not approve the policy of a hard peace which would reduce the population "until there are only 40 million Germans left out of the 70 million now alive," writes an American newspaper correspondent.[18] He adds grimly that "most Americans would not enjoy watching the process." Who but men perverted in mind and in heart would want to see people going to their death through a slow process of starvation? The policy of calculated starvation was condemned by the Colmer Congressional Report. "If a hard peace requires the elimination of eight to ten million Germans, it would be much more humane to eliminate them at once. The Committee does not feel that the American people can face the responsibility for permitting wide-spread starvation in Germany." It should be noted that William M. Colmer, Representative from Mississippi, headed a Committee of eighteen Congressmen who, on a trip to Germany, saw with their own eyes the shocking situation that arose out of a studied and designed policy of vengeance. General Eisenhower in his testimony before a Congressional Committee expressed himself quite bluntly when he asked whether the horrible conditions in Germany would not make "men wonder if it was worth while to have taken up arms against the Nazis." As Americans we must condemn a policy of vengeance because it besmirches our fair name for just and generous dealing with a fallen foe, and also because it endangers the peace for which we fought. To make a Hitlerian peace would destroy the faith of people in democracy. The indictment of an entire nation can not be justified in the light of principles of democracy. We expressed our horror when the Nazis proclaimed the doctrine of racial guilt against all the Jews. Rightly we condemned such a doctrine. Shall we now profess it in the kind of peace we are making? "What incentive under this plan," asks the Colmer Committee on Postwar Economic Policy, "exists for Germany to turn to democratic ways?" Justice Robert H. Jackson, prosecutor of the Nazis at Nürnberg, repudiated the notion of collective responsibility. He said in his address opening the trial: "We know that the Nazi party was not put in power by a majority of the German vote. We know that it came to power by an evil alliance between the most extreme of the Nazi revolutionaries, the most unrestrained of the German reactionaries, and the most aggressive of the German militarists."[19] In truth, it would be unjust to indict all the German people, women and children, who had no voice in domestic politics, as well as to indict the countless numbers of anti-Nazis, many of whom suffered for years in concentration camps. Resistance to the Hitler movement was stronger than the American people generally know. In its leading editorial *Petrusblatt*, Berlin's first Catholic newspaper in seven years, declared that the paper's predecessor "would not bow before the spiritual terror of Nazi socialism. For five long years, from 1933 to 1938, we waged a journalistic battle against race hatred, lies, and injustice. Persecutions of Christians, oral and written warnings, interrogations, threats—nothing deflected us from the course charted for us by our Bishops." An amazing story will be told when the facts of the underground movement against Nazidom during the war are brought to light. Measures of reeducation in ideals of democracy will fail in both Germany and Japan if to the terrible sufferings consequent upon the war, new ones are added deliberately in cold blood by advocates of a hard, vengeful peace. Instead of shattering the faith of the conquered nations in the basic principles of democracy, we should leave nothing undone to strengthen [these principles] by reaffirming, in both word and deed, democracy's fundamental teaching. The inalienable rights of man, among which are life, liberty, and pursuit of happiness, and his birth in equality, are endowments, not of governments or of men, but of the Creator. A policy of mercilessness leads to cruelty, and therefore to injustice. Men will not carry for long burdens of injustice. They will take up arms and fight. The history of reparations after World War I gives us a warning lesson. Reparations were atrocious in their injustice. "In reality," wrote Ambassador William C. Bullit, "they were so unworkable that they produced financial and economic chaos, and had to be revised."[20] In 1923 Pius XI issued words of warning but his voice was drowned out by the shrill clamor of the hate-hawkers of that day. He was accused of wanting a soft peace for the enemy. Now in retrospect we see that he was right when he urged statesmen to join social charity with justice lest intolerable burdens of reparations create bitterness and hatred, and lead to another war.[21]

Far-seeing men recognize that a policy of revenge acts as a boomerang, and will in the end harm our interests. In despair, starving people become fertile soil for Fascism and Communism, or in their hunger they turn to banditry and immorality. Under conditions of disorder peace can not thrive, and how then can world prosperity result of a kind such as men now plan? To strip a people, not only of its household goods, but also of its tools and machinery of production impoverishes them. "If the whole future recovery of Europe is to be geared to fear of the bogey of Germany, reduced in its boundaries and stripped of its war-making capacity as Germany is, the recovery of Europe becomes a hopeless problem."[22] Poor people are poor markets for the goods we produce in field and factory. We shall hurt our own farmers and industrial workers, if, by a stupid, indeed insane, policy of a hard peace, we destroy one of our biggest markets. Full employment will become a phantom which men will chase but never overtake; it will serve as an election slogan to deceive the worker, but will not fatten his pay envelope. In the light of cool facts one can see the sanity of the comment made by the London *Economist* on Mr. Baruch's plan to make Germany a nation of goat-herders and foresters. "Unfortunately, very few voices have been raised to state the simple fact that Mr. Baruch's plan is immoral, uneconomic, and unworkable." A more devastating statement could hardly have been delivered in such few words. Europe will become a great liability to the American taxpayers, as the lend-lease plan was despite solemn pledges to the contrary when it was enacted, if hate prevents recovery on the European continent. It will serve the best interests of American taxpayers if all the people of Europe are put on a self-help basis as fast as possible. The propaganda charge of war guilt must be revised, reparations must be scaled down to reasonable levels, pledges given to nations large and small, conquerors and conquered, must be scrupulously kept, humility must replace the farcical righteousness of "peace-loving" nations. In this way only will an era of full employment be made a reality. A policy of mercy that casts bread on the waters will prove to be the best policy in the long run. "Cast thy bread on running waters," advises the Sacred Writer, "for after a long while thou shalt find it again."[23] Like a ship heavily laden with precious goods, deeds of mercy assure a large return to their doer. To create One World in Charity through such a policy must be the chief task of statesmen. If they fail in this, they will have failed mankind.

With Malice towards None

Charity is needed to rebuild a broken world. If millions starve to death, and if more millions eke out a pitiful existence, are robbed, and raped, and fall prey to disease, it is bad for order, recovery, morale, the freedoms of democracy, and prosperous security. If the continent of Europe becomes a slum of tens of millions of pauperized people, neither prosperity nor peace can prevail. Charity must spearhead the way to a new and better order. Charity must not be exclusive, else it is no longer charity. For, charity is universal; it embraces all men, friend and foe. True charity forbids the exclusion of enemies from deeds of beneficence. To the Jews of old the Lord said: "If thy enemy be hungry, give him to eat: if he thirst give him water to drink, for thou shalt heap hot coals upon his head and the Lord will reward thee."[24] Vengeance is definitely dammed. "He that seeks to revenge himself, shall find vengeance from the Lord. Forgive thy neighbor if he hath hurt thee, and then shall thy sins be forgiven to thee when thou prayest. . . . He that hath no mercy on a man like himself, how does he beg mercy for his own sins?"[25] Indeed, how will a hateful and vengeful man dare ask God for mercy on account of his sins—his atrocities, if, hating his enemy, he will not show him mercy? The Psalmist prays a curse on his own soul should he be vengeful to them who had done him evil. "If I have rendered evil to them that paid me evil, let me deservedly fall empty before my enemies. Let the enemy pursue my soul, and take it, and tread down my life on the earth, and bring down my glory to the dust."[26] Victor nations could reflect with much profit on these words. Will their glory be brought down to the dust, will they be trampled upon, on some other day, by other powerful nations because in their pride of victory they dealt mercilessly with their enemy? The history of nations can easily answer these questions. Once mighty in their valor and proud in their glory, they are no more. The decline and fall of nations fill the pages of history with many doleful tragedies. To Christians, too, come commands of mercy and love to a fallen foe. "But I say to you who are listening," cried out Christ in His Sermon on the Mount, "love your enemies, do good to those who hate you . . . And if you love those who love you, what merit have you? And if you do good to those who do good to you, what merit have you? For, even sinners do that."[27] Who would dare call himself a Christian and yet willfully cast aside these commandments of Christ? St. Paul re-echoed the teaching of the Divine Master in these words: "Be not wise in your own conceits. To no man render evil for evil, but provide good things not only in the sight of God but also in the sight of men . . . Do not avenge yourselves, beloved, but give place to the wrath, for it is written, Vengeance is mine, I will repay, says the Lord. But if thy enemy is hungry, give him food: if he is thirsty, give him drink, for, by so doing thou wilt heap coals of fire upon his head. Be not overcome by evil but overcome evil with good."[28] How does this teaching apply to our conquered enemies? Good Christians know the answer. Happily few in numbers are those who reject this teaching of the God of Israel and of His Christ. Theirs is a law of revenge. They are blind to the fact that, in rejecting the law of love of enemy, they really accept the teachings of Nazidom. Cruelly they advocate the decimation of Germany because "she is relatively too strong and too large population-wise."[29] Brutal, is it not? Surely such a one is not a Christian, but may he even call himself an American? Another writes: "We have been told that if we don't give to Europe there will be mass starvation, and Europe will go Communist. Well, what's so bad about that—for Europe. Both things are the best that could happen—for Europe."[30] Not all brutal men lived in Germany or Japan. Such utterances explain how Hitler could find men to execute his cruel policies of extermination of what he called inferior races and peoples. To our shame we must admit that we also have proud master-race advocates in our country. The hearts of these depraved overlords are left cold, possibly even rejoice with hell-born glee, that our policy in Japan may result in the death of 8,000,000 by starvation and exposure.[31] Their lust for vengeance is sated when they are told that "the unhappy continent of Europe faces one of the blackest, saddest winters since the chaos of the Thirty Years War. Cold, famine, and misery vie with each other in the ruins of last's battlefields, and the terrible specter of potential epidemic, already creeping in the gutted ruins of great cities, threatens to sweep out across a frightened world. More than 20,000,000 desperate and homeless people are now milling east and west, north and south across the Continent. Tuberculosis is rife. The very young and the very old especially are beginning to die in droves as the autumn leaves fall."[32] Many months have passed since this was written, and winter is now almost gone, but in the meantime death reaped its huge harvest, and sickness fed on undernourished bodies, and black despair gripped the hearts of countless millions. Gluttons for hate and revenge are having their fill. Propaganda has done its deadly work. On the one hand, it has fixed on entire nations collective responsibility and war-guilt, and, on the other, it has created in victor nations a pharisaical attitude of righteousness. The Lord's parable of the Pharisee and the publican who went up to the temple to pray, the one proud and boastful, the other meek and humble, could be well applied to the present-day international situation. Fortunately, there are those who remember Edmund Burke's dictum: "I know no way of indicting a whole people." There are men in Congress who, refusing to join in the hymn of hate, courageously declare after a calm appraisal of the facts: "Those Germans who suffer will in the main be the very old who generally opposed Hitler, and the very young who are hardly responsible for him."[33] There are those in our land who recall the brave words of the immortal Lincoln: "With malice toward none and charity toward all," and ask that they be applied to international relations. Statesmen would be sure of creating a better world if they gave heed to the sage words of Pius XII. "Do not ask from any member of the family of peoples, however small or weak, for the renunciation of substantial rights or vital necessities which you yourselves, if it were demanded of your people, would deem impractical." If we would serve our country well, we must not be cowards. Fearlessly we must proclaim Christ's law of love of enemy. It may bring us reproach and condemnation from those who know not Christ, but realizing that a peace based on justice and inspired by charity is the only kind of peace that is sensible, why should we be disturbed about what men will say? As Christians we have no choice but to be on the side of Christ, and we may be confident of this, that being on His side we are on the right side. The history of two thousand years bears testimony to the fact that where men sincerely followed the teaching of Christ, there peace became a fact. Hitler held up to scorn Christ's teaching on meekness, kindness, mercy, and charity. He and his partners in crime declaimed that these are "soft" virtues and may no longer be preached. Arrogance, pride, and hatred have once more crashed into ruin. Shall we follow their leadership by now trying to build one world on foundations of "hard" vices—on ill will, malice, and hate? Shall we allow his ideas to prevail in the work of postwar reconstruction? Shall we make ourselves partners of vindictive, inhuman, immoral and unchristian treaty provisions that will be nothing less than spawning grounds of another war? To us Christians comes the duty to speak out. We must breach the wall of silence that shuts out the voice of Christ. With malice toward none we must put forth every effort to build One World in Charity. As in St. Paul's day, so still in ours, charity is the greatest of all virtues, the motive-force for all other virtues, the golden bond of perfection.

The New Order in Christ

We entered the war with high ideals. We were assured by the late President Roosevelt that the war would not be one of vengeance but to establish a new order in the spirit of Christ. Mr. Churchill spoke of the war as a crusade for the preservation of the rights of men. Peoples were cheered by these assurances. The events since the close of hostilities, however, justify the gloom that has settled over the minds of men. Even before the end of the war it became clear that solemn pledges and promises would not be kept. What dismal fate the Atlantic Charter suffered is known to all the world. Right has not become might. On the contrary, might is extolled as the only means for the preservation of peace. "Peace must rest on power," is the crisp, clipped statement of the head of our government. Instead of taking the leadership among nations to bring about progressive disarmament and abolition of peacetime military training in a powerful machine of propaganda is put to work urging the maintenance of armies and navies on a scale larger than ever before. The race of armaments that would be started thereby among nations receives little consideration. Backbreaking taxes would be loaded on the common people of all lands. The standard of living would necessarily be lowered, or certainly it could not be raised because of the expenditure of money for guns and ships. The flower of youth would be torn from wholesome home surroundings and from the peacetime arts of education, vocation, and culture, and would be subjected to the poisonous atmosphere of immorality and irreligion associated, unfortunately, with life in army barracks. Like an octopus militarism would begin to coil its tentacles around our democratic institutions.

This is not the new order in Christ which people were encouraged to envision. Instead of stating principles for a good peace plan "we have compromised and sought to make mere piece-meal settlements. Instead of honest, promising discussion even on diverging plans, we are witnessing a return of the tragedy of power politics and the danger of balance of power arguments which, with the substitution of mere expediency for justice, have begotten war after war."[34] Small nations have been sacrificed on the alter of expediency. Brave little Finland has been mutilated. Lithuania, Estonia, and Latvia have been absorbed by force into the Union of Soviet Republics. The Balkan States in southeastern Europe have been made the stooges and allies of a scheming totalitarian government. Rebel governments have been set up, as in Iran, in defiance of pledges given the Allied Powers, and presented to them as accomplished facts; and tragic Poland partitioned by her own Allies can not call her soul her own. This is not the new order in Christ for which we fought. Might is made right. Indeed, peace is made to rest on power, but it is not peace. The atomic bomb will shatter such a peace. Two billion dollars were spent to erect atomic bomb plants. If that sum of money were spent to build in the lives of men, through church and school, strong principles of justice and charity, a power would be released in mankind so tremendous that a lasting peace would be ensured. We still have faith in moral and spiritual values, because we have faith in man if he is given a chance for good against the terrific odds of evil in the world. But instead of promoting interests of religion evil forces push them into the background and even completely stifle them. In all Russia there is but one Catholic priest, and he is there because he enjoys the extraterritorial rights and privileges of the French Embassy. Polish bishops of the Byzantine Rite have been driven into exile, or are languishing in prison. Of the Latin Metropolitan Sees in Poland only two still have their Ordinaries. Poland today has less than half of its full total of fifty-one bishops. The Church is allowed to do her work only under severe limitations. Catholic schools are practically non-existent. The Church has no right to exist except as a stooge of the State. Conditions in the Baltic States are no less horrible. Russian Communists "promoted beliefs and practices incompatible with Christian teaching, sought to subvert the influence of the churches over the people, expelled the teaching of religion from all schools, and reshaped the educational system and particularly the education and training of Lithuanian, Latvian, and Estonian youths. [They did so] on a progressively militarized footing and for the object of maintaining a dictatorship of one, single Communist Party."[35] Similar treatment is accorded religion in the Balkan States. The news of religious persecution that succeeds in escaping from there over the walls of censorship is shocking. Important above all other things of importance, religion is given no consideration in any of the conferences of the Big Powers. Statesmen seem not to realize that, instead of building a solid mansion of peace, they are but erecting a tower of Babel. Much is said of the need of re-educating the enemy in democracy, but it hardly occurs to the advocates of such a program that education without religion will not serve the cause of democracy well. Much is said, too, of re-conversion in the business world, but hardly a word is breathed of the need of re-conversion to moral and spiritual values. Occasionally men of affairs call attention to the need of a return to God, but their voice is like that of one crying in the wilderness. How can there be a new order in Christ, if in the affairs of nations there is not even as much as a thought of Christ? Secularism, divorcing religion from the affairs of men, yesterday sowed the wind, and today reaps the whirlwind. Ruins are piled up everywhere. For building a new order in Christ, good will, reciprocal confidence in all peoples, and collaboration of all, are the imperative need of the present hour. Therefore, "motives of hate, vengeance, rivalry, antagonism, unfair and dishonest competition must be kept out of political and economic debates and decisions."[36] This demands that fairness toward all nations, big and small, must be observed. Apt are the words of the Sacred Writer: "Who can say, my heart is clean, I am pure from sin? Diverse weights and diverse measures, both, are abominable before God."[37] The different standards of justice used in international relations are one of the abominations of the times, a real menace to peace. For building a new order in Christ, respect for truth must be restored. Lying propaganda and arbitrary censorship have created one-sided judgements and false assertions, and have misled public opinion so that the electorate sways in its ideas like reeds shaken by the wind."[38] War propaganda tells only one side of the story; it is at best a half-truth. In other instances, it deliberately uses untruths to mislead the enemy, or to build up home morale, or to cover up blunders in administration. Another species of untruth is based on a misuse of words for the purpose of confusing and thinking of men. Lenin advocated this method as a device of revolution, and his present-day followers are using it with no little effect in foreign policy negotiations. For the building of a new order in Christ, finally, the totalitarian state, whose strength is "cruel and bloody tyranny" must be eliminated. Such a state lowers man to a mere pawn in the game of politics and makes him a cipher in economic calculations. In relations with other nations, it changes frontiers with the stroke of a pen. [It] deprives people of natural outlets for the products of their industry, and drives millions of men from homes and lands, tearing them out by the roots and wrenching them from a civilization and a culture which they had striven generations to cultivate. Arbitrarily it sets bounds to the desire of men to migrate to other lands and to colonize them. "All this constitutes a policy contrary to the dignity and welfare of the human race."[39] If men submitted themselves to the law of love of God and of neighbor, evil forces such as have destroyed peace on earth would be disarmed of their strength. In his Christmas Tree address President Truman rightly remarked: "In love, which is the very essence of the message of the Prince of Peace, the world would find a solution of all its ills." We must all work harder than ever to make Christ's law of love prevail in our hearts and in the hearts of others so that through it we may help to create One World in Charity.

Appendix D

One World in Charity, *Illegal German Text* (*French Zone, 1947*)

Über die Einwelt der Liebe
Hirtenbrief** des Hochwürdigsten Bischofs *Aloysius Münch,* Fargo, USA.

** Mit Weglassung weniger Stellen.
Eure Geliebte in Christo! Zum 1. Mal in der Geschichte christl. Völker versuchen machtvolle Männer und Regierungen die Ausübung der christl. Caritas unmöglich zu machen! Es wird uns gesagt, dass es falsch sei, unsere Feinde zu lieben und denen Gutes zu tun, die uns Übles angetan haben. Der christlichen Liebe soll es nicht erlaubt werden, dem Beispiel des barmherzigen Samariters zu folgen. Die Lebensmittelrationen für den Feind sollen nach einer "Krankheits- und Unruheformel" bemessen werden und nicht in Übereinstimmung mit den Gewichten und Massen der christ. Liebe. Schreckliche Meldungen über Hunger, Krankheit, und Tod erreichen uns immer noch aus europäischen und asiatischen Ländern. Die Barbarei, die der Krieg in den Herzen der Menschen wachgerufen hat, ist unglaublich. Das Wort der Alten: "Homo homini lupus" (Der Mensch ist für den Menschen ein Wolf) ist wieder wahr geworden. Wir dürfen nicht länger schweigen. Wenn wir Christus nicht unsere Stimme erheben, werden die Heiden in unserer

Mitte es tun. In dieser hasserfüllten Zeit müssen wir es wagen, mutig zu sein und unumwunden unserer Überzeugung Ausdruck zu geben, damit die Furcht nich zur stillschweigenden Dulderin oder Förderin der Grausamkeit werde. . . . Kein Zeitalter verzeichnet ähnliche Brutalitäten. Die Scheusslichkeiten, wie sie in der Kriegs- und Eroberungsgeschichte der Griechen und Römer oder in der Invasionsgeschichte der Hunnen oder Goten oder in der Geschichte des schrecklichen Dschingiskan geschildert werden, verblassen neben den Ungeheuerlichkeiten unserer Zeit. Wir sollten uns nicht wundern, wenn die Geschichtsschreiber, — nachdem sie einmal vollen Einblick in die schwarzen und blutigen Ereignisse dieser Zeit genommen haben werden, —unser Zeitalter als das der Barbaren bezeichnen werden! Zu unserer Schande werden wir bekennen müssen, dass es unser Schicksal war, im dunkelsten Zeitalter der Menschheitsgeschichte gelebt zu haben. Auch die Inquisition oder die Bartholomäusnacht können nicht im entferntesten zum Vergleich herangezogen werden! Maidanek, Belsen, Dachau, Buchenwald, Lidice, Hiroshima und Nagasaki werden ihren Opfern immer wieder zurufen sich zu erheben und ihre grauenhaften Erlebnisse zu erzählen!—Dann kam das Ende des Krieges, aber nicht das Ende weiterer Greultaten: Stehlen und Plündern, Aushungerung und Tod aus überlegter Be- rechnung, erzwungene Abwanderung von Millionen von Heim und Besitz. -Schandtaten gegen die Frauenwelt und sogar gegen die auser- wählten Lämmer Gottes, Entweihung der Heiligtümer und andere Exzesse der Gottlosigkeit! Die Menschen, die nur in einem geringen Abstand von den Engeln erschaffen wurden, haben sich durch ihr wildes Tun unter das Niveau der Bestien des Dschungels erniedrigt? Der Krieg ist grausam und macht die Menschen brutal. Wir erinnern uns nur zu gut an die verbrecherischen und schrecklichen Episoden der Gangsterei in unserem Lande. Ohne Rücksicht auf Leben und Eigentum war ihnen nichts heilig. Um wieviel mehr bleiben eine ewige Schande die schreck- lichen Dinge, von denen die Zivilbevölkerung von Warschau und Rotterdam, von Coventry, Belgrad, Köln, London, Berlin und Dresden bis Hiroshima und Nagasaki befallen wurden! Indes ist noch nicht alles vorbei! Hinter einem geheimen Schleier werden die Grausamkeiten auch heute noch fortgesetzt! Immer noch sind Hunderttausende, ja Millionen von Frauen und Kindern getrennt, in Minen und Fabriken zur Arbeit unter Umständen einer Skaverei gezwungen, die sich nicht sehr von der- jenigen unterscheidet, die die Römer bei den von ihnen unterjochten Völkern anwandten. Machen wir uns nicht zu Teilnehmern an den

Verbrechen Hitlers, indem wir jetzt genau dasselbe tun, was wir einst
verurteilten? Die Heuchelei ist riesengross! Die Tatsache, dass diese
Zwangsarbeit jetzt als "menschliche Reparation" bezeichnet wird,
ändert nichts an der Tatsache, dass es nichts anderes als Sklavenarbeit ist!
Wir sind erbärmliche Heuchler, wenn wir nicht auch das Verbrechen
brandmarken, was wir zu rügen uns beeilten, als es vom Feinde verübt
wurde. Das Gebot der Gerechtigkeit hat keinen doppelten Massstab!

Nie aber hat sich eine Tragik von solch riesigem Umfang ereignet,
als sie sich in unseren Tagen vollzieht. Die Zunge verstummt bei dem
Versuch, die Leibes- und Seelennot der dem Untergang geweihten
zwangsausgewiesenen Menschen zu schildern! Sogar die Tinte will in
der Feder, während die Hand die führt, zu Eis gefrieren, wenn sie diese
schrecklichen Dinge erzählen soll! Welch ein grausames Elend! Ein
Zeitungs-kommentator, der wegen seiner humanen Gefühle bekannt ist,
schrieb unter dem Eindruck des Geschauten: "Wenn die amerikanischen
Nachrichtenphotographen ihre Erlebnisse ehrlich berichten, dann wird
das amerikanische Volk sehr bald Filme von verhungerten deutschen
Männern und Frauen und Kindern zu sehen bekommen, die in ihrer
Grauenhaftigkeit mit den Bildern vom Konzentrationslager Buchenwald,
wo Deutsche von Deutschen gefoltert wurden, gut rivalisieren können!
Aber, das werden gültigkeit oder gar der irregeführten Rache oder des
reinen Unverstandes auferlegt werden!" Zitiert von David Lawrence on
Brooklyn Tablet (15.12.1945).

Schrecklicher aber als Worte es auszudrücken vermögen, ist die
Tatsache, dass durch eine Kalt-berechnende Rachepolitik Leid und Not
über Millionen von Menschen verhängt werden, die zum grössten Teil
weder für den Ausbruch des Krieges, noch für seine Schrecken verantwortlich sind! Welche Verantwortung kann zum Beispiel Kindern auferlegt werden? Wie kann ein Krieg gege hilflose Menschen, vor allem
gegen alte Leute, gegen Frauen und Kinder gerechtfertigt werden?
Warum müssen sie so bitter leiden und eines elenden Todes sterben?—
Nur weil einige Menschen in führenden Stellungen die Ziele und
Methoden unserer Politik bestimmen, die das *Mosaische Gesetz* des
"Auge um Auge und Zahn um Zahn" wieder neu belebt haben. Wir ver-
werfen diese Rachepolitik, weil Christus sie verworfen hat (Matthew 5,
38-41), weil er uns gelehrt hat, unsere Mitmenschen zu lieben—sogar
unsere Feinde, denen Gutes zu tun, die uns hassen und für jene zu beten,
die uns verfolgen! Wir holen usere Lehre bei Christus und wir werden
sie und nie bei den Hasspredigern in unserer Mitte holen, den *anderen*

Hitlern, die—wie er—aus einer ganzen Nation ein kriechendes Belsen machen möchten! In dieser Sache sind wir bei Christus und an seiner Seite *wissen* wir, dass wir uns auf dem richtigen Weg befinden . . . . Wenn wir für die Besiegten ein Gutes Wort für Erbarmung einlegen, dann soll das nicht heissen, dass wir in Bezug auf nachgewiesene Kriegsverbrechen die Forderung der Gerechtigkeit ausschalten wollten! Noch soll es heissen, dass das besiegte Volk *vor* den notleidenden hungrigen Menschen in den befreiten Ländern bevorzugt werden sollte? Aber als Christen und *Amerikaner* erheben wir entrüstet unsere Stimme gegen eine *amtliche* Unmenschlichkeit, die es der UNRRA nicht gestattet, von ihren Unterstützungsvorräten weder nach Deutschland noch nach Japan zu schicken und ausserdem es nicht einmal privaten Hilfsagenturen erlaubt, Lebensmittel, Kleidungsstücke und Medizin an die vom Krieg heimgesuchten Menschen zu senden, die in den Ruinen ihrer zerbrochenen Städte ein Leben des Elends führen. Wir verurteilen diese unmenschlichen und grausamen Verordnungen des "War Relief Control Board." Wie können wir ruhig bleiben, und nicht die Abscheulichkeiten verurteilen, die unter amtlichen Directiven begangen werden, nachdem wir die Schandtaten der *Nazis* verurteilt haben?!

Wir machen die Frage eines Leitartikels zu der unsrigen: "Werden wir nicht eines Tages nach unserer eigenen Apathie (Gefühllosigkeit) gerichtet werden, wenn wir den einzelnen Deutschen dafür verantwortlich machen, dass er Belsen nicht untersuchte und nichts dagegen getan hat?" (Leitartikel in *Life* vom 24.12.1945). Wir haben über die gemeinen Schandtaten, die von den Nazi-Verbrechern begangen wurden, streng zu Gericht gesessen. Sollten wir da nicht auch zu Gericht sitzen über die Schändlichkeiten, die im Rahmen der vergeltenden Gerechtigkeit begangen werden, die jedoch in der Tat garkeine Gerechtigkeit ist, sondern die reinste *Rache?* Lasst uns die Worte des göttlichen Richters über die Völker beachten: "Mit welchen Urteil ihr richtet, mit werdet auch ihr gerichtet werden und mit welcherlei Mass ihr messet, mit dem wird auch Euch wieder gemessen werden.

Wir verurteilen eine Verschwörung des Stillschweigens seitens eines grossen einflussreichen Teiles userer Presse, dass sie dem amerikansichen Volk die wirkliche Not Der Menschen in Europa nicht bekannt macht. Unser Volk ist grossherzig, -es würde mit vollen Händen antworten: es würde sogar von demjenigen abgeben, das es selbst benötigt, um den notleidenden Menschen zu helfen. Ganz bestimmt würde user Volk nicht weniger tun als das Volk Grossbritanien, das sogar auf Kosten der eigenen magern Rationen eine Hilfe für seine ehemalige Feinde organisiert hat. Würde dem amerikanischen Volk ein genaues Bild von dem Leid und dem Elend dieser Menschen gegeben, es würde seine Regierung dazu zwingen zu tun, was die Regierung von Dänemark—trotz der Erinnerung an die Härten unter der Nazi-Besetzung getan hat, indem sie Lebensmittel und Kleider für mehr als 200 000 Zivilisten schickte, die aus dem östlichen Deutschland geflohen waren, um dem Ansturm der roten Armee am Ende des Krieges zu entgehen.

Brot übers Wasser hinüber, -die Barmherzigkeit kann sicher nicht ausschliesslich auf dem Boden des Eigennutzes oder des Gewinnes gegründet werden. Mit schmerzlich bewegten Herzen hörten wir Christen die amtliche Erklärung des Staatdepartments über die Richtschnur der "United States Aid to Germany." Die gegenwärtige Norm der Belieferung Deutschlands wird, -soweit die Vereinigten Staaten in Betracht kommen, immer noch von der "Krankheits-und Unruheformel" bestimmt, m.a.W., Die Belieferung wird nur dann gewährt, wenn die verhungerten Menschen durch Krankheit zu einer Gefahr für *unsere* Leute in der Besatzungsarmee werden und wenn sie durch Unruhen den Frieden bedrohen, sonst nicht! Wir lehnen ein so herzloses Verhalten ab. Es kann zu nichts Gutem führen. Es vergisst den Segen, der denjenigen versprochen wurde, die barmherzig sind: "Selig sind die Barmherzigen, denn sie werden Barmherzigkeit erlangen." Eine humane Politik der Barherzigkeit würde den besiegten Völkern den Beweis liefern, dass wir entschlossen sind, das Versprechen einzulösen, das zu Weihnachten '44 von dem verstorbenen Präsidenten Roosevelt gegeben wurde: "Unser Land hat kein Verlangen danach, das deutsche Volk zu zermalmen oder zu vernichten!" -Im Gedanken an dieses Versprechen können wir die Politik eines harten Friedens nicht willigen, der die Bevölkerung verkleinern würde" bis von den jetzt lebenden 65 Millionen nur noch 40 Millionen übrigbleiben," schreibt ein amerikanischer Zeitungskorrespondent (Russell Hill, *New York Herald Tribune*). Er fügt bezeichnend hinzu, dass "die meisten Amerikaner wohl einer solchen Prozedur *nicht* gern zusehen möchten" -Wer würde auch ausser einigen an Geist und Gemüt perversen Personen zusehen wollen, wie Menschen durch einen langsamen Prozess der Aushungerung ihrem Tode entgegensehen? -

Die Politik des Aushungerne ist übrigens vom Colmerschen Kongress verurteilt worden m.d.W.[mit den Worten]: "Wenn ein harter Friede die Ausmerzung von 8-10 Mill. Deutschen mit sich bringt, dann wäre es viel humaner, sie mit *einem* Schlage auszumerzen. Das Komitee glaubt nicht, dass das amerikanische Volk die Verantwortung auf sich zu nehmen gewillt ist, in Deutschland eine weitverbrreitete Hungersnot zu gestalten!" -Als Amerikaner müssen wir eine Politik der Rache verdammen, denn sie würde unseren guten Namen beschmutzen, mit dem wir in früheren Zeiten für unsere gerechte und grossmütige Behandlung eines besiegten Feindes bekannt sind, und sie würde auch den Frieden gefährden, für den wir gekämpft haben. Der Abschluss eines Hitlerfriedens würde den Glauben der Völker an die Demokratie zerstören. Eine ganze Nation unter Anklage zu stellen, kann im Lichte demokratischer Prinzipien nie gerechtfertigt werden. Der Widerstand gegen die Hitlerbewegung war stärker als das amerikanische Volk im allgemein weiss. . . . . Es führt auch zur Verarmung und Proletarisierung eines Volkes, wenn man es nicht nur seiner Haushaltungsgüter, sonder auch seiner Werkzeuge und seiner Produktionsmaschinerie beraubt. Ein verarmtes Volk ist zudem ein schlechter Markt für die von uns in Feld und Fabrik produzierten Güter. Es wird unsere eigenen Farmer und Fabrikarbeiter schädigen, wenn wir durch die stupide, ja wahnsinnige Politik eines harten Friedens einen unserer grössten Märkte zerstören . . . . Im Lichte kalter Tatsachen kann jeder die gesunde Vernunft in dem Kommentar des *London Economist* zu dem *Plan des Herrn Baruch erkennen, aus Deutschland ein* Volk von Schlafhirten und Waldbewohnern zu machen, -in welchem festgestellt wird: "Leider haben sich sehr wenig Stimmen erhoben die einfache Tatsache zu konstatieren, dass der Plan des Herrn Baruch unmoralisch, unwirtschaftlich und undurchführbar ist!" -Ein vernichtendere Erklärung hätte in so wenigen Worten kaum gegeben werden können. Es gibt eben Menschen, die sich lediglich an das Gebot der Rache halten. Sie sind blind gegenüber der Tatsache, dass sie mit der Ablehnung der Feindesliebe tatsächlich die Lehren des Nazitums annehmen. Sie befürworten grausam die Dezimierung Deutschlands, weil es "relativ zu stark und bevölkerungsmässig zu gross ist!" (Brief: "On Feeding the Germans," Congressional Records [dated] 18.12.1945 A 6027). Brutal, nicht war? -Ganz sicher, so einer ist kein Christ, aber . . . auch kein wahrer Amerikaner! Ein anderer schreibt: "Man hat uns gesagt, dass ein Massverhungern einsetzen wird, wenn wir Europa nichts geben, und dass Europa dem Kommunismus verfalle. Nun, was wäre denn das Schlimmes für Europa? Beides wäre das Beste, was für dasselbe eintreten könnte" (Brief: "Charity should begin at home," ibid. A 6053). Man sieht also: Nicht *alle* brutalen Menschen haben nur in Deutschland oder Japan gelebt! Zu unserer Schuld müssen wir gestehen, dass *auch wir* solche Meisterrassenverteidiger" in unserem Lande haben. -Die Herzen dieser verdorbenen Machthaber bleiben kalt, finden vielleicht sogar noch höllische Freude daran, dass unsere Politik in Deutschland und Japan zum Tode von Millionen von Menschen durch Hunger und Kälte führen mag (*Life*, 3.12.45). Die Rachelust ist befriedigt, wenn man ihnen sagt, dass der unglückliche Kontinent Europa seit dem Chaos des 30. jähr. Krieges einer der schwärzesten und jammervollsten Zeiten entgegensieht. Kälte, Hunger, Krankheit und Elend wetteifern miteinander in den Ruinen der letztjährigen Schlachtfelder ohnehin schon grausig genug. Die Propaganda hat ihr tödliches Werk getan. Auf der einen Seite hat sie ganzen Völkern die Kollektive Verantwortung und Kriegesschuld aufgebürdet und auf der andern hat sie bei den Siegernationen eine widerliche heuchlerische, pharisäische Haltung der Selbstgerechtigkeit erzeugt . . . Als Christen haben wir keine andere Wahl, als uns auf die Seite Christi zu stellen und wir können davon überzeugt sein, dass wir uns bei Ihm auf der rechten Seite befinden! Die Welt und unser Volk können nur durch seine heiligen Gebote noch gerettet werden. ——Sollen wir uns zu Teilnehmern an rachsüchtigen, unmenschlichen und unchristlichen Friedensbedingungen machen, die nichts anderes als die Brutstätten eines *neuen* Krieges sein werden?

Uns Christen fällt die Aufgabe zu, vernehmlich zu reden. Wir müssen die Mauern des Schweigens durchbrechen, die die Stimme Christi ausschliessen. Mit Groll gegen nieman im Herzen müssen wir jede Kraft daran setzen, die "Einwelt++ in der Liebe" zu bauen.

Wie in den Tagen des hl. Paulus, so ist die Liebe auch in den unsrigen die grösste Tugend, die bewegende Kraft für alle übrigen Tugenden, das "goldene Band der Vollkommenheit."—Amen! Aloysius, Bischof von Fargo, USA.

Notes

Introduction: Aloisius Muench and the Question of Guilt and Responsibility

1. Muench recounts this audience in both a letter and in his diary. See diary entry dated 21 May 1957, vol. 21, p. 287. In: the Aloisius Muench Collection (hereafter cited as HM 37), box 1, folder 1 (hereafter cited as HM 37/1/1), The American Catholic History Research Center & University Archives, Catholic University of America (hereafter ACUA), Washington, D.C. See also letter from Muench, Bad Godesberg, to Monsignor Joseph Adams, Chicago, 29 May 1957. HM 37/11/7, ACUA.

2. Letter from Elisabeth Baumgart, Selingen, to Muench, Kronberg, 24 July 1947. HM 37/20/10, ACUA.

3. Letter from Theodor Lebeda, Limburg, to Muench, Kronberg, 7 October 1947. HM 37/116/15, ACUA.

4. Letter from Thea Brack, Reichenbach am Heuberg, to Muench, Kronberg, 24 September 1947. HM 37/128/3, ACUA. A copy of Muench's reply is not available.

5. Letters to Muench from German Catholics support Robert Moeller's argument that "one of the most powerful integrative myths of the 1950s emphasized not German well-being but German suffering. It stressed that Germany was a nation of victims, an imagined community defined by the experience of loss and displacement during the Second World War. . . . Largely absent were the most obvious victims of the Nazi state itself." See Robert Moeller, *War Stories:*

The Search for a Usable Past in the Federal Republic of Germany (Berkeley: University of California Press, 2001), 6–7.

6. Letter from Father Gerald Weber, Bad Godesberg, to Bishop Leo Dworschak, Fargo, 20 June 1956. HM 37/64/4, ACUA.

7. Aloisius Muench, *One World in Charity: A Pastoral*, 7. I thank the librarians of the Aloisius Cardinal Muench Seminary in Fargo, North Dakota, for sending me a copy of the pastoral letter's original edition. A second edition version of *One World* is available in HM 37/93/4, ACUA.

8. Ibid. Here, Muench quoted the second and third books of the Old Testament, Exodus 21:24 ("eye for eye, tooth for tooth, hand for hand, foot for foot") and Leviticus 24:20 ("fracture for fracture, eye for eye, tooth for tooth").

9. Muench, *One World,* 7.

10. The Private Diary of Aloisius Muench, 21 April 1953, vol. 17, pp. 43–44; hereafter cited as "Muench diary entry dated [ ], vol. [ ], p. [ ]." All volumes can be found in HM 37/1/1; this citation will therefore not be repeated.

11. Muench diary entry dated 29 June 1951, vol. 14, p. 45.

12. Jeffrey Herf demonstrates this phenomenon in postwar West German political life. Adenauer, who argued that a "re-Christianization" of Germany was necessary, used religious themes to stress "forgiveness" and "mercy" over justice. In May 1946, he told a Wuppertal audience, "the duty of the victors and the right of the defeated rest on divine mercy and divine justice, and no one who breaks the commandment of divine justice will go unpunished." In his 1949 speech "Courage to Love" (*Mut zur Liebe*), Theodor Heuss, president of the Federal Republic from 1949 to 1959, used terms with religious connotations as well, focusing on "love" as opposed to "justice." See Jeffrey Herf, *Divided Memory: The Nazi Past in the Two Germanys* (Cambridge: Harvard University Press, 1997), 221, 312.

13. Letter from Joseph Hering, Amberg, to Muench, Bad Godesberg, 1 August 1957. HM 37/131/4, ACUA.

14. Letter from Bishop (Dr.) Joseph Freundorfer, Augsburg, to High Commissioner John J. McCloy, Frankfurt, 11 January 1951. HM 37/139/2, ACUA.

15. Letter from Muench, Bad Godesberg, to Father Peter Leo Johnson, Milwaukee, 14 April 1951. HM 37/10/2, ACUA.

16. "Memorandum for Judge Advocate File" by Colonel James L. Harbaugh, Judge Advocate Division, 19 November 1948, in folder entitled "Execution File—1948—Part I," box 12. RRPTA, WC, JAD, USAREUR, RG 338, NARA.

17. Letter from Frings, Cologne, to Muench, Kronberg, 22 November 1948. HM 37/140/11, ACUA.

18. Letter from Muench to Frings, Cologne, 27 November 1948. HM 37/140/11, HUA.

19. Letter from (unspecified) personal secretary to Bishop A. J. Muench, Kronberg, to Father Franz Lövenstein, S.J., Erlangen, 14 September 1948, HM 37/9/5, ACUA.

20. Ibid.

21. Letter from Muench, Kronberg, to Frings, Cologne, 27 November 1948. HM 37/140/11, ACUA.

22. James J. Weingartner, *A Peculiar Crusade: Willis J. Everett and the Malmedy Massacre* (New York: New York University Press, 2000), 159. Weingartner also understands clearly the anti-Semitic implications of Muench's language (see pp. 216–17).

23. Muench does not relay Marimpolski's first name.

24. According to Muench, Marimpolski worked for the War Crimes Commission in Poland, and extradition meant that Germans accused of war crimes committed in Poland would be tried in Poland, not Germany.

25. Letter from Aloisius Muench, Kronberg, to Terry Muench, Milwaukee, 15 January 1947, HM 37/32/2 and diary entry dated 10 January 1947, vol. 5, p. 46.

26. See Rolf Lindner, *Freiherr Ernst Heinrich von Weizsäcker, Staatssekretär Ribbentrops von 1938 bis 1943* (Lippstadt: Zeitgeshichte im ROBE-Verlag, 1997); Telfred Taylor, *Military Tribunals: Case No. 11: The United States of America against Ernst von Weizsäcker* (Nürnberg: Office of Military Government for Germany, U.S., 1948); and Ernst Weizsäcker, *Memoirs of Ernst Weizsäcker*, translated from the German by John Andrews (London: V. Gollancz, 1951).

27. Letter from Father Ivo Zeiger to Muench, Kronberg, 21 October 1950. HM 37/73/16, ACUA.

28. "Your visit brought joy to our house [in Kronberg]. I hope sincerely that we shall have the pleasure of another good chat before too many weeks speed by. I prize highly the friendship with which you have blessed me," Muench wrote to Magee. See letter from Muench, Kronberg, to Mr. Warren Magee, Nuremberg, 30 April 1949, HM 37/72/11a, ACUA. The *Zentrale Rechtsschutzstelle* (Main Office for the Legal Protection of War Criminals), part of the Federal Republic of Germany's Justice Department and headed by Hans Gawlik, subsequently hired Magee to work in the United States on behalf of the five remaining "red jackets" scheduled for execution in February 1951. See Hilary Earl, "Accidental Justice: The Trial of Otto Ohlendorf and the *Einsatzgruppen* Leaders in the American Zone of Occupation, Germany, 1945–1958" (Ph.D. diss., University of Toronto, 2002), 501–5.

29. Letter from Muench, Kronberg, to Substitute Secretary of State Monsignor John B. Montini, Rome, 30 April 1949, HM 37/72/11a, ACUA.

30. Muench diary entry dated 8 April 1948, vol. 8, p. 5.

31. Muench diary entry dated 23 April 1948, vol. 8, p. 14.

32. Muench diary entry dated 30 June 1948, vol. 8, p. 59.

33. The Society for the Prevention of World War III, Inc., was a nonprofit organization based out of New York City whose directors were Rex Stout (president), Lyle Evans Mahan (vice president), Rudolph Fluegge, Frederick W. Foerster, C. Montieth Gilpin, Julius L. Goldstein, Isodore Lipschutz, Emil Ludwig, Eric Mann, Peter B. Olney, and Harry L. Selden. Its

advisory council consisted of Louis K. Anspacher, George Biddle, Rev. L. M. Birkhead, Rev. R. H. Brooks, D.D., Cecil Brown, Struthers Burt, Mary Ellen Chase, Thomas Craven, George Creel, James S. Cushman, Jo Davidson, John R. Davies, Walter D. Edmonds, Maj. George Fielding Elliot, Clifton Fadiman, Douglas S. Freeman, Christopher La Farge, Maurice Leon, Clarence H. Low, Mrs. Harold V. Milligan, Herbert Moore, Allan Nevins, Louis Nizer, Quentin Reynolds, Dean Wm. F. Russel, William L. Shirer, Booth Tarkington, R. J. Thomas, Sigrid Undset, Mark Van Doren, Mrs. Benjamin P. Watson, Maj. Malcolm Wheeler-Nicholson, and Paul Winkler. For its stated goals, see T. H. Tetens, *Know Your Enemy* (New York: Society for the Prevention of World War III, 1944), 123–27.

34. See Weingartner, *Peculiar Crusade*, 216-17, and Muench diary entry dated 16 February 1956, vol. 21, p. 88. Muench might have been referring to Isodore Lipschutz, one of the society's directors.

35. Roosevelt's successor, continued Kling's letter, "Harry *Salomon* Truman, was the business partner of the Jew Jacobson in his hometown in Missouri for more than twenty years." Letter from Otto Kling, Munich, to Cardinal Michael Faulhaber, Munich, 25 September 1947. HM 37/138/2, ACUA. Faulhaber apparently sent Kling's letter to Muench, to whom he was very close. No evidence of Faulhaber's or Muench's response, or the possible discussion that ensued, is available. Kling also referred specifically to Muench's pro-German and anti-Jewish pastoral letter, *One World in Charity*.

36. Muench diary entry dated 15 February 1947, vol. 5, p. 66. See also Joseph W. Bendersky, *The "Jewish Threat": Anti-Semitic Politics of the U.S. Army* (New York: Basic Books, 2000), 366.

37. Letter from Muench, Bad Godesberg, to Monsignor Paul Tanner, Washington, 17 March 1950. HM 37/114/6, ACUA.

38. Letter from Anton Rupert Sittl, Munich, to Muench, Kronberg, 21 January 1948. HM 37/128/4, ACUA.

39. Letter from Fasnacht, Chicago, to Muench, Kronberg, 27 December 1949. HM 37/97/11, ACUA.

40. Muench diary entry dated 3 December 1953, vol. 19, p. 24.

41. Letter from Muench to Father James "Boots" Nellen, 28 March 1951. HM 37/13/8, ACUA. Defined simply, a nuncio is an ambassador of the pope to secular governments. His task is twofold: to maintain diplomatic relations between the Holy See and the respective government, and to superintend church affairs within his assigned territory. He does the latter by relaying papal instructions to bishops in the territory. See memorandum entitled "Nunciature," 3 June 1946. In folder entitled "Muench, Bishop," box 181, RA, ECA, Record Group 260: Office of Military Government–United States (hereafter RG 260-OMGUS), National Archives II, College Park, Maryland (hereafter NARA).

42. Letter from Johannes B. Dietl, Regensburg, to Muench, Kronberg, 14 February 1947. HM 37/92/2, ACUA.

43. Letter from Curate Alfons Haslberger, Bad Adelholzen, to Muench, Kronberg, 25 November 1949. HM 37/92/9, ACUA.

44. Muench mentions this fact a number of times in his diary.

45. Letter from Father Gerald Weber, Bad Godesberg, to Monsignor Howard Smith, Fargo, 29 October 1953. HM 37/64/1, ACUA.

46. Letter from Muench, Bad Godesberg, to Helen and Jack Crowley, Algiers, 30 October 1958. HM 37/17/3, ACUA.

47. Letter from Aloisius Muench, Kronberg, to his mother Theresa Kraus Muench, 9 November 1950. HM 37/30/11, ACUA.

48. Muench diary entry dated 16 April 1953, vol. 17, p. 41.

49. Muench diary entry dated 5 June 1954, vol. 20, p. 64. Pius XII's preoccupation with communism is a major argument in Michael Phayer's 2000 study on the Catholic Church and the Holocaust. For the most recent study of Eugenio Pacelli's fight against communism, see Peter C. Kent, *The Lonely Cold War of Pope Pius XII* (Montreal and Kingston: McGill-Queen's University Press, 2002).

50. Letter from Muench, Kronberg, to Stritch, Chicago, 3 November 1948. HM 37/6/6, ACUA.

51. Muench diary entry dated 7 November 1949, vol. 11, p. 38.

52. Professor Foerster was author of several dozens of books that wrestled with ethical, political, social, religious issues as well as with human sexuality. See Max Pascal, *Pädagogische und politische Kritik im Lebenswerk Friedrich Wilhelm Foersters* (Stuttgart: Ibidem-Verlag, 1999).

53. *Autorität und Freiheit* first appeared in 1920, published by J. Kösel Verlag (Kempten, Germany).

54. Michael Phayer, *The Catholic Church and the Holocaust, 1930–1965* (Bloomington: Indiana University Press, 2000), 32–40.

55. Letter from Professor Friedrich Wilhelm Foerster to a "Herr Rössler," Vita Nova Verlag, Lucerne, Switzerland, 6 June 1947. HM 37/20/10, ACUA.

56. Letter from Aloisius Muench, Kronberg, to F. W. Schuchard, Dickinson, North Dakota, 3 October 1947. HM 37/20/10, ACUA.

57. Letter from Muench, Kronberg, to Monsignor Sebastian Bernard, Milwaukee, 30 August 1947. HM 37/9/2, ACUA.

58. Letter from Muench, Kronberg, to Monsignor Edward Kersting, Burlington, Wisconsin, 13 May 1947. HM 37/9/2, ACUA.

59. Muench diary entry dated 18 February 1947, vol. 5, p. 71.

60. Muench diary entry dated 7 October 1948, vol. 8, p. 97.

61. Letter from Monsignor Joseph Adams, Chicago, to Muench, Kronberg, 8 April 1947. HM 37/9/2, ACUA.

62. Letter from Auxiliary Bishop Johannes Neuhäusler, Munich, to Muench, Kronberg, 7 November 1949. HM 37/69/27, ACUA.

63. Letter from Aloisius Muench, Bad Godesberg, to his sister Terry Muench, Milwaukee, 15 March 1951. HM 37/32/6, ACUA.

64. Muench diary entry dated 11 February 1947, vol. 5, p. 63.

65. Letter from Muench, Kronberg, to Monsignor Richard Smith, Religious Affairs, 2 January 1947. HM 37/124/3, ACUA.

66. Muench diary entry dated 16 July 1952, vol.15, p. 78.

67. Muench diary entry dated 25 May 1952, vol. 15, p. 33.

68. *Catholic Bulletin* (Saint Paul, Minn.), 6 May 1960. HM 37/29/2, ACUA.

69. See Norbert Frei, *Vergangenheitspolitik: Die Anfänge der Bundesrepublik und die NS-Vergangenheit* (Munich: Beck, 1996), for discourse about the Nazi past among prominent politicians in East and West Germany and in West German legislation.

70. See Hannah Arendt, *Eichmann in Jerusalem: A Report on the Banality of Evil* (New York: Penguin Books, 1964), 298. See also Friedrich Meinecke, *Die deutsche Katastrophe; betrachtungen und erinnerungen* (Zürich: Aeo-Verlag e.g., 1946).

71. Omer Bartov, "Defining Enemies, Making Victims: Germans, Jews and the Holocaust," *American Historical Review* 103; 3 (June 1998): 787.

72. Ibid.

73. Herf, *Divided Memory*, 226.

74. Ibid.

75. Frei, *Vergangenheitspolitik*, 13–14. See also Maria Mitchell, "Materialism and Secularism: Christian Democratic Union Politicians and National Socialism, 1945–1949," *Journal of Modern History* 67 (June 1995): 278–308. Mitchell argues that the CDU understood National Socialism to be part of the "age-old battle between Christianity and materialism." The CDU defined itself in opposition to "materialism," meaning it rejected "capitalism, statism, liberalism, militarism, nationalism, secularism, socialism, Prussianism, and Protestantism" (284).

76. Herf, *Divided Memory*, 282.

77. Ibid., 209.

78. Rebecca Boehling, *A Question of Priorities: Democratic Reform and Economic Recovery in Postwar Germany* (Providence, R.I.: Berghahn Books, 1996), 19.

79. "Policy [on] German Guilt," included in "Basic Policy for Information and Information Control in Germany," dated 17 January 1946. In folder 4 entitled "History," box 69. Records of the Information Control Division Headquarters: Central Decimal File of the Executive Office 1944–1949 (hereafter ICD-HQ-CDF Executive Office), RG 260-OMGUS, NARA.

80. General Robert A. McClure, "Special Guidance—German Guilt" dated 17 January 1946. In folder 45 entitled "German Attitudes," box 69. ICD-HQ-CDF Executive Office, RG 260-OMGUS, NARA. The "Basic Policy" memorandum (see n. 79 above) lists the author of "Special Guidance-German Guilt" as General Robert A. McClure and its recipients as "lower [Army] units."

81. Ibid.

82. Ibid.

83. Herf, *Divided Memory*, 208.

84. Norbert Frei, "Von deutscher Erfindungskraft oder: Die Kollektivschuldthese in der Nachkriegszeit," in *Hannah Arendt Revisited: Eichmann in Jerusalem und die Folgen*, Gary Smith, ed. (Frankfurt/Main:

Suhrkamp Verlag, 2000), 163–76. Frei argues that "collective guilt" became an ideal rhetorical device for proponents of amnesty and obstructed further judicial action against Nazi criminals. See also Thomas Schwartz, "John J. McCloy and the Landesberg Cases," in *American Policy and the Reconstruction of West Germany, 1945–1955*, ed. Jeffrey M. Diefendorf, Axel Frohn, and Hermann-Josef Rupieper (Washington, D.C: German Historical Institute and Cambridge University Press, 1993), 433–54. Schwartz argues that popular resentment in West Germany at notions of "collective" guilt mixed with a form of "psychological denial" acted to reduce support for war crimes trials.

85. Ernst Christian Helmreich, *The German Churches under Hitler: Background, Struggle, and Epilogue* (Detroit: Woyne State University Press, 1979), 421.

86. The standard work on the Evangelical Church in the immediate postwar years is Clemens Vollnhals, *Evangelische Kirche und Entnazifierung, 1945–1950: die Last der nationalsozialistischen Vergangenheit* (Munich: R. Oldenbourg, 1989). An excellent recent work on the subject is Matthew D. Hockenos, *A Church Divided: German Protestants Confront the Nazi Past* (Bloomington: Indiana University Press, 2004).

87. "Die bayerischen Bischöfe: Erstes gemeinsames Hirtenwort nach dem Krieg, Eichstätt, 28 June 1945," in *Dokumente deutschen Bischöfe: Hirtenbriefe und Ansprachen zu Gesellschaft und Politik 1945–1949*, ed. Wolfgang Löhr, vol. 1 (Würzburg: Echter Verlag, 1985), 31. The pervasive rumors about gassing in the East as well as the conspicuous presence of Jewish labor camp inmates and evacuees in Germany during the last months of the war belie this statement. Telling is a comment by one German woman interviewed by Alison Owings: "we all knew there were KZ's and so on, but my husband after he saw it with his own eyes, only then did he really know it. We knew that Jews were somehow being gassed, but we repressed it. We did not [allow ourselves to] picture it. One did know, but one did not *realize* it fully. One could not, because we would have gone insane." See Owings, *Frauen: German Women Recall the Third Reich* (New Brunswick, N.J.: Rutgers University Press, 1993), 353.

88. For the full text of the Fulda pastoral, see "Die deutschen Bischöfe: Erster gemeinsamer Hirtenbrief nach dem Krieg, Fulda, 23 August 1945," in Löhr, *Dokumente deutschen Bischöfe*, 40–45. Phayer's research indicates that the German bishops debated several drafts of the Fulda pastoral before agreeing to the version that appeared in the public domain. The first draft "glossed over the Holocaust," calling it only a "dark chapter" in German history. But Bishop Konrad Preysing of Berlin demanded revisions, and Phayer credits Preysing for the sentences noted above. The bishops also edited certain passages out of the final draft, such as a section denying that Germans knew about specifics concerning atrocities, because, argues Phayer, Germans did know. Finally, the bishops avoided the issues of anti-Semitism and Catholic enthusiasm for the war. See Phayer, *Catholic Church and the Holocaust*, 135–39.

89 "Die deutschen Bischöfe: Erster gemeinsamer Hirtenbrief nach dem Krieg, Fulda, 23 August 1945," in Lohr, *Dokumente deutscher Bischöfe*, 40–41.

90. Pius XII (Eugenio Pacelli) had specific reasons for protecting the Concordat, which is still in effect today. As papal nuncio in Munich and Berlin during the 1920s, Pacelli sought to bring the newly drafted Code of Canon Law (1917) to Germany on a state-by-state basis. The 1917 Code, a pyramidal model culminating in supreme papal authority, gave the Catholic Church a universal and comprehensive law book. John Cornwell argues convincingly that "in light of the 1917 Code, the Vatican's concordat policy was transformed. Thenceforward the Concordat was to become an instrument of consensus by which the lives of bishops, clergy, religious, and faithful were regulated, top-down, everywhere in the world on an equal basis." Secretary of State Pacelli worked for the passage of the 1933 Reich Concordat, drafted after the principles of the new Code of Canon Law, to ensure the Vatican's right to regulate Church affairs in Germany. As pope, Pacelli successfully fought to keep the Concordat in place, again in order to secure uniformity and the Vatican's superior position. While Cornwell's book is criticized for its implication of Pius XII as Hitler's willing accomplice (a point Cornwell cannot prove), his work is on target regarding Pius XII's lifelong concern for centralization of Vatican influence and its physical protection during the war. See John Cornwell, *Hitler's Pope: The Secret History of Pius XII* (New York: Penguin Books, 1999), 42, 84–85.

91. See Ludwig Volk, "Der Heilige Stuhl und Deutschland 1945–1949," *Stimmen der Zeit* 194 (1976): 802-3. See also letter from Muench, Bad Godesberg, to Monsignor Joseph Adams, 12 March 1956, HM 37/11/3, ACUA.

92. See "Address of the Apostolic Nuncio Archbishop A. J. Muench," 4 April 1951. HM 37/70/5, ACUA.

93. Letter from Muench, Bad Godesberg, to General Frank L. Howley, 2 March 1953, HM 37/135/3, ACUA.

94. Ibid.

95. See Aloisius Muench, untitled memorandum (no date; contents place it as having been written in August 1946); Chancery Correspondence files under the letter "M" (hereafter cited as CC/M), Joseph Cardinal Bernardin Archives & Records Center, Chicago, Illinois (hereafter cited as Archdiocesan Archives Chicago). Muench repeated this argument to Robert Murphy in 1949. See Muench diary entry dated 15 July 1949, vol. 10, pp. 42-43.

96. For the most recent work on von Galen, see Beth Griech-Polelle, *Bishop Von Galen: German Catholicism and National Socialism* (New Haven, Conn.: Yale University Press, 2002). Her study examines von Galen's use of Catholic values, theology, and ideology to selectively oppose certain elements of National Socialism, such as the euthanasia project, while choosing to remain silent on issues concerning the discrimination, ghettoization, deportation, and murder of Jews. Unlike earlier studies that place von Galen in the pantheon of resisters to Nazism, Griech-Polelle's research reveals a more complex figure who moved between the boundary of dissent and complicity during the Nazi regime. Alternatively, see

Joachim Kuropka, ed., *Clemens August Graf von Galen: Neue Forschungen zum Leben und Wirken des Bischofs von Münster* (Muenster, 1999); and Joachim Kuropka and Maria-Anna Zumholz, eds., *Clemens August Graf von Galen: Sein Leben und Wirken in Bildern und Dokumenten* (Cloppenburg, 1992).

97. See Appendix A, "Historiographical Essay: Pope Pius XII and the Holocaust." See also Guenther Lewy, *The Catholic Church and Nazi Germany* (New York: McGraw-Hill, 1964); and Gordon Zahn, *German Catholics and Hitler's Wars* (New York: E.P. Dutton, 1969). Important work thereafter includes Gerhard Besier, "Anti-Bolshevism and Anti-Semitism: The Catholic Church in Germany and National Socialist Ideology, 1936–1937," *Journal of Ecclesiastical History* 43 (July 1992): 447–56; Ernst Klee, *Persilscheine und falsche Pässe* (Frankfurt: Fischer Verlag, 1991); and Sarah Gordon, *Hitler, Germans, and the "Jewish Question"* (Princeton, N.J.: Princeton University Press, 1984), 247–49. One documented and important exception can be cited. Bishop Konrad Preysing of Berlin (1880–1950) was unique among the German bishops in that he was the only one who intervened for *all* Jews, not just those who converted to Catholicism. Preysing's cousin was the famous Clemens August Count von Galen, the so-called "lion of Münster." Preysing came to see the 1933 Concordat as "a mistake," a view markedly different than that of Pius XII. Preysing supported the work of Margarete Sommer, head of the *Hilfswerk beim Ordinariat Berlin*, a diocesan rescue operation for Berlin Jews (the only Catholic organization of its kind). In March 1943, Preysing wrote to Pius XII to describe the final roundup of Jews in Berlin (February 27–March 1), indicating that their deportation likely meant their death. In a series of thirteen letters in fifteen months (1943–44), he repeatedly urged Pius XII to recall Vatican Nuncio Orsenigo, break off diplomatic relations with the Nazis, and condemn the murder of the Jews. See Phayer, *Catholic Church and the Holocaust*, 18, 49–50, 57, 69, 74, 81, 152.

98. Colman Barry, O.S.B., *American Nuncio: Cardinal Aloisius Muench* (Collegeville, Minn.: Saint John's University Press, 1969), 77. Barry, Muench's biographer, was a Catholic priest belonging to the Order of Saint Benedict (O.S.B.). He does not give a source for this comment. There are several possibilities. Barry conducted interviews over a period of eight years (1961–69) with Muench, his family members, and friends and associates in Fargo, Milwaukee, Germany, and Rome. Barry wrote the book in Fargo. Bishop of Fargo Leo F. Dworschak granted Barry full permission to use the papers. One can only speculate that an archival official in Fargo told Barry about the weight of Muench's papers. See *American Nuncio*, v–vi.

99. Barry had access to Muench's correspondence and thus could have seen letters referring to direct transfer of records from Bad Godesberg to Fargo, but does not mention it. Perhaps Barry did not consider this fact important.

100. Letter from Father Gerald Weber, Bad Godesberg, to Bishop Leo Dworschak, Fargo, 20 June 1956. HM 37/64/4, ACUA.

101. Despite sharing their last name, Aloisius Muench and Charlie Muench were not related.

102. Letter from Muench, Rome, to Charlie Muench, New York, 5 February 1960. HM 37/33/15, ACUA.

103. Barry, *American Nuncio*, 326. According to Barry, "Sister Ilga spent a year in Fargo during 1962 and 1963 arranging the Muench Papers in the chancery archives. She translated over fifty interviews with representatives of Church and State who worked with Cardinal Muench during his years in Germany, organized and translated . . . his extensive speeches and writings, and supplied information on his procedures in Germany." This comment reveals the extent to which Sister Ilga Braun helped Barry prepare materials for his subsequent biography of Muench. Again, Barry does not note a source. Presumably, these comments were simply a reflection of his personal experience or direct commentary from Sister Braun herself, who (alongside many of his oral sources) was his contemporary at the time of *American Nuncio*'s publication in 1969.

104. Barry obtained his Ph.D. in history at the Catholic University of America (hereafter CUA) in 1953. Father Barry became a respected historian of American Catholicism. After earning his Ph.D., Barry taught history at Saint John's Abbey in Collegeville, Minnesota, later becoming its president. Letter from Colman Barry, Collegeville, to Muench, Kronberg, 28 October 1953. HM 37/10/5, ACUA. David O'Brien, review of *American Nuncio*, by Colman Barry, *Church History* 40, 2 (June 1971): 246–47.

105. Ellis was managing editor of the *Catholic Historical Review* from 1941 until 1962.

106. Letter from Reverend John Tracy Ellis, Washington, to Muench, Bad Godesberg, 1 July 1953. HM 37/27/6, ACUA. Catholic University of America Press in Washington, D.C. published *The Catholic Church and German Americans* in 1953.

107. Letter from Muench to Ellis, 23 July 1953. HM 37/27/6, ACUA.

108. A draft of Muench's review is available in HM 37/27/6, ACUA.

109. Letter from Father Colman Barry, Saint John's Abbey, Collegeville, to Muench, 28 October 1953. HM 37/10/5, ACUA.

110. Letter from Muench to Reverend Ulric Beste, O.S.B., Collegio Sant' Anselmo, Rome, 7 October 1957. HM 37/11/8, ACUA.

111. Leo Dworschak, review of *American Nuncio*, by Colman Barry, *Catholic Action News* (hereafter *CAN*), 32, 6 (June 1969): 2. *CAN* was the Catholic monthly periodical for the diocese of Fargo, North Dakota. See also Colman Barry, "Cardinal Muench: Mission of Charity," *American Benedictine Review* 19, 4 (December 1968): 403.

112. Letter from Colman Barry, Collegeville, to Muench, Rome, 4 October 1961. HM 37/19/2, ACUA. Audio tapes of all persons interviewed by Barry are available at Catholic University archives. While unique, they are of limited value in that Barry is uncritical of Muench or the Church and unfamiliar with German history or the role of the Catholic Church and individual Catholics in Nazi crimes.

113. For Phayer's comments on it, see "Pope Pius XII, the Holocaust, and the Cold War," *Holocaust and Genocide Studies* 12, 2 (Fall 1998): 253 n. 64.

114. Letter from Bishop Justin A. Driscoll, Fargo, to Father Blasé Dixon, Archives, Catholic University, 7 January 1974. HM 37/29/1, ACUA. The finding guide to the collection dates the presentation of the papers to 17 November 1972.

115. Letter from Director of Archives Lloyd F. Wagner to Driscoll, Fargo, 18 January 1974. HM 37/37/1, ACUA.

116. See Barry, *American Nuncio*, 160–88 (on displaced persons), 200–215 (on the Concordat), and 121–35 (on the school issue). Barry's sources include oral interviews with Muench's contemporaries as well as diary entries and a series of letters from the Muench Papers. For example, Barry reproduces correspondence between Muench, Bavarian *Land* Commissioner Murray D. Van Wagoner, and General Lucius Clay in appendices 3 (296–99) and 4 (299–309). The letters explicate the nature of Muench's struggle with American *Land* officials over school reform in Bavaria.

117. Spotts and Phayer do discuss Muench's penchant for anti-Semitic stereotypes. See Frederic Spotts, *The Churches and Politics in Germany* (Middletown, Conn.: Wesleyan University Press, 1973), 83–84, 86; Phayer, *Catholic Church and the Holocaust*, 152–57. See Phayer, 111–13, 139–42, on the case of Muench and SS concentration camp physician Hans Eisele. With these exceptions, Muench's role in postwar guilt dialogue has escaped the attention of historians.

118. David O'Brien, review of *American Nuncio*, by Colman Barry, *Church History*, 40, 2 (June 1971): 246–47.

119. Archbishop H. E. Cardinale, review of *American Nuncio*, by Colman Barry, *Catholic Historical Review* 56, 1 (April 1970): 202–3; Thomas Joyce, C.M.F., "*American Nuncio*: Americans in the Service of Rome," *American Benedictine Review* 20, 4 (December 1969): 472–80; Monsignor John S. Kennedy, "Balancing the Books: Far from Fargo," *Our Sunday Visitor* (Huntington, Ind., 22 June 1969); and George Shuster, "The Nuncio from North Dakota in Post-war Germany," *Catholic Messenger* 87, 33 (Davenport, Iowa: Catholic Messenger Publishing), 10.

120. Franklin Littell, review of *American Nuncio*, by Colman Barry, *Journal of Ecumenical Studies*, 7, 3 (Summer 1970): 581–82.

1. The Life and Career of Aloisius Muench

1. Phayer, *Catholic Church and the Holocaust*, 2–4, 13. For the story of this encyclical, see Georges Passelecq and Bernard Suchecky, *The Hidden Encyclical of Pius XI*, translated from the French by Steven Randall (New York: Harcourt Brace, 1997).

2. David W. Southern, *John LaFarge and the Limits of Catholic Interracialism, 1911–1963* (Baton Rouge: Louisiana State University Press, 1996), xiii–xiv.

3. Phayer, *Catholic Church and the Holocaust*, 12–13.

4. Letter from Alfred Haas, New York, to Muench, Kronberg, 21 June 1948. HM 37/14/9, ACUA.

5. Letter from Muench, Kronberg, to Haas, New York, 16 July 1948. HM 37/14/9, ACUA.

6. Letter from Muench, Kronberg, to LaFarge, New York, 16 July 1948. HM 37/14/9, ACUA.

7. For the case "Jewish Restitution Successor Organization versus *Kirchengemeinde* Hassfurt, and Muench's involvement on behalf of *Domkapitular* Johannes Kötzner (1951), see HM 37/130/2, ACUA. For Muench's intervention on behalf of Catholic Friedrich Pflüger of Munich (1953), see HM 37/126/5, ACUA. The most documentation exists for Muench's extensive efforts on behalf of Catholic Joseph Weishäupl of Munich (1955). See HM 37/5/9; 110/5; and 110/7, ACUA.

8. See Muench diary entry dated 27 January 1955, vol. 20, p. 182.

9. Letter from Muench, Kronberg, to Robert McGovern, Education and Religious Affairs (no date). HM 37/23/2, ACUA.

10. Letter from Anthony Schuller, Kemnath, to Muench, Kronberg, 9 September 1946. HM 37/23/2, ACUA.

11. Letter from Muench, Kronberg, to Father Henderson, Regensburg, September 1946. HM 37/9/1, ACUA.

12. Letter from Father John F. Orzel, Bayreuth, to Muench, Kronberg, 7 October 1946. HM 37/23/2, ACUA.

13. Letter from Anni Schuller, Kemnath, to Muench, Kronberg, 7 October 1946. HM 37/23/2, ACUA.

14. Diary entry dated 26 October 1946, vol. 5, p. 3.

15. Letter from Muench, Kronberg, to J. M. Ferguson, Property Control, Munich (no date). HM 37/124/1, ACUA.

16. Letter from Muench, Kronberg, to Father John F. Orzel, Bayreuth, 30 December 1946. HM 37/23/2, ACUA.

17. Letter from Muench, Kronberg, to his sister Terry Muench, 25 August 1950. HM 37/32/5, ACUA.

18. Letter from Anni Schuller, Kemnath, to Muench, Bad Godesberg, 4 June 1954. HM 37/23/2, ACUA.

19. Dr. E. Herbrich, *Alois Kardinal Muench: Ein Lebensbild*, vol. 12, *Schriftenreihe des Sudetendeutschen Priesterwerk Königstein-im-Taunus* (Limburg: Pallottinerdruck, 1969), 10. This essay is brief and meant as a tribute to the cardinal. The Saint Albertus Magnus Seminary at Königstein-im-Taunus (Hesse) was an expellee and refugee seminary founded in November 1947 located only three miles from the Villa Grosch in Kronberg. Bishop Muench was a major financial donor. The seminary trained Catholic refugees and expellees from Silesia, Sudeten, Breslau, Ermland, and Prague. Limburg-an-der-Lahn, located northwest of Kronberg on the Rhineland Palatinate-Hesse border, was Muench's "favorite cathedral and diocesan center." These two facts explain interest in Muench on the part of Königstein's Sudeten priest-academicians and Limburg

Catholic publishers, and explain also the essay's uncritical and brief nature. See Barry, *American Nuncio*, 175, 188–89. Barry's source for this biographical detail is an interview with Monsignor Albert Büttner, Bonn/Beul, 18 October 1963.

20. Barry, *American Nuncio*, 5–7. Barry's source is his interview with Muench's family and their spouses, Milwaukee, 26 June 1962: Mary (Muench) Herrick, Frank Herrick, Mrs. Frank (Doris) Muench, Frank Muench, Teresa Muench, Dorothy (Muench) Ott, Barbara Ott.

21. Herbrich, *Alois Kardinal Muench*, 13.

22. Barry, *American Nuncio*, 14–17.

23. "Eulogy of His Eminence Cardinal Muench," *In Memory of His Eminence Aloisius Joseph Cardinal Muench* (Rome: Arti Grafiche Scalia, 1962), 13. According to Barry, Muench enjoyed academic life at Wisconsin and planned to pursue his doctorate at the University of Innsbruck (Austria) in preparation for a seminary professorship. Because that university suffered severe damage during World War I, the Swiss-born archbishop of Milwaukee Sebastian Messmer recommended that Muench go to the University of Fribourg instead. Muench left for Fribourg in 1919. See Barry, *American Nuncio*, 16–17. Barry's source is an interview with Cardinal Muench, Fargo, summer 1961.

24. Barry, *American Nuncio*, 18. Barry does not provide Muench's personal recollections of the meeting. Barry's source is an interview with Cardinal Muench, Fargo, summer 1961.

25. *A Tribute on the Occasion of the Silver Jubilee of Aloisius Joseph Cardinal Muench: Episcopal Consecration 1935–1960* (Diocese of Fargo, N.D., 1960).

26. Steven Avella, who characterizes Muench as an "orderly and purposeful man," calls the former professor's assumption of the rectorship a "faculty coup d'etat" in which "Muench took over the reigns of the seminary and resumed the process of seminary modernization begun earlier by [Archbishop] Messmer." See Steven M. Avella, ed., *Saint Francis Seminary: Sesquicentennial Essays* (Saint Francis, Wis.: Saint Francis Seminary, 1997), 70. Avella's treatment of Muench is brief.

27. Steven M. Avella, *This Confident Church: Catholic Leadership and Life in Chicago, 1940–1965* (Notre Dame, Ind. University of Notre Dame Press, 1992), 17–18.

28. "Eulogy," 15.

29. Barry, *American Nuncio*, 30–31.

30. For a good if uncritical summary of Muench's work as bishop of Fargo, see Father Robert Laliberte, "Muench as Bishop: Actions and Words," *Scattered Steeples: The Fargo Diocese, a Written Celebration of Its Centennial*, ed. Jerome D. Lamb, Jerry Ruff, and Father William Sherman (Fargo: Burch, Longergan and Lynch, 1988), 104–10.

31. (Father) James Hennesey, S.J. *American Catholics: A History of the Roman Catholic Community in the United States* (New York: Oxford University Press, 1981), 194, 129.

32. Philip Gleason, *The Conservative Reformers: German-American Catholics and the Social Order* (Notre Dame, Ind.: University of Notre Dame Press, 1968), 2.

33. Especially strong during the 1930s, the Rural Life Movement was a midwestern Catholic phenomenon that stressed economic and social aspects as well as perceived virtues of rural living. It addressed the distinct needs of western and midwestern Catholics, geographically separated from the Catholic "establishment" on the industrial belt of the Great Lakes and in eastern seaboard cities. See Michael Zöller, *Washington and Rome: Catholicism in American Culture*, translated from the German by Steven Rendall and Albert Wimmer (Notre Dame, Ind.: University of Notre Dame Press, 1999), 158. Muench was extremely active in the National Catholic Rural Life Conference while bishop of Fargo because of its popular support in his rural diocese. See Barry, *American Nuncio*, 42–44.

34. German-American Catholics founded the CCVA in 1854. It was one of the first national organizations for lay Catholics. After 1901, the CCVA made social study, social criticism, and social reform its leading concerns. Muench attended CCVA annual conventions as a student-seminarian and carried its work with him abroad to Europe. After he returned to the United States in 1922, he gave regular addresses at the CCVA annual convention. Barry, *American Nuncio*, 44–45.

35. For instance, despite its interest in social reform, the CCVA was a severe critic of the welfare state and post–New Deal American liberalism. See Gleason, *Conservative Reformers*, 4.

36. This outlook was captured in Muench's comment about U.S. diplomat Walter Dowling in 1954. In describing his fellow dinner guests to his sister Terry, Muench said, "Mr. Walter Dowling and his wife [were among the guests]. [They are] Southerners, and non-Catholic, but fine people." See letter from Aloisius Muench, Bad Godesberg, to Terry Muench, Milwaukee, 31 March 1954. HM 37/32/9, ACUA.

37. Muench established the monthly publication of *Catholic Action News* in 1939, so that the diocese of Fargo might have "a historical record." For further detail on the *CAN*, Diana Deats-O'Reilly, *The Bishops of Fargo: Biographical Sketches of the Shepherds of the Diocese of Fargo, 1889–1985* (Grand Forks, N.D., privately published by Diana Deats-O'Reilly, 1985), 7. Deats-O'Reilly provides useful factual information but no critical analysis. Muench's intentions aside, *CAN* was a conservative and pro-Catholic parochial religious publication.

38. See Hennesey, *American Catholics*, 188, and John Tracy Ellis, *American Catholicism*, 2nd edition (Chicago: University of Chicago Press, 1969), 146.

39. Muench, "The Bishop Writes," *CAN* (February 1940).

40. Aloisius Muench, "The Outstretched Hand of Communism" (pamphlet; Saint Louis: Central Bureau Press, 1938), 3.

41. Muench, "The Bishop Writes," *CAN* (July 1942). Muench was not alone in his belief that the influence of communism should be minimized post-

war. It was a concern shared by the State Department as well. See Boehling, *Question of Priorities*, 19.

42. See Carol Rittner and John K. Roth, eds., *Pope Pius XII and the Holocaust* (London: Leicester University Press, 2002), 3–5.

43. Defenders of Eugenio Pacelli would deny this statement regarding Pius XII's Christmas message. While Pacelli might not have used specific language (the words "Jew" and "antisemitism" were absent), argue his defenders, his words were meant and interpreted by Catholics and the Nazi regime alike as a strong protest. Perhaps we should rely on the interpretation of Italian fascist dictator Benito Mussolini, who purportedly told his son-in-law, Count Galeazzo Ciano, "this is a speech of platitudes which might better be made by the parish priest of Predappio" (Mussolini's native village); in Richard L. Rubenstein, "Pope Pius XII and the Shoah," in Rittner and Roth, eds., *Pope Pius XII and the Holocaust*, 177.

44. Muench, "The Bishop Writes," *CAN* (February 1943).

45. Muench, "The Bishop Writes," *CAN* (October 1943).

46. For coverage of Holocaust-related issues in the American press, Deborah Lipstadt, *Beyond Belief: The American Press and the Coming of the Holocaust, 1933–1945* (New York: Free Press, 1986), is the standard work. For a similar study of the American Protestant press in particular, see Robert Ross, *So It Was True: The American Protestant Press and the Nazi Persecution of the Jews* (Minneapolis: University of Minnesota Press, 1980). For the purposes of understanding Muench's later years in Germany, especially pertaining to the Catholic clemency campaign on behalf of German war criminals, it is worth noting that the Holy See in Rome knew of the extermination camps in Poland. Vatican officials, including Pope Pius XII, were among the first to learn about the Holocaust in 1942. See Phayer, *Catholic Church and the Holocaust*, 41–66.

47. Muench, "The Bishop Writes," *CAN* (June 1943).

48. Muench, "The Bishop Writes," *CAN* (January 1944).

49. Muench, "The Bishop Writes," *CAN* (March 1944).

50. Muench and Ryan, "Church, Fascism, and Peace," 14.

51. Ibid., 8.

52. Ibid., 13.

53. Muench, "The Bishop Writes," *CAN* (July 1940).

54. Muench and Ryan, "Church, Fascism, and Peace," 9–11.

55. See James E. McNutt, "Adolf Schlatter and the Jews," *German Studies Review* 26, 2 (May 2003): 355–58.

56. Muench and Ryan, "Church, Fascism, and Peace," 42–43.

57. Daniel Jonah Goldhagen, *Hitler's Willing Executioners: Ordinary Germans and the Holocaust* (New York: Alfred A. Knopf, 1996).

58. Donald Warren, *Radio Priest: Charles Coughlin, the Father of Hate Radio* (New York: Free Press, 1996), 1–3.

59. Ronald H. Carpenter, *Father Charles H. Coughlin, Surrogate Spokesman for the Disaffected* (Westport, Conn.: Greenwood Press, 1998), 13.

60. When Gallagher died in 1937, his replacement, Archbishop Edward Mooney, supported the long-standing efforts of Vatican officials (including Secretary of State Pacelli and Pope Pius XI) to curb Coughlin. Warren, *Radio Priest*, 204–7.

61. Aloisius Muench, "Father Coughlin's Money Program," *Salesianum*, 30, 2 (April 1935): 9, 11, 21.

62. Ibid.

63. Barry, *American Nuncio*, 28–29.

64. Letter from James D. Hagarty, Chicago, to Monsignor Aloisius Muench, Saint Francis, Wis., 27 May 1935. HM 37/53/2, ACUA.

65. Barry, *American Nuncio*, 30. The Muench-Coughlin correspondence is not among the Muench papers.

66. Letter from Aloisius Muench, Fargo, to Samuel Stritch, Chicago, 24 December 1945. CC/M, Archdiocesan Archives Chicago.

67. Letter from Stritch to Muench, 31 December 1945, CC/M, Archdiocesan Archives Chicago.

68. Born in Olginate, Italy, Cesare Orsenigo was appointed Apostolic Nuncio to the Netherlands on 23 June 1922 and subsequently Apostolic Nuncio to Hungary in 1925. On 25 April 1930, he succeeded Eugenio Pacelli as apostolic nuncio to Germany. He died on 1 April 1946.

69. Ludwig Volk, "Der Heilige Stuhl und Deutschland," 795.

70. Barry, *American Nuncio*, 67.

71. See Spotts, *Churches and Politics in Germany*, 29, and Muench diary entry dated 7 November 1949, vol. 11, p. 38.

72. Volk, "Der Heilige Stuhl und Deutschland," 795–96.

73. These national groups included Lithuanians, Latvians, Estonians, Ukrainians, Slovenians, Romanians, Hungarians, Poles, Croatians, Yugoslavs, and Slovaks. See memorandum entitled "Attachment of approved delegates of Vatican Group to USFET," no date. HM 37/69/4, ACUA.

74. Barry describes the 10 November 1945 meeting between the head of the third Vatican mission (Archbishop) Carlo Chiarlo and Army General Dwight D. Eisenhower as a "comedy of errors." Barry, *American Nuncio*, 56–58.

75. Muench diary entry dated 28 February 1947, vol. 5, p. 83.

76. Barry, *American Nuncio*, 51–52.

77. Spotts, *Churches and Politics in Germany*, 33.

78. Volk, "Der Heilige Stuhl und Deutschland," 797.

79. Muench diary entry dated 3 July 1946, vol. 4, p. 7.

80. Letter from Aloisius Muench, Kronberg, to Howard Smith, Fargo, 5 November 1946. HM 37/55/2, ACUA. Muench also confided to his mother that Stritch had been the one to recommend him to the pope in February 1946. See letter from Muench, Kronberg, to Theresa Muench, Milwaukee, 15 November 1946, HM 37/30/6, ACUA. Several years later, upon his nomination as nuncio to the Federal Republic, Muench remarked to a friend that "Cardinal Stritch felt proud of [Muench's] latest promotion . . . because he was really the one to push [Muench] ahead whenever possible." See letter from

Muench to Monsignor Joseph Adams, Chicago, 29 March 1951. HM 37/10/2, ACUA.

81. Barry, *American Nuncio*, 59. A front-page report in the *CAN* confirmed that "Bishop Muench received an audience with the Pope and made a report on the state of the diocese of Fargo." See article entitled "Bishop Muench in Audience, Reports to Holy Father," *CAN* (March 1946). We do not know further details about their private discussion on 23 February.

82. Letter from Aloisius Muench, Fargo, to his sister Terry Muench, Milwaukee, 29 May 1946. HM 37/32/1, ACUA.

83. Letter from Aloisius Muench, Bad Godesberg, to his mother Theresa Muench, Milwaukee, 5 November 1952. HM 37/30/13, ACUA. The date of this letter is significant. Muench kept the early date of his selection (3 March 1946) from his mother until years later. He did so because of his almost simultaneous appointment as liaison representative to the American army.

84. Letter from Aloisius Muench to Terry Muench, 29 May 1946. The date of this letter is significant because American occupation officials were still unclear as to Muench's Vatican assignment, and the obvious conflict of interest it represented.

85. Letter from Secretary of War Robert Patterson, Washington, to Monsignor Howard J. Carroll, Washington, 21 March 1946. HM 37/55/1, ACUA.

86. Barry, *American Nuncio*, 60–61.

87. Letter from Aloisius Muench, Fargo, to Apostolic Delegate Amleto Cicognani, Washington, 30 May 1946, CC/M, Archdiocesan Archives Chicago.

88. Letter from Patterson to Carroll, 19 April 1946. HM 37/55/1, ACUA.

89. Letter from Aloisius Muench, Fargo, to Monsignor Howard Carroll, Washington, 7 May 1946. HM 37/69/3, ACUA.

90. Letter marked "confidential" from Aloisius Muench, Fargo, to Bishop William T. Mulloy, Covington (Kentucky), 17 May 1946. HM 37/69/3, ACUA.

91. Letter from Robert Patterson, Washington, to Aloisius Muench, Fargo, 7 June 1946. HM 37/124/1, ACUA.

92. Muench's Berlin office was located on *Dohlstrasse* in the suburb Berlin-Dahlem. It was staffed with one priest, two domestics, and one automobile. It was the official headquarters of Muench's business as liaison consultant to the military government. See memorandum entitled "Expenses of Bishop Muench in Germany," April 1947. HM 37/69/3, ACUA.

93. Report entitled "Religious Affairs" dated August 1946, 25–25. In "Basic Documents" folder, box 158, RA, ECR, RG 260-OMGUS, NARA.

94. Monsignor Walter Carroll, originally from Pittsburgh, was head of the English language desk at the Vatican secretariat of state, which handled Vatican diplomatic relations. Msgr. Carroll was also chosen as the head of the first and second Vatican missions to Germany (June and September 1945). Barry, *American Nuncio*, 53.

95. Report entitled "Religious Affairs," dated August 1946; Basic Documents, box 158, RA, ECR, RG 260, NARA, pp. 24–25.

96. Officer Robert Alexander of Internal Affairs and Communications–Berlin replied to Arndt quoting from the August 1946 Religious Affairs
report. See letter from Dr. Karl Arndt, Chief, Religious Affairs Branch, Stuttgart,
to Robert Alexander, Chief, Internal Affairs and Communications, Berlin,
6 November 1947. Alexander replied on 21 November. Both letters in "Religious
Affairs Miscellaneous Part II," box 164, RA, ECR, RG 260-OMGUS, NARA.

97. Historian Joseph Bendersky cites evidence showing that both Military
Governor Lucius Clay and his political advisor in the State Department, Robert
Murphy, viewed Jewish colleagues as untrustworthy. See Bendersky, *"Jewish
Threat,"* 364–71. Bendersky persuasively shows that many high ranking-officers
and officials in postwar Germany and back in the United States believed that
"Jewish refugees in American uniforms unduly affected American policy toward
Germany in a variety of detrimental ways," 364.

98. Ibid., 370. Some suspected him of anti-democratic and even "fascist" sympathies. Other studies describe him as "an outspoken Catholic suspected of exhibiting favoritism toward Catholics" and as being "greatly
mistrusted" by Treasury Secretary Morgenthau. See Boehling, *Question of
Priorities*, 44.

99. Muench diary entry dated 16 September 1946, vol. 4, p. 74.

100. Letter from Muench, Kronberg, to Bishop Vincent J. Ryan, Bismarck,
15 November 1946. HM 37/8/4, ACUA.

101. See Letter from Douglas Waples, Chief, Publications Control Branch,
to General Robert McClure, 21 December 1946. Series 1, box 3, John O. Riedl
Collection, Marquette University.

102. Muench's notions about involving himself in things beyond spiritual
care are clear in a long memorandum to Archbishop Samuel Stritch written in
late 1946. Muench reported that on his first meeting with Clay and Murphy on
August 3, he requested the privilege of a diplomatic pouch and cipher code. See
"Memorandum," undated, CC/M, Archdiocesan Archives Chicago. Extensive
documentation of the *Lilliput* scandal and other Muench-related documentation
regarding the bishop's opinion on "good" or "bad" publications, usually
depending on its religious versus secular, "socialistic," or "communistic" content
exists in the folder "Muench, Bishop," box 247; ICD-Publications Control
Branch; RG 260-OMGUS, NARA. Muench approached fellow Catholic Robert
Murphy to push the cause of Catholic publications and paper allocation, and
Murphy cooperated. See folder entitled "Muench, Bishop," box 181, RA, ECR,
RG 260-OMGUS, NARA. On school policy, see also folder entitled "Muench,
Bishop," box 181, RA, ECR, RG 260-OMGUS, NARA. On restitution,
Muench participated in at least four cases on behalf of Catholic Germans fight-
ing against the return of property to former Jewish German owners. See HM
37/5/9; 126/5; and 130/2.

103. Cable from OMGUS/signed Clay to AGWAR for WARCAD/for
Echols, 29 May 1946. Document 24, folder 4: AG 000.3 (Religion). Box 2. Office
of the Adjutant General: General Correspondence & other Records ("Decimal
File"). Records of the Executive Office. RG 260-OMGUS, NARA.

104. Muench diary entry dated 3 August 1946, vol. 4, p. 35. It is unclear at what point Muench openly acknowledged his role as apostolic visitor (July 1946–February 1947) to military government authorities, but apparently he had not done so by August 1946.

105. Letter from Muench to Cicognani, 30 May 1946.

106. Volk, "Der Heilige Stuhl in Deutschland," 795.

107. Letter from Aloisius Muench, Rome, to Terry Muench, Milwaukee, 18 February 1947. HM 37/32/2, ACUA.

108. Letter from Muench, Kronberg, to Archbishop Samuel Stritch, Chicago, 25 September 1946. HM 37/69/3, ACUA.

109. Volk notes, "der Visitator konnte seine Werk nicht auf offizielle Weise angehen." See Ludwig Volk, "Bilanz einer Nuntiatur 1946–1959: Schlussbericht des ersten Nuntius in der Nachkriegszeit," *Stimmen der Zeit* 195 (1977): 149.

110. Barry, *American Nuncio*, 67. Though Barry does not footnote this specific comment, I assume his source is his interview with Monsignor Bernhard Hack (Rome, 23 November 1963).

111. Letter from Muench, Kronberg, to Martin Salm, Chilton (Wis.), 17 November 1949. HM 37/15/1, ACUA.

112. Volk, "Bilanz einer Nuntiatur," 152. Pope Pius XII gave Muench the title of archbishop in 1950.

113. In addition to his Vatican duties in Germany and his three-year stint as liaison representative for the American occupation, Muench also remained bishop of Fargo. He kept up with its business through correspondence, visits, and a close working relationship with the auxiliary bishop of Fargo, Leo Dworschak. Muench's appointment to the College of Cardinals in Rome at the end of 1959 marked the end of his career as nuncio to Germany and also as archbishop of the diocese of Fargo. In Rome, Muench was given curial assignments as a regular member of the Congregations of Religious, Rites, and Extraordinary Affairs, three of the permanent commissions of cardinals functioning in the central Vatican administration. He died in 1962, at the age of seventy-three.

2. *Excusing the Holocaust: The Sensation of* One World *in Charity*

1. For the full original text of *One World* as first published (by the Diocese of Fargo, North Dakota) in the early spring of 1946, see appendix C.

2. See "Viewpoints," *CAN* (July 1946): 1–3.

3. Barry discusses Muench's controversial pastoral letter *One World in Charity* briefly (*American Nuncio*, 77–80), and ignores its anti-Semitic implications. He uncritically accepts Muench's questionable claim (in 1947) to have known nothing of *One World*'s distribution beyond the diocese of Fargo. Barry calls the pastoral letter "forthright and fearless." He uncritically repeats Muench's assertion in *One World* that U.S. policy toward Germany was a "planned conspiracy of revenge by persons who had infiltrated Washington and

the military occupation in Germany." If Barry was aware of Muench's veiled reference to Jews here, he ignored it and repeated it. Barry also glosses over Muench's cooperation with the Holy See and certain German bishops to commute the sentences of some German Catholic war criminals convicted of Holocaust-related crimes (see chapter 4). In the works of Spotts, Volk, and Phayer, *One World* is not mentioned.

4. For a discussion of how Berlin seminarians trained during the Weimar period understood the concept "who is neighbor," that is to say, who was included in the category "neighbor" and who was excluded, see (Father) Kevin Spicer, C.S.C., *Resisting the Third Reich: The Catholic Clergy in Hitler's Berlin* (De Kalb: Northern Illinois University Press, 2004).

5. Walter Zwi Bacharach's characterization of Catholic-Jewish relations provides a good summary of the established canon on this subject. Christians were interested in the survival of the Jews in order to convert them to Christianity, and they rejected racist theories. Nazism called for the physical annihilation of the Jews and the eradication of Judaism. Under the Nazis, protection of Christians and promotion of the interests of the Catholic Church took precedence for the Church over humanitarian concern for the fate of Jews. Bacharach notes that it is difficult to prove the existence of a direct link between Catholic anti-Judaism and Nazi anti-Semitism. But ideological continuity between Nazism and Catholic anti-Judaism existed nonetheless, in that Catholics played an important part in "disseminating the negative image of the Jew (417)." See Walter Zwi Bacharach, "The Catholic Anti-Jewish Prejudice, Hitler, and the Jews," In *Probing the Depths of German Antisemitism: German Society and the Persecution of the Jews, 1933–1941,* ed. David Bankier (New York: Berghahn Books, 2000), 415–30.

6. See James Carroll, *Constantine's Sword: The Church and the Jews* (Boston: Houghton Mifflin, 2001), 22; 40.

7. Olaf Blaschke argues that anti-Semitism infecting the German Catholic milieu during the *Kaiserreich* was far *more* damaging than that practiced by small antisemitic political parties, an argument already appearing in David Blackbourn, *Marpingen: Apparitions of the Virgin Mary in Bismarckian Germany* (New York: Knopf, 1994); Olaf Blaschke, *Katholizimus und Antisemitismus im Deutschen Kaiserreich* (Göttingen: Vandenhoeck und Ruprecht, 1997); James F. Harris, *The People Speak! Anti-Semitism and Emancipation in Nineteenth-Century Bavaria* (Ann Arbor: University of Michigan Press, 1994); and Helmut Walser Smith, *German Nationalism and Religious Conflict: Culture, Ideology, Politics, 1870–1914* (Princeton, N.J.: Princeton University Press, 1995).

8. Aloisius Muench, *One World in Charity: A Pastoral,* 1.

9. *One World,* 2.

10. Ibid., 3.

11. Ibid., 4.

12. Leni Yahil, *The Holocaust: The Fate of European Jewry,* translated from the Hebrew by Ina Friedman and Haya Galai (New York: Oxford University Press, 1990), 274–75.

13. Dina Porat, "Vilna," *The Holocaust Encyclopedia,* ed. Walter Laquer, editor (New Haven, Conn.: Yale University Press, 2001), 664.

14. *One World,* 5.

15. It was titled "Intervention of Mercy."

16. *One World,* 9.

17. Ibid., 10–11.

18. Ibid., 13.

19. Jackson stated: "We have no purpose to incriminate the whole German people. We know that the Nazi party was not put in power by a majority of the German vote. We know that it came to power by an evil alliance between the most extreme of the Nazi revolutionaries, the most unrestrained of the German reactionaries, and the most aggressive of the German militarists." See "Policy [on] German Guilt," included in "Basic Policy for Information and Information Control in Germany," dated 17 January 1946. In folder 4 entitled "History," box 69. Records of the Information Control Division Headquarters: Central Decimal File of the Executive Office 1944–1949.

20. *One World,* 14.

21. The historical record on German Catholic resistance to Nazism between 1933 and 1945 has been told. See, among others, Helmreich, *German Churches under Hitler,* 237–96, 347–68; Heinz Boberbach, ed., *Berichte des SD und der Gestapo über Kirchen und Kirchenvolk in Deutschland, 1934–1944* (Mainz: Grünewald Verlag, 1971); John Conway, *The Nazi Persecution of the Churches 1933-1945* (New York: Basic Books, 1968); Kurt Nowak, *Geschichte des Christentums in Deutschland* (Munich: Beck Verlag, 1995), 243–90.

22. *One World,* 15.

23. Muench does not specify his source further.

24. Here, Muench quotes from the Old Testament book of Proverbs 25:21–22. These words are accredited to David's son and successor Solomon (ca. 961–922 B.C.E.). Quoted in *One World,* 17.

25. From the New Testament Gospel of Luke 6:27–34. Quoted in *One World,* 18.

26. This is consistent with Muench's outlook on religious and practicing Jews, which was often favorable, especially when compared to his views of Jews he considered "materialistic," "communist and socialistic," "vengeful," or "greedy."

27. *One World,* 20.

28. Ibid., 21.

29. Ibid., 22.

30. Ibid., 23–25.

31. Ibid., 4.

32. Ibid., 13–14.

33. Ibid., 5.

34. Letter from "Father Markert," Techny, to Muench, c/o Reverend A. Memmesheimer, Chicago, 7 June 1946. HM 37/9/1, ACUA.

35. "Eine Welt in der Liebe," *Nord-Dakota Herold* (Dickinson, North Dakota), 8 March 1946. I thank the State Historical Society of North Dakota for making the *Herold* available to me.

36. Letter from Cornelius Sittard, Dickinson, to Muench, Kronberg, 18 November 1946. HM 37/14/5, ACUA.

37. Founded in Saint Paul, Minnesota, in 1867, *The Wanderer* was in the editorial hands of the Matt family since 1899. Joseph Matt, who took it over at that time, was one of the principal leaders of the CCVA and remained greatly interested in its social reform projects. *The Wanderer* was highly conservative on political and religious issues. Gleason, *Conservative Reformers,* 4.

38. Letter from Alphonse J. Matt, Saint Paul, to Muench, Kronberg, 16 April 1947. HM 37/25/1, ACUA. Muench replied that the idea of mass distribution in Germany was acceptable, the only question being that he "would not know who would foot the bill . . . [would] the CCVA (Catholic Central Verein of America)? Or would the [American] bishops? Or, maybe a group of donors—friends of the Church in Germany?" See letter from Muench to Matt, 24 April 1947. HM 37/25/1, ACUA.

39. In the *Saint Josefsblatt* case, the translator is unknown. The first installment of *One World* appeared in German on 15 July 1946; the second on 22 July; the third on 29 July; the fourth on 5 August; and the fifth and final installment on 12 August 1946. My thanks to the University of Oregon for making microfilm copies of the *Saint Josefsblatt* available to the University of Maryland.

40. Barry, *American Nuncio,* 79. Barry does not provide a source here. The Muench-Regnery correspondence available in the Muench collection does not mention this incident. I am unable to discern to whom Regnery distributed these copies.

41. Letter from Mary Filser Lohr, New York, to Muench, Kronberg, 9 April 1947. HM 37/26/10, ACUA.

42. Muench diary entry dated 21 January 1947, vol. 5, p. 50.

43. Lauter did not include a copy of this particular "sixteen single-spaced" version, and, to my knowledge, no copy of this version exists elsewhere. Depending on typesetting and paper size, this version may have been a complete translation.

44. Letter from Franz Lauter, Cologne, to Muench, 2 January 1947. HM 37/23/4, ACUA.

45. We know that Muench granted permission to the U.S. German-language newspaper *Familienblatt* some time prior to 7 June 1946.

46. The Catholic imprimatur, literally a word placed at the beginning or end of a published document, grants "permission to print." It is the license required of all writings that treat doctrine, morality, canon law, or scripture. Imprimatur is issued by a diocese and requires approval of the diocesan bishop.

47. Letter from Gabriel Vollmar, Bonn, to Muench, Kronberg, 17 March 1947. HM 37/96/7, ACUA.

48. Letter from Muench to Vollmar, 15 April 1947. HM 37/96/7, ACUA.

49. Under occupation, all publications distributed in the American zone of Germany needed the approval of the Information Control division (ICD).

50. Letter from John O. Riedl to Karl Arndt, 24 April 1947. In: John O. Riedl Collection, series 1, box 3, Marquette University. No copy of the version referenced by Riedl is available, hence it is not clear whether Riedl refers to the sixteen-page version circulated in Cologne or to another version.

51. Letter from Vollmar, Bonn, to Muench, Bad Godesberg, 23 April 1952. HM 37/90/3, ACUA.

52. Letter from Monsignor Joseph Kamps, Beuren, to Muench, Kronberg, 25 January 1948. HM 37/92/5, ACUA.

53. Letter from Sister Maura, Dortmund, to Muench, Kronberg, 3 April 1947. HM 37/37/6, ACUA. Her letter does not clarify who actually copied the letter.

54. Letter from Sister Alodia, Dortmund, to Muench, Kronberg, 18 April 1947. HM 37/37/1, ACUA.

55. Letter from Hedwig Rohmer, Munich, to Muench, Kronberg, 14 January 1947. HM 37/9/2, ACUA.

56. News clippings saved by Muench. HM 37/162/7, ACUA.

57. Letter from Muench, Chicago, to Francis Cardinal Spellman, New York, 17 November 1947. HM 37/69/13, ACUA. No record of Murphy's response is available. Bishop Muench's explanation was addressed to Cardinal Spellman due to the fact that Murphy approached the cardinal regarding *One World* that fall, prompting Cardinal Spellman to ask Muench for a written explanation.

58. Muench diary entry dated 13 June 1947, vol. 6, p. 19.

59. Letter from Muench to Spellman, 17 November 1947.

60. Letter from Muench, Kronberg, to Georg Meixner, Bamberg, 21 June 1947. HM 37/139/4, ACUA.

61. Letter from Father John LaFarge, New York, to Muench, Kronberg, 11 July 1947. HM 37/9/3, ACUA.

62. John LaFarge, *The Manner Is Ordinary* (Garden City, NY: Image Books, 1957), 278–79.

63. Letters from Muench to LaFarge, 3 September 1951 and 27 November 1952, HM 37/10/3 and 10/4, ACUA.

64. Letter from Picard de la Vacquerie, French Zone, to Muench, Kronberg, 5 September 1947. HM 37/69/13, ACUA. De la Vacquerie attached a copy in French, which came to only five typeset, single-spaced pages.

65. Letter from Muench to de la Vacquerie, 30 September 1947. HM 37/69/13, ACUA.

66. Letter from Muench, Kronberg, to Sister Maura, Dortmund, 19 July 1948. HM 37/37/6, ACUA.

67. Weekly Intelligence Report for Schwabach, 12 September 1947. Folder "Intelligence Reports," box 1479, Correspondence of Schwabach Resident Liaison & Security Office, 1945-9, Records of the Field Operations Division, RG-260-OMGUS, NARA.

68. Muench diary entry dated 30 August 1947, vol. 6, p. 46.

69. Letter from *Stadtpfarrer* Ruh, Oberkirch, to Muench, Kronberg, 6 September 1947. HM 37/92/4, ACUA. This particular twelve-page version is not available in the Muench collection or in the National Archives.

70. Letter from General Pierre J. Koenig, French Zone headquarters, to General Lucius Clay, Berlin, 23 September 1947. In folder 9 (entitled "December 1947"), box 37 (October–December 1947), CGCPA, OPAG-B, RG 84-State Department, NARA.

71. Letter from John Riedl, Religious Affairs, to Muench, Kronberg, 8 October 1947. In folder entitled "Religious Affairs Miscellaneous part II," box 164, RA, ECR, RG 260-OMGUS, NARA.

72. Muench diary entry dated 6 October 1947, vol. 6, p. 79. See also Phayer, *Catholic Church and the Holocaust,* 155.

73. Muench diary entry dated 21 December 1947, vol. 7, pp. 30–31.

74. Muench heard of this later, both from Spellman and from Murphy. In a private conversation dated 29 January, Murphy told Muench of Clay's ultimate decision to remain silent about the complaint on the 6 October plane ride. When Muench inquired as to why Clay did not simply approach him then, directly, Murphy replied that Clay had a "complex mind," and, further, it was inappropriate in that Muench was Clay's guest on the trip. See Muench diary entry dated 29 January 1948, vol. 8, pp. 66–67.

75. Muench diary entry dated 21 December 1947.

76. Telegram, Spellman to Murphy, 9 October 1947. In folder 7 (entitled "October 1947"), box 7 (October–December 1947), CGCPA, OPAG-B, RG 84-State Department, NARA.

77. Zöller, *Washington and Rome,* 171; Hennesey, *American Catholics,* 276.

78. Letter from Spellman to Murphy, 25 November 1947. In folder 9 (entitled "December 1947"), box #37 (October–December 1947), CGCPA, OPAG-B, RG 84-State Department, NARA.

79. Letter from Muench to Stanley Bertke, 13 October 1947. HM 37/55/6, ACUA.

80. Muench diary entry dated 12 November 1947, vol. 6, pp. 97–99.

81. Letter from de la Vacquerie to Muench, 24 October 1947. HM 37/69/13, ACUA.

82. Muench diary entry dated 17 November 1947, vol. 7, p. 4.

83. Muench diary entry dated 12 November 1947.

84. Letter from Murphy to Spellman, 24 October 1947. In folder 9 (entitled "December 1947"), box 7 (October–December 1947), CGCPA, OPAG-B, RG 84-State Department, NARA.

85. Muench diary entry dated 17 November 1947.

86. Letter from Muench to Spellman, 17 November 1947, appendixes to letter from Spellman to Murphy, 25 November 1947, in folder 9 (entitled "December 1947"), box 37 (October–December 1947), CGCPA, OPAG-B, RG 84-State Department, NARA.

87. No other documents mention a request from a "publication in Bonn."

88. Spellman asked Muench's permission to do so. See letter from Spellman to Muench, 25 November 1947. HM 37/69/13, ACUA.

89. Murphy wrote to Spellman, "I have taken the liberty of showing the enclosure to General Clay. I believe this satisfactorily closes the matter. This is an interesting example of what may happen when words are taken out of their context and detached from the date on which they were used . . . I shall look forward to Bishop Muench's return [to Germany] and will acknowledge his memorandum when I see him." Letter from Murphy to Spellman, 16 December 1947, in folder 9 (entitled "December 1947"), box 7 (October–December 1947), CGCPA, OPAG-B, RG 84-State Department, NARA. This letter is also available in the private papers of Francis J. Cardinal Spellman, Archives, Archdiocese of New York (AANY), Saint Joseph's Seminary, Yonkers, New York. See Robert Murphy, London, to Francis Spellman, New York, 16 December 1947; in AANY, S/D-12, folder 21, Fargo. I thank Archivist Sister Marguerita Smith for making a photocopy of this letter available to me. The Spellman papers are closed, though the archive will allow individual requests.

90. Letter from Muench to de la Vacquerie, 30 September 1947.

91. Letter from Muench, Kronberg, to Mary Filser Lohr, New York, 10 May 1947. HM 37/26/10, ACUA.

92. Letter from Muench to "*Stadtpfarrer* Ruh," 13 September 1947. HM 37/92/4, ACUA.

93. Muench diary entry dated 12 November 1947.

94. Weekly Intelligence Report for Schwabach, 12 September 1947. In folder entitled "Intelligence Reports," box 1479, Correspondence of Schwabach Resident Liaison & Security Office, 1945-9; Records of the Field Operations Division, RG 260-OMGUS, NARA.

95. Muench diary entry dated 21 January 1947.

96. Letter from Muench, Kronberg, to his sister Terry Muench, Milwaukee, 18 February 1947. HM 37/32/2, ACUA.

97. Letter from *Stadtpfarrer* Ruh to Muench, 6 September 1947.

98. Letter from *Weihbischof* (Auxiliary Bishop) Höcht, Regensburg, to Muench, Kronberg, 1946. HM 37/142/6, ACUA.

99. Letter from Sister M. Chrysanthus, Holy Cross, Indiana, to Muench, Kronberg, 24 July 1946. HM 37/38/1, ACUA.

100. Letter from Sister Crescentia, Holy Cross, Indiana, to Muench, Kronberg, 11 July 1946. HM 37/38/1, ACUA.

101. Letter from Sister M. Chrysanthus to Muench, 24 July 1946.

102. Letter from Franz Lauter to Muench, 2 January 1947.

103. Letter from Franz Münnich, Ostlutter, to Muench, Kronberg, 26 April 1947. HM 37/20/9, ACUA.

104. Letter from Franz Grübert, Furth, to Muench, Kronberg, 2 January 1947. HM 37/83/1, ACUA.

105. Letter from Elisabeth Baumgart to Muench, 24 July 1947.

106. Letter from H. Mertens, Hersfeld, to Muench, Kronberg, 26 September 1947. HM 37/128/3, ACUA.

107. Letter from Wilhelm Heinrich Ewald, Freiherr von Freyberg, to Muench, Kronberg, 27 April 1947. HM 37/20/9, ACUA.

108. Ibid.

109. Letter from Barbara Vincenz, Koblenz, to Muench, Kronberg, 5 February 1947. HM 37/20/9, ACUA.

110. Letter from Therese Wagner, Munich, to Muench, Kronberg, 5 March 1947. HM 37/20/9, ACUA.

111. Letter from Hedwig Rohmer, Munich, to Muench, Kronberg, 14 January 1947. Two copies, one in German and one translated copy, exist in the collection. See HM 37/9/2 and 55/3, ACUA.

112. Letter from Vollmar to Muench, 3 December 1951. HM 37/96/8, ACUA.

113. Letter from Vollmar to Muench, 23 April 1952. HM 37/90/3, ACUA.

114. Letter from H. Hassenbach, Frankfurt/Main, to Muench, Kronberg, 22 December 1952. HM 37/21/8, ACUA.

115. Letter from Father Howard Smith, Bad Godesberg, to a "Dave," Fargo, 29 December 1952. HM 37/63/6, ACUA.

116. "Cardinal Muench Asked to Testify for Eichmann," *Chicago Daily Tribune,* 22 April 1961. HM 37/30/5, ACUA.

117. When Muench heard of the clipping, he was indignant. "If this Wechtenbruch, assistant of the lawyer Servatius, comes here [to Villa Salvator Mundi, Vatican City] to see me, I would refuse to see him because no matter what I say it will be twisted," Muench wrote to his sister Terry. See letter from Muench, Rome, to his sister Terry, Milwaukee, 29 April 1961. HM 37/30/5, ACUA.

118. "Cardinal Never Met Eichmann," *Daily News,* 5 May 1961. HM 37/60/10, ACUA.

119. Letter from Grübert to Muench, 2 January 1947.

120. Letter from Father Franz Weimar to Muench, Kronberg, 11 October 1947. HM 37/53/7, ACUA.

121. Letter from Father Franz Schmal, Todtnauberg, to Muench, Kronberg, 18 April 1947. HM 37/92/3, ACUA.

122. "Freund und Anwalt der Deutschen," *Kirchliche Nachrichten Agentur (KNA) Beilage.* HM 37/45/2, ACUA.

123. Letter from Barbara Muschweck, Nuremberg, to Muench, Kronberg, 7 July 1947. HM 37/20/10, ACUA.

3. Comfort and Consensus: Muench and the German Catholic Hierarchy, Clergy, and Laity

1. Letter from Bishop Michael Keller, Münster, to Muench, Bad Godesberg, 29 January 1952. HM 37/141/9, ACUA.

2. Letter from Muench to Keller, 1 February 1952. HM 37/141/9, ACUA.

3. Ibid.

4. Ibid.

5. "Der Standpunkt der Katholischen Kirche bezüglich des Antisemitismus dürfte der Conference hinreichend bekannt sein und bedarf meine Ermeinung keines besonderes Hinweises," wrote Muench. He did not elaborate. Perhaps he referred to the Church's explicit and public rejection of racism in *Mit Brennender Sorge*. Ibid.

6. Ibid.

7. See, for example, letter from Muench, Bad Godesberg, to Monsignor Paul Tanner, Washington, 17 March 1950. HM 37/114/6, ACUA.

8. "Conrad Gröber, Erzbischof von Freiburg: Schreiben an den Diözesanklerus nach dem Ende des Weltkriegs, 21 June 1945," in Löhr, *Dokumente deutscher Bischöfe*, 21.

9. "Gröber, Erzbischof von Freiburg: Hirtenbrief über die Anklagen gagen das deutsche Volk, 21 September 1945," in Löhr, *Dokumente deutscher Bischöfe*, 21. 45–55.

10. Lewy, *Catholic Church and Nazi Germany*, 288.

11. He responded by helping Jewish converts to Catholicism to emigrate through the Saint Raphael's Verein, for which the general secretary of the Verein suffered imprisonment. Unlike Frings (Cologne), he supported the efforts of Gertrud Luckner and the Freiburg circle to improve Christian-Jewish relations after the war's end. Heinz Hürten, *Deutsche Katholiken* (Munich: Schöningh Verlag, 1992), 510–11; Phayer, *Catholic Church and the Holocaust*, 67–81.

12. Converted Catholic Gertrud Luckner was born in 1900 in Liverpool, England, but raised in Germany. She studied economics and social welfare at the universities of Königsberg, Birmingham (at the Quaker College for Religious and Social Work), Frankfurt, and Freiburg. She obtained her doctorate from the University of Freiburg in 1938, where she completed her dissertation entitled "Self-Help Among the Unemployed in England and in Wales based on English History of Ideas and Economics." In 1933, she began working with the Catholic Caritas Association in Freiburg. After the outbreak of the war in 1939, she organized (with the blessing of Gröber) the Office for Religious War Relief (*Kirchliche Kriegshilfsstelle*) within the Caritas Association. Her office in effect became an instrument for helping racially persecuted "non-Aryans," both Christian and Jewish. Using monies she received from Archbishop Gröber, she smuggled Jews over the Swiss border and passed information to Jews outside of Germany. On 5 November 1943, as she was about to transfer monies to the last remaining Jews in Berlin, she was arrested by the Gestapo and incarcerated in Ravensbrück until 3 May 1945. See Hans-Josef Wollasch, *Betrifft, Nachrichtenzentrale des Erzbischofs Gröber in Freiburg: Die Ermittlungen der Geheim Staatspolizei gegen Gertrud Luckner, 1942–1944* (Konstanz: UVK, 1999). After the war, she and her associates Franz Böhm, Hans Lukaschek, and Karl Thieme established a center for Catholic-Jewish reconciliation in Freiburg and founded the journal-newsletter *Freiburger Rundbrief*. Luckner also spearheaded relief efforts for Holocaust survivors.

See Phayer, *Catholic Church and the Holocaust*, 184. On Hans Lukaschek, former *Oberpräsident* (1929–1933) for Upper Silesia and Federal Minister for Expellees in Adenauer's first cabinet, see Frank Buscher, "The Great Fear: The Catholic Church and the Anticipated Radicalization of Expellees and Refugees in Postwar Germany," *German History: The Journal of the German History Society* 21, 2 (2003): 212.

13. Letter translated by Muench from Archbishop Conrad Gröber, Freiburg, to Archbishop Samuel Stritch, Chicago, 30 November 1946. HM 37/114/1, ACUA. Gröber first sent the letter to Muench, with instructions to forward it to Stritch. See letter from Gröber to Muench, 30 November 1946. HM 37/140/3, ACUA.

14. Phayer, *Catholic Church and the Holocaust*, 189–90.

15. Ibid.

16. Handwritten note from Muench, Kronberg, to Stritch, Chicago, 18 December 1946, CC/M, Archdiocesan Archives Chicago.

17. Letter from Archbishop John T. McNicholas, Cincinnati, to Muench, Kronberg, 31 December 1946. HM 37/114/1, ACUA.

18. Letter from Muench, Kronberg, to Bishop John Mark Gannon, Erie, Pennsylvania, 25 January 1947. HM 37/114/1, ACUA.

19. Luckner initiated (in 1948) and edited (until 1973) the newsletter *Freiburger Rundbrief*, which had both Christian and Jewish contributors. It was dedicated to the theme of correcting Christian misconceptions about Judaism and bringing about better understanding between Christians and Jews. See Michael Phayer, "The German Catholic Church after the Holocaust," *Holocaust and Genocide Studies* 10, 2 (Fall 1996): 151–65.

20. Letter from Muench, Kronberg, to Frau Dr. Gertrud Luckner, Freiburg im Breisgau (hereafter Freiburg), 15 May 1949. HM 37/102/4, ACUA.

21. "Wir möchten auch diesmal biten, dass Sie . . . das 2. Exemplar an Ihr Seelsorgeamt weiterleiten," she wrote. Letter from Luckner, Freiburg, to Muench, Kronberg, June 1949. HM 37/102/4.

22. "Wir haben nämlich auch auf diesem grossen Gebiete nur 75.000 Katholiken. Deswegen haben wir auch kein besonderes Seelsorgsamt und kann darum nicht Ihrem Wunsche entsprechen ein Exemplar Ihres Rundbriefes an unser Seelsorgsamt weiterzuleiten," Muench wrote. Letter of reply from Muench to Luckner, 19 September 1949. HM 37/102/4, ACUA.

23. Letter from Secretary Robert Deubel, Bad Godesberg, to Luckner, Freiburg, 24 January 1952. HM 37/102/7, ACUA.

24. Letter from Secretary Robert Deubel, Kronberg, to Luckner, Freiburg, 10 May 1950. HM 37/102/5, ACUA.

25. Phayer, *Catholic Church and the Holocaust*, 192.

26. Letter to Luckner, c/o Dr. Karl Borgmann, from Muench, Rome, 18 July 1960. HM 37/19/12, ACUA.

27. "Kardinal Joseph Frings, Erzbischof von Köln: Hirtenbrief über seine Romfahrt nach seiner Ernennung zum Kardinal, 11 March 1946," in Löhr, *Dokumente deutscher Bischöfe*, 93.

28. Muench diary entry dated 10 November 1946, vol. 5, p. 12.

29. Frings may have been referring to the activities of the SS Race and Settlement Main Office (*Rasse-und Siedlungshauptamt*) or to those of the Ethnic German Central Office (*Volksdeutsche Mittelstelle*, or Vomi), under the direction of Catholic SS-Gruppenführer Werner Lorenz.

30. Report entitled "The Catholic Bishops and Dr. [Eugen] Kogon," from Richard G. Akselrad to ICD-Hesse, 23 August 1947. In folder entitled "Anti-Nazi Church Activity," box 169. RA, ECR, RG 260-OMGUS, NARA. Michael Phayer also discusses the Akselrad interview in "German Catholic Church After the Holocaust," *Holocaust and Genocide Studies*, 155–56.

31. For the controversy in West Germany over Globke's appointment in Adenauer's cabinet, see Herf, *Divided Memory*, 289–92.

32. Muench diary entry dated 15 May 1956, vol. 21, p. 133.

33. Muench diary entry dated 8 May 1956, vol. 21, p. 126.

34. Letter from Dr. Hans Globke, Bonn, to Muench, Rome, 9 March 1960. HM 37/19/3, ACUA.

35. "Wilhelm Berning, Bischof von Osnabrück: Fastenhirtenbrief über Familie, Volk und Kirche, 23 January 1947," in Löhr, *Dokumente deutscher Bischöfe*, 168.

36. Letter from Bishop Michael Buchberger, Regensburg, to Muench, Kronberg, 10 February 1947. HM 37/142/6, ACUA.

37. Letter from Buchberger to Muench, 4 June 1948. HM 37/142/6, ACUA. Letter from Muench, to Buchberger, Regensburg, 9 July 1948. HM 37/142/6.

38. See Eugen Kogon, *Der SS Staat: Das System der deutschen Konzentrationslager* (Munich: Karl Alber Verlag, 1946); and Kogon, *The Theory and Practice of Hell: The German Concentration Camps and the System Behind Them*, translated from the German by Heinz Norden (London: Secker and Warburg, 1950), based on 1949 German edition.

39. "Kirchliche Kundgebungen von politischer Bedeutung," *Frankfurter Hefte* 7 (July 1947): 633–38.

40. Report entitled "The Catholic Bishops and Dr. [Eugen] Kogon," 6.

41. "Lorenz Jäger, Erzbischof von Paderborn: Fastenhirtenbrief über die Rettung des menschlichen Gemeinschaftslebens," 26 January 1947, in Löhr, *Dokumente deutscher Bischöfe*, 183. For the best recent study of Jäger, see Wolfgang Stücken, *Hirten unter Hitler: Die Rolle der Paderborner Erzbischöfe Caspar Klein und Lorenz Jäger in der NS-Zeit* (Essen: Klartext-Verlag, 1999). Stücken examines the moral stewardship of Klein (1865–1941; archbishop of Paderborn 1920–41) and Jäger (1892–1975; archbishop of Paderborn 1941–73) during the Nazi era. Both placed church political strategy and, as threats to the Church increased, the continued existence of the Church and Church life within the Nazi state above the fate of Jewish Germans or other victims. Commenting on the Fulda pastoral of 1943, which explicitly condemned the killing of "innocent persons of foreign races and ancestry," Jäger insisted that the Church's proper concern should be limited

to "our German brothers and sisters, who are of one blood with us" (165). Then and thereafter, Jäger preached support for the German war as an epic defense of Christian civilization against bolshevism.

42. Report entitled "Catholic Bishops and Dr. [Eugen] Kogon," 5.

43. Richard L. Merrit, *Democracy Imposed: U.S. Occupation Policy and the German Public, 1945–1949* (New Haven, Conn.: Yale University Press, 1995), 140–45.

44. Letter from Dr. Otto Hipp, Munich, to Cardinal Michael Faulhaber, Munich, 28 June 1948. HM 37/92/6, ACUA. Johannes Dietl of Munich sent a copy of Hipp's letter to Muench. Otto Hipp was the pre-1933 lord mayor (*Oberbürgermeister*) of Regensburg, former chairperson of the Bavarian assembly of cities (*Städtetag*), and a member of the *Bayerische Volkspartei* (BVP). On 3 May 1945, he was appointed deputy mayor of Munich. He was sixty years old at the time and a native of Munich. Six weeks later, he accepted the post of Bavarian minister for culture and education. See Boehling, *Question of Priorities*, 111–12.

45. See Michael H. Kater, *The Nazi Party: A Social Profile of Members and Leaders, 1919–1945* (Cambridge, Mass.: Harvard University Press, 1983).

46. Letter from August Hardick, Kirchen, to Muench, Kronberg, 23 January 1947. HM 37/127/9, ACUA.

47. Merrit, *Democracy Imposed*, 140–45.

48. Muench diary entry dated 10 December 1947, vol. 7, pp. 18–19.

49. Ibid.

50. In Catholic farm areas, the Nazi party rarely gained so much as 10 percent of the vote, due to the fact that in Catholic regions the NSDAP faced opposition from the Church, Catholic parties (the Center Party, or, in Bavaria, the Bavarian People's Party), and local Catholic notables and press. See Richard F. Hamilton, "The Rise of Nazism: A Case Study and Review of Interpretations— Kiel, 1928–1933," *German Studies Review* 26, 1 (February 2003): 43. See also Martin Broszat et al, *Bayern in der NS-Zeit*, 6 vols. (Munich: Oldenbourg, 1977–83).

51. See Oded Heilbronner, *Catholicism, Political Culture, and the Countryside: A Social History of the Nazi Party in South Germany* (Ann Arbor: University of Michigan Press, 1998).

52. Mann relied upon *Justiz und NS-Verbrechen: Sammlung deutscher Stafurteilte wegen national-sozialistischer Tötungsverbrechen 1945–1966*, ed. Fritz Bauer (Amsterdam: University Press, 1968–81), 22 vols., among other sources. For his discussion of religion as a factor in likelihood to become a perpetrator, see Michael Mann, "Were the Perpetrators of Genocide 'Ordinary Men' or 'Real Nazis'? Results from Fifteen Hundred Biographies," *Holocaust and Genocide Studies* 14, 3 (Winter 2000): 347–49.

53. In 1940, the total SS staff members in Auschwitz did not exceed 500. On 15 January 1945, one day before the camp's evacuation, the number of SS personnel reached its peak of 4,481 SS men and 71 SS women supervisors. Throughout the camp's entire history, a total of 6,800 SS men and about 200 SS women supervisors (total population under study) served in the camp. See

Aleksander Lasik, "Historical-sociological Profile of the Auschwitz SS," in *Anatomy of the Auschwitz Death Camp,* ed. Israel Gutman and Michael Berenbaum (Bloomington: Indiana University Press in association with the United States Holocaust Memorial Museum, 1994), 274, 279–80.

54. Letter from Franz Burger, Munich, to Muench, Kronberg, November 1946. HM 37/125/9, ACUA.

55. See Robert Gellately, *Backing Hitler: Consent and Coercion in Nazi Germany* (Oxford: Oxford University Press, 2001). Gellately debunks the myth of acquiescence due solely to the regime's terror methods.

56. Letter from unnamed curate in Wies, to Muench, Kronberg, 18 December 1950. HM 37/81/8, ACUA.

57. Letter from Georg Kretschner, Baden-Baden, to Muench, Bad Godesberg, 11 June 1951. HM 37/21/7, ACUA.

58. Letter from Hipp to Faulhaber, 28 June 1948.

59. Letter from Wilhelm Zimmermann, Karlsruhe, to Pope Pius XII, Rome, 18 October 1955. HM 37/84/11. The letter was sent to the Bad Godesberg nunciature by Father Wilhelm Ritter of Orsingen, and Muench was to forward it to the Vatican.

60. Letter from Felise Book, Borken, to Muench, Kronberg, 25 September 1947. HM 37/83/1, ACUA.

61. Letter from Heinz Krämer, Rüsselheim, to Lucius Clay, Berlin, 1 September 1947. In folder 1 (document 65), box 116 (AG 000.1 through AG 000.3: Religion, January–June 1947), Office of the Adjutant General: General Correspondence and Other Records (Decimal File) 1945–1949, Records of the Executive Office (hereafter REO), RG 260-OMGUS, NARA.

62. Letter from Josefa Reiter, Bad Tolz, to Muench, Kronberg, 9 February 1947. HM 37/69/6, ACUA.

63. Otto Karl Kiep (1886–1944) was a high-ranking German diplomat who withdrew from active service in 1933 due to ideological differences with Nazism. In 1939, he joined the Foreign Division of the *Wehrmacht* High Command. He was arrested and executed by the Gestapo in July 1944 for his contacts with opposition circles in the *Abwehr* (Wehrmacht Intelligence). Eugenie Kiep (born von Rath) was related to Ernst von Rath (1909–38), famous for his death at the hands of Herschel Grynspan on 7 November 1938. Grynspan mistook von Rath, legation secretary for the German embassy in Paris, for the ambassador.

64. Muench diary entry dated 20–21 March 1957, vol. 21, p. 263.

65. Letter from Dr. Leisler Kiep, Kronberg, to Muench, Bad Godesberg, 16 February 1954. HM 37/22/3, ACUA.

66. Letter from Kiep, Kronberg, to Muench, Bad Godesberg, 17 December 1953. HM 37/15/8, ACUA.

67. Muench diary entry dated 6 August 1946, vol. 4, p. 39.

68. Letter from Maria Unseld (sister to August Unseld), New York, to Muench, Kronberg, 26 September 1947. HM 37/14/7, ACUA.

69. Muench diary entry dated 6 August 1946, vol. 4, p. 39.

70. Other selected sources on this debate include: Vera Bücker, *Die Schulddiskussion im deutschen Katholismus nach 1945* (Bochum: Studienverlag Brockmeyer, 1989); Konrad Repgen, "Die Erfahrung des Dritten Reiches und das Selbstverständniss der deutschen Katholiken nach 1945," in *Die Zeit nach 1945 als Thema kirchlicher Zeitgeschichte*, ed. Victor Conzemius, M. Gneschat, and H. Kocher (Göttingen: Vandenhoeck und Ruprecht, 1988), 127–80; and Karl Dietrich Bracher, "Problems of the German Resistance," in *The Challenge of the Third Reich*, ed. Hedley Bull (Oxford: Clarendon, 1986), 57–76.

4. Granting Absolution: Muench and the Catholic Clemency Campaign

1. In his diary, Muench recorded a conversation with a German monsignor in the Vatican secretariat of state. The monsignor described Montini as "sympathetic to Germans." Muench diary entry dated 4 September 1952, vol. 16, p. 18.

2. Muench diary entry dated 6–7 December 1948, vol. 9, pp. 60–61. Beyond their imprisonment in Landsberg and Spandau, Muench did not specify further as to which convicted German war criminals were under discussion specifically.

3. "HQ European Command Staff Message Control Incoming Message, UEP Secret, E UCOM 43/160 Operational Priority TOO 161605Z TOR 161743Z, Secretary of the Army from Draper to OMGUS, 16 December 1948," in folder entitled "General Clemency File—1951—Volume II," box 4, RRPTA, WC, JAD, USAREUR, RG 338, NARA. The memorandum was transmitted from Cicognani to Draper via Father Edmund Walsh, S.J.

4. Letter from Muench, Kronberg, to General Thomas Handy, Heidelburg, 27 February 1950, in folder entitled "General Clemency File, January 1950 to April 1951," box 3, Clemency Files for 1947–1950, RRPTA, WC, JAD, USAREUR, RG 338, NARA.

5. See Jan Erik Schulte, *Zwangsarbeit und Vernichtung: das Wirtschaftsimperium der SS: Oswald Pohl und das SS-Wirtschafts-Verwaltungshauptamt, 1933–1945* (Paderborn: F. Schöningh, 2001).

6. The best recent work on the Wirtschafts- und Verwaltungshauptamt includes Michael Thad Allen, *The Business of Genocide: The SS, Slave Labor, and the Concentration Camps* (Chapel Hill: University of North Carolina Press, 2002); and Walter Naasner, *SS-Wirtschaft und SS-Verwaltung: Das SS-Wirtschafts-Verwaltungshauptamt und die unter seiner Dienstaufsicht stehenden wirtschaftlichen Unternehmungen und weitere Dokumente* (Düsseldorf: Droste Verlag, 1998).

7. Document entitled "Summary of Clemency Requests," in folder entitled "General Clemency File, volume one, folder one, 1951," box 3, RRPTA, WC, JAD, USAREUR, RG 338, NARA.

8. See Records of the United States Nürnberg war crimes trials: United States of America *v.* Oswald Pohl et al. (case IV), 13 January 1947–11 August

1948; National Archives microfilm publications M 890, National Archives Collection of World War II Crimes Records, RG 238, NARA.

9. The "general clemency files," part of Record Group 338 (United States Army-Europe, USREAUR) at the National Archives in College Park, Maryland, contain thousands of letters to American authorities from Germans of all stripes, all begging for or demanding clemency. I thank Dr. Katharina von Kellenbach for directing me to these records.

10. Phayer, *Catholic Church and the Holocaust*, 138–39. Phayer found no published version of *Rechtsbewusstsein und Rechtsunsicherheit* but did find a manuscript copy marked "Rome, March 1946" in the city library of Munich (256). Rumors about poor conditions in Landsberg prison were as popular as they were untrue. See *Landsberg: Ein dokumentarischer Bericht* (Munich: Information Services Division, Office of the U.S. High Commissioner for Germany, 1951), translated from the February 1951 Information Bulletin of the U.S. High Commissioner for Germany.

11. In the German Protestant churches, the vanguard of the clemency movement included Theophil Wurm (Stuttgart), Otto Dibelius (Berlin), Hanns Lilje (Hannover), and Hans Meiser (Munich).

12. For the Protestant clemency campaign, see Ronald Webster, "Opposing 'Victors' Justice': German Protestant Churchmen and Convicted War Criminals in Western Europe after 1945," *Holocaust and Genocide Studies* 15, 1 (Spring 2001): 47–69.

13. Henry Friedlander, *The Origins of Nazi Genocide: From Euthanasia to the Final Solution* (Chapel Hill: University of North Carolina Press, 1995), 39–40.

14. Ibid.

15. See Records of the United States Nürnberg war crimes trials: United States of America v. Karl Brandt et al. (case I), 21 November 1946–20 August 1947; National Archives microfilm publications M 8887, National Archives Collection of World War II Crimes Records, RG 238, NARA. See also Ulrich-Dieter Oppitz, *Medizinverbrechen vor Gericht: das Urteil im Nürnberger Ärzteprozess gegen Karl Brandt und andere sowie aus dem Prozess gegen Generalfeldmarschall Milch* (Erlangen: Palm & Enke, 1999).

16. Servatius served as Adolf Eichmann's defense attorney in 1961.

17. Letter from Sister M. Peregrina Recknagel, Berlin, to Dr. Robert Servatius, Nuremberg, 3 January 1947. HM 37/128/3, ACUA. A copy of this and additional letters supporting Brandt as well as a number of other convicted war criminals can be found in the Muench papers. We can assume that copies came to be in Muench's possession due to his open involvement and publicly perceived interest in the clemency campaign.

18. Letter from Sister M. Castella Blöckl, Munich, to Servatius, 12 December 1946. HM 37/128/3, ACUA.

19. Letter from Sister M. Sebalda, Berchtesgaden, to Servatius, 13 December 1946. HM 37/128/3, ACUA.

20. Letter from Dr. Robert Servatius, Nuremberg, to Muench, Kronberg, 15 September 1947. HM 37/128/3, ACUA.

21. On 16 July 1945, General Dwight D. Eisenhower instructed the commanders of the 3rd and 7th U.S. Armies to establish military courts for the purpose of trying cases "involving offenses against the laws and usages of war or the laws of the occupied territory or any part thereof commonly known as war crimes, together with such other related cases within the jurisdiction of Military Government courts as may from time to time be determined by the Theater Judge Advocate, committed prior to 9 May 1945" in their respective Military Districts (Bavaria, Hesse, Württemberg-Baden, and Bremen). See Frank M. Buscher, "To Punish and Reeducate: U.S. War Crimes Policy in Germany After the Second World War," manuscript-in-progress, 21. Do not cite without permission of Frank Buscher.

22. Ordinance No. 2 (September 1944) described three types of courts: General Military Courts, with authority to impose all sentences including the death penalty; Intermediate Military Courts, able to impose all sentences except death or imprisonment of more than 10 years or fines of more than $10,000; and Summary Courts, able to impose all sentences except death or imprisonment of more than 1 year or fines of more than $1,000. All three had jurisdiction over "all offenses against the laws and usages of war." Each Military District had "one or more" General Military Court, each *Regierungsbezirk* and some large cities and subdivisions within the District had "one or more" Intermediary Military Court. See Buscher, "To Punish and Reeducate," 21, citing Holger Lessing, *Der Erste Dachauer Prozess, 1945–1946* (Baden-Baden: Nomos, 1993), appendices 4 and 8. The first Army trial took place during the summer of 1945. The U.S. Army trials officially ended on 31 December 1947, with a total of 489 cases. See "Brief on War Crimes Affairs," 27 August 1952, in General Administration files, box 12, RG 338, NARA. I thank Elizabeth Yavnai for bringing this document to my attention.

23. The Dachau trials are the subject of a dissertation-in-progress entitled "Military Justice: The U.S. Army's Investigation and Prosecution of Nazi War Criminals in Germany, 1944–1948" by Elizabeth Yavnai, Ph.D. candidate at the London School of Economics. I thank Ms. Yavnai for her clarifications on this section of my manuscript.

24. Buscher, "To Punish and Reeducate," 21.

25. The accepted general work on the SS is Helmut Krausnick, Hans Buchheim, Martin Broszat, and Hans-Adolf Jacobsen, *Anatomy of the SS State*, translated from the German by Elizabeth Wiskemann (New York: Walker and Company, 1968). It appeared under the title *Anatomie des SS-Staates* in 1965.

26. Buscher, "To Punish and Reeducate," citing Norman E. Tutorow, *War Crimes, War Criminals, and War Crimes Trials—An Annotated Bibliography and Source Book* (New York: Greenwood Press, 1986), 477.

27. For a thorough treatment of the review process in the Army trials, see Buscher, "To Punish and Reeducate," 27–30.

28. Yavnai, "Military Justice," and Weingartner, *Peculiar Crusade*, 163.

29. See "Brief on War Crimes Affairs," 27 August 1952, pp. 9–14, General Administration files, box 12, RG 338, NARA. I thank Elizabeth Yavnai for

bringing this document to my attention. See also Buscher, "To Punish and Re-educate," 32–33.

30. Buscher, *The U.S. War Crimes Trial Program in Germany, 1946–1955* (New York: Greenwood Press, 1989), 38.

31. Buscher, "To Punish and Reeducate," 14.

32. Ibid. For these statistics, Buscher cites Thomas Alan Schwartz, *America's Germany: John J. McCloy and the Federal Republic of Germany* (Cambridge, Mass.: Harvard University Press, 1991), 162–64.

33. Ibid. Buscher quotes Thomas Alan Schwartz, "Die Begnadigung Deutscher Kriegsverbrecher. John J. McCloy und die Häftlinge von Landsberg," *Vierteljahrshefte für Zeitgeschichte* 38, 3 (1990): 375–414.

34. Schwartz, "John J. McCloy and the Landsberg Cases," 433–43.

35. Buscher, "To Punish and Reeducate," 38.

36. Schwartz, "John J. McCloy and the Landsberg Cases," 439, 453.

37. Buscher, "To Punish and Reeducate," 43.

38. Schwartz, "John J. McCloy and the Landsberg Cases," 453.

39. Muench diary entry dated 17 August 1952, vol. 16, pp. 1–2.

40. Muench diary entry dated 20 November 1950, vol. 13, pp. 49–50. Both McCloy and Muench seemed to have troubled consciences on the matter. McCloy happened to have dinner with Muench on the eve of his controversial January 1951 amnesty of Landsberg inmates convicted in one of the twelve Nuremberg successor trials. McCloy, General Thomas Handy (who made equivalent decisions in the Dachau trials cases), and other "brass" attended the investiture of one Father Kelly, which took place in Saint Anne's Chapel of Heidelburg. ("Investiture" means the ceremony by which a priest receives the honorary title of "monsignor," attached to the newly achieved rank of "domestic prelate"). McCloy purportedly said to Handy, "I want to appear before Saint Peter [in heaven] with a clean conscience." McCloy wished for "no executions except in cases where evidence was beyond dispute." Muench defended McCloy and Handy on their decision to give amnesty only to some Landsberg criminals. Upon hearing that young Benedictine monks in Beuron denounced the two Americans on this count, Muench described himself as an "especially vehement" listener. He told one monk to "get the facts before passing judgement" on McCloy and Handy. See diary entry dated 1 April 1951, vol. 13, p. 91.

41. Hans Eisele, "Memorandum: Audiatur et Altera Pars," September 1947, Landsberg-am-Lech, 56. Folder not marked; box 454; War Crimes Case Files #000-50-9, War Crimes Branch, USAREUR RG 338, NARA. I would like to thank Dr. David Hackett for bringing Eisele's NARA file to my attention.

42. French L. MacLean, *The Camp Men: The SS Officers Who Ran the Nazi Concentration Camp System* (Atglen, Pa.: Schiffer, 1999), 68.

43. Letter from Hans Eisele to "War Crimes Group, revisions section," September 1947. HM 37/131/11, ACUA. Muench received copies of all Eisele clemency correspondence from Auxiliary Bishop Johannes Neuhäusler.

44. *The Buchenwald Report*, translated by David A. Hackett (Boulder: Westview Press, 1995), 63–64. The report is a translation of the complete text of

the original report *Bericht über das Konzentrationslager Buchenwald bei Weimar* prepared in April–May 1945 by the Intelligence Team of the Psychological Warfare Division, Supreme Headquarters, Allied Expeditionary Force (SHAEF), which included 168 eyewitness accounts by former Buchenwald prisoners.

45. Ibid.

46. This list is available in box 453; War Crimes Case Files #000-50-9, War Crimes Branch, RG 338-USAREUR, NARA; and HM 37/131/11, ACUA.

47. Letter from Elisabeth Bronberger, Munich, to Aloisius Muench, National Catholic Welfare Conference War Relief Services, Washington, D.C., 29 November 1947. HM 37/20/10. She used the official letterhead of Gebrüder Bronberger Spedition und Lagerhäuser Spezialfirma für Maschinentransporte (Brothers Bronberger Shipping and Warehouses Firm for Machinery Transportation) of Munich.

48. Letter from Elisabeth Bronberger, Munich, to Colonel Dwinell, Frankfurt, 25 November 1947. She used private stationary. In folder "Eisele, Hans," box 454, War Crimes Case Files #000-50-9, War Crimes Branch, USAREUR, RG 338, NARA.

49. Phayer, *Catholic Church and the Holocaust,* 141–42.

50. Ernst Klee, *Persilscheine und falsche Pässe,* 78–80, cited in Earl, "Accidental Justice," 470–71.

51. For a complete list of Aschenauer's clients, see letter from Dr. Rudolf Aschenauer, Nuremberg, to General Thomas Handy, Heidelberg, 27 March 1950. In folder entitled "Clemency Files 1949–1950," box 2, Clemency Files 1947–1950 (hereafter CF), Records Related to Post-Trial Activities 1945–1957 (hereafter RRPTA), War Crimes Branch (hereafter WC), Division of the Judge Advocate (hereafter JAD), USAREUR, RG 338, NARA.

52. Letter from Neuhäusler, Munich, to the United States Congress, Washington, 23 March 1948. In folder entitled "Neuhäusler," box 11, RRPTA, WC, JAD, USAREUR, RG 338-Army Files, NARA.

53. Neuhäusler sent Muench a full copy of his 1948 petition to American military government officials. See HM 37/133/8, ACUA.

54. Letter from Muench, Kronberg, to Neuhäusler, Munich, 18 November 1948. HM 37/133/4, ACUA. Michael Phayer makes note of this exchange between Muench and Neuhäusler, interpreting it as a "warning" meant to restrain Neuhäusler. See "Pope Pius XII, the Holocaust, and the Cold War," *Holocaust and Genocide Studies* 12, 2 (fall 1998): 244, and *Catholic Church and the Holocaust,* 143.

55. Letter from Muench, Kronberg, to Neuhäusler, Munich, 23 April 1949. HM 37/141/6, ACUA.

56. Letter from Muench, Kronberg, to Father James Nellen, Milwaukee, 18 February 1948. HM 37/13/5, ACUA.

57. Letter from Aloisius Muench, Bad Godesberg, to Terry Muench, Milwaukee, 15 May 1954. HM 37/32/9.

58. *Trials of War Criminals Before the Nürnberg Military Tribunals under Control Council Law No. 10,* vol. 11, Nürnberg, October 1946–April 1949 (Buffalo: William S. Hein, 1997), 764.

59. Ibid., 776–77.

60. On 9 June 1941, Hitler issued directive No. 31, by which he appointed Field Marshal List armed forces commander (*Wehrmachtbefehlshaber*) southeast. The order directed List to report directly to Hitler through the Wehrmacht High Command (*Oberkommando der Wehrmacht*). See Geoffrey P. Megargee, *Inside Hitler's High Command* (Lawrence: University of Kansas Press, 2000), 96.

61. *Trial of War Criminals*, 766.

62. Ibid., 804.

63. Letter from Cardinal Josef Frings, Cologne, to Muench, Kronberg, 18 September 1947. HM 37/133/2, ACUA.

64. *Trials of War Criminals*, 802.

65. Hitler had been pressing List, Army group commander of Army Group A, to push a spearhead through a particularly mountainous area, and List responded that his forces would be made too vulnerable by such a move. On 9 September 1942, Hitler had the head of the Wehrmacht High Command Wilhelm Keitel contact commander of the Army General Staff Franz Halder to say that List should resign his post. List did so the next day. See Megargee, *Inside Hitler's High Command,* 180.

66. Letter from Frings, Cologne, to General Thomas T. Handy, 27 April 1950, in folder entitled "Frings," box 10. RRPTA, WC, JAD, USAREUR, RG 338, NARA.

67. "Josef Kardinal Frings, Cologne, to the Judge Advocate," 27 May 1951, unmarked folder, box 4. GCF, RRPTA, WC, JAD, USAREUR, RG 338, NARA.

68. Letter from Commissar (Bishop) Heinrich Wienken to General Lucius Clay, Berlin, 19 September 1947. HM 37/133/5, ACUA.

69. Ibid.

70. Letter from Thea Brack, Reichenbach am Heuberg, to Muench, Kronberg, 24 September 1947. HM 37/128/3, ACUA. A copy of Muench's reply is not available.

71. Letter from Thea Brack to Bishop Heinrich Wienken, Berlin, 29 December 1947. HM 37/133/5, ACUA.

72. German industrialist Gustav Krupp von Bohlen und Halbach (1870–1950) married Bertha Krupp, sole heiress of Friedrich Krupp, Inc., and became its chairman in 1909. Krupp served as a trustee of the Adolf Hitler Donation of German businessmen and put the company in the service of German rearmament. In 1943, he handed over direction of the company to his son, Alfried Krupp. In subsequent postwar trials, Gustav Krupp was deemed unable to stand trial, and his son Alfried stood accused in his stead. See Lothar Gall and Burkhard Beyer, *Krupp im 20. Jahrhundert: die Geschichte des Unternehmens vom Ersten Weltkrieg bus zur Gründung der Stiftung* (Berlin: Siedler, 2002).

73. See Records of the United States Nürnberg war crimes trials: United States of America *v.* Alfried Krupp et al. (case XI), 16 August 1947–31 July 1948; National Archives microfilm publications M 896, National Archives Collection of World War II Crimes Records, RG 238, NARA.

74. Letter from Muench to Robert Murphy, 22 November 1948, in folder 20 entitled "M," box 8 (1948), CGCPA, USPAG-B, RG 84-State Department, NARA.

75. See letter from Murphy to Muench, 26 November 1948, in folder 20 entitled "M," box 8 (1948), CGCPA, USPAG-B, RG 84-State Department, NARA.

76. See S. Jonathan Wiesen, *West German Industry and the Challenge of the Nazi Past, 1945–1955* (Chapel Hill: University of North Carolina Press, 2001).

77. See Hilary Camille Earl, "Accidental Justice: The Trial of Otto Ohlendorf and the Einsatzgruppen Leaders in the American Zone of Occupation, Germany, 1945–1958" (Ph.D. dissertation, University of Toronto, 2002); and Records of the United States Nürnberg war crimes trials: United States of America *v.* Otto Ohlendorf et al. (case IX), 15 September 1947–10 April 1948; National Archives microfilm publications M 895, National Archives Collection of World War II Crimes Records, RG 238, NARA.

78. Translation of "In the Red Jackets," *Münchner Merkur* no. 324, 28 December 1950, in folder entitled "General Clemency File, January 1950 to April 1951," box 3, Clemency Files 1947–1950, RRPTA, WC, JAD, USAREUR, RG 338, NARA.

79. Letter from Helene Elisabeth Princess von Isenburg, Munich, to Muench, Kronberg, 7 December 1950. HM 37/133/2, ACUA.

80. Letter from Dr. Rudolf Aschenauer, Munich, to Muench, Kronberg, 23 December 1950. HM 37/133/3, ACUA.

81. Sladek referred to Rudolf Aschenauer's essay entitled "Otto Ohlendorf: Ein Versuch, Gegebenheiten wahrheitsgemäss darzustellen," attached to the letter from Father Paulus Sladek, Munich, to Muench, Kronberg, 10 January 1951. HM 37/133/2, ACUA.

82. Letter from Sladek to Muench, 10 January 1951.

83. Letter from Sladek to Muench, 19 January 1951. HM 37/133/3, ACUA.

84. Letter from Robert Deubel, Kronberg, to Sladek, Munich, 23 January 1951. HM 37/133/3, ACUA.

85. Muench diary entry dated 9 August 1952, vol. 15, p. 94. In 1953, their previous conversations about Ohlendorf apparently forgotten, Muench sent Pope Pius XII a glowing report on the activities of the *Ackermann Gemeinde*. Father Sladek later thanked Muench for the "letter of praise and commendation [Sladek] received from the Holy Father" for his work with Sudeten expellees. See diary entry dated 21 February 1953, vol. 17, pp. 11–12.

86. The *Kirchliche Hilfsstelle,* with offices in Munich and Frankfurt, was an agency working "primarily but not exclusively with expellees from southeastern Europe" (Hungary, Romania, Yugoslavia), directed by Monsignor Alfred Büttner. In 1950, acting on the recommendation of the Fulda Bishops' Conference, the Catholic Refugee Council (*Katholischen Flüchtlingsrates*) established the *Arbeitsgemeinschaft Kirche und Heimat*, intended as "a replacement for the *Kirchliche Hilfsstelle.*" Prelate Franz Hartz, member of the Catholic

Refugee Council and the Holy See's appointee in charge of pastoral care for refugees and expellees (1949–53), was appointed the new organization's president. See Buscher, "Great Fear," 209, 216–17.

87. *Der Volksbote* had financial support from the episcopate and also from *Caritas*. See Buscher, "Great Fear," 217.

88. Letter from Aloisius Muench, Kronberg, to Giovanni Battista Montini, Rome, 24 February 1951. HM 37/133/2, ACUA. I thank Jane Klinger, Chief Conservator, Conservation Services, Collections Division, United States Holocaust Memorial Museum, for translating this letter from Italian to English. On this particular letter, see also Phayer, *Catholic Church and the Holocaust,* 162–63.

89. Ibid.

90. Letter from Aloisius Muench, Bad Godesberg, to his sister Terry Muench, Milwaukee, 21 August 1952. HM 37/32/7, ACUA.

5. The Longest Hatred

1. Letter from Muench, Bad Godesberg, to Monsignor Paul Tanner, Washington, 17 March 1950. HM 37/114/6, ACUA.

2. Muench diary entry dated 7 May 1951, vol. 13, p. 120.

3. Muench diary entry dated 12 January 1948, vol. 7, p. 46.

4. Muench diary entry dated 9 August 1946, vol. 4, p. 42.

5. Germans, especially in Munich, also frequently perceived Special Branch officers, who were in charge of denazification on the local level, as "Jewish avengers." A number of regular military government detachment officers propagated such views as well. See Boehling, *Question of Priorities,* 20–25.

6. Ibid., 45.

7. Muench diary entry dated 12 September 1946, vol. 4, p. 71.

8. The conflict concerned rights to a particular building in the internment camp, which Neuhäusler wished to designate as a chapel for Christian internees.

9. Muench diary entry dated 21 May 1949, vol. 10, p. 4.

10. Earl F. Ziemke, *The U.S. Army in the Occupation of Germany, 1944–46,* Army Historical series (Washington, D.C.: U.S. Army Center of Military History, 1990), 86, 102–6.

11. Kempner was a Jewish German born in Freiburg-im-Breisgau. From 1928 to 1933, Kempner, a jurist, lectured at the Berlin College for Politics and acted as legal advisor to the Prussian Interior Ministry. In 1933, the Gestapo arrested Kempner for his efforts to prosecute the NSDAP on charges of conspiracy for high treason. Kempner emigrated through Italy and France to the United States, where he became a U.S. government attorney. In 1945, he was assigned to staff of American Chief Prosecutor Robert H. Jackson. See the Robert M.W. Kempner Papers, 1935–1993, Archives, United States Holocaust Memorial Museum, Washington, D.C.

12. Muench diary entry dated 2 March 1953, vol. 17, pp. 16–17.

13. *Der Monat* was the Berlin-based monthly periodical co-founded in 1948 by New York native Melvin J. Lasky and funded by the Ford Foundation. Its contributors included Hannah Arendt, George Orwell, Ernest Hemingway, Aldous Huxley, Thomas Mann, and other contemporary luminaries. The first issue appeared in October 1948, and the last in March 1971. See Marko Martin, *"Eine Zeitschrift gegen das Vergessen." Bundesrepublikanische Traditionen und Umbrüche im Spiegel der Kulturzeitschrift "Der Monat"* (New York: P. Lang, 2003) and Martin, *Orwell, Koestler und all die anderen: Melvin J. Lasky und "Der Monat"* (Asendorf: Mut-Verlag, 1999).

14. See letter from Kempner, Landsdowne, Pennsylvania, to Muench, Kronberg, 6 December 1949. HM 37/15/1, ACUA.

15. Letter from Muench, Kronberg, to Father (Major) Thomas Corcoran, Chaplain Division, Heidelburg, 20 June 1949. HM 37/136/4, ACUA.

16. We do not know if "Urman, Schlechter, Fleischer, and Langerfeld" were Jews, leftists, communists, socialists, vengeful, or all five. See Muench Diary entry dated 11 July 1949, vol. 10, p. 38.

17. Letter from Muench, Kronberg, to Howard Smith, 4 February 1947. HM 37/55/3, ACUA.

18. See article entitled "Gefängnis im Tarnnetzprozess," *Die Welt* (8 January 1957). HM 37/23/6, ACUA.

19. Muench diary entry dated 7 April 1953, vol. 17, pp. 37–38.

20. Letter from Muench, Bad Godesberg, to Dr. Osco N. Cole, Memphis, Tennessee, 13 February 1953. HM 37/15/6, ACUA.

21. Muench diary entry dated 4 December 1956, vol. 21, p. 225.

22. Letter from Muench to Rev. Dr. Peter Leo Johnson, Milwaukee, Wisconsin, 14 April 1951. HM 37/10/2, ACUA.

23. Letter from Muench, Bad Godesberg, to Joseph Hering, Amberg (Upper Palatinate region of Bavaria), 27 August 1957. HM 37/131/4, ACUA.

24. Robert Wistrich, *Antisemitism: The Longest Hatred* (New York: Pantheon Books, 1991).

25. Although the exact number of Jewish Germans on the eve of Hitler's rise to power is not known, estimates range from 510,000 to 525,000, a mere 0.9 percent of the country's population, in the winter of 1932–33. See Yahil, *Holocaust*, 21.

26. Charles Herbert Stember was a well-known figure in the field of survey research. Under the auspices of the American Jewish Committee, Stember conducted opinion polls concerning American attitudes toward Jews from 1937 to 1962. See Stember, ed., *Jews in the Mind of America* (New York: Basic Books, 1966), 9–10.

27. See Idith Zertal, *From Catastrophe to Power: Holocaust Survivors and the Emergence of Israel* (Berkeley: University of California Press, 1998).

28. See Werner Bergmann and Rainer Erb, *Anti-Semitism in Germany: The Post-Nazi Epoch Since 1945*, translated from the German by Belinda Cooper and Allison Brown (New Brunswick, N.J.: Transaction, 1997).

29. Michael Brenner, *After the Holocaust: Rebuilding Jewish Lives in Postwar Germany*, translated by Barbara Harshav (Princeton, N.J.: Princeton University Press, 1997), 139.

30. Herf, *Divided Memory*, 204. See also Merrit, *Democracy Imposed*, 132–40.

31. Bernstein referred to the fact that a number of Jewish DPs refused to work. Polish-Jewish DP Arno Lustiger—a survivor of Auschwitz, Gross-Rosen, and Buchenwald—recalled that the American army tried to involve the Jewish DPs in the German economy. The army "thought the DPs shouldn't loaf around without work, but should participate in the construction of the German economy," remembered Lustiger. He and others rejected army overtures in this regard. "That was an abstruse idea that we should help the Germans built their economy, when they themselves destroyed it with their own guilt and their own crimes." See Brenner, *After the Holocaust*, 90–95.

32. Memorandum entitled "A Program to Deal with Anti-Semitism in Germany," from Rabbi Phillip S. Bernstein to General Joseph McNarney, commander in chief, USFET, 16 July 1947 (document 13), in folder 1, box 117, OAG-GC, REO, NARA.

33. Yehuda Bauer, *Out of the Ashes: The Impact of American Jews on Post-Holocaust European Jewry* (Oxford: Pergamon Press, 1989), 45. Excellent scholarly work exists regarding the experience of Jewish displaced persons in postwar Germany. Selected works include Angelika Eder, *Flüchtige Heimat: jüdische displaced persons in Landsberg am Lech, 1945 bis 1950* (Munich: Kommissionsverlag UNI-Drück, 1998); Jael Geis, *Übrig sein–Leben danach: Juden Deutscher Herkunft in der Britischen und amerikanischen Zone Deutschlands, 1945–1949* (Berlin: Philo Verlagsgessellschaft, 2000); Angelika Königseder and Juliane Wetzel, *Waiting for Hope: Jewish Displaced Persons in Post-World War II Germany* (Evanston: Northwestern University Press, 2001); Zeev W. Mankowitz, *Life Between Memory and Hope: The Survivors of the Holocaust in Occupied Germany* (Cambridge: Cambridge University Press, 2002); Michael R. Marrus, *The Unwanted: European Refugees in the Twentieth Century* (New York: Oxford University Press, 1985), reprinted as *The Unwanted: European Refugees from the First World War through the Cold War* (Philadelphia: Temple University Press, 2002); and Mark Wyman, *DPs: Europe's Displaced Persons, 1945–1951* (Ithaca, N.Y.: Cornell University Press, 1998).

34. The standard work is Hagit Lavsky, *New Beginnings: Holocaust Survivors in Bergen-Belsen and the British Zone in Germany, 1945–1950* (Detroit: Wayne State University Press, 2002).

35. Brenner, *After the Holocaust*, 135–37.

36. After 15 May, Jewish displaced persons emigrated to Israel from Germany and Austria at the rate of 4,000 per month. See "Interim Report of Advisor on Jewish Affairs" William Haber to Kenneth Royall, Army Secretary, 28 October 1948. In folder 17 (H), box 8 (1948 A–Z), CGCPA, OPAG-B, RG 84-State Department, NARA.

37. See William B. Helmreich, "Against All Odds: Survivors of the Holocaust and the American Experience," in *The Holocaust and History: The Known, the Unknown, the Disputed, and the Reexamined*, ed. Michael Berenbaum and Abraham J. Peck, eds. (Bloomington and Washington: Indiana University Press in association with the United States Holocaust Memorial Museum, 1998), 750–51.

38. Brenner, *After the Holocaust*, 41.

39. Letter from Otto Kling, Munich, to Cardinal Michael Faulhaber, Munich, 25 September 1947. HM 37/138/2, ACUA. Faulhaber apparently sent Kling's letter to Muench, to whom he was very close. No evidence of Faulhaber's or Muench's response, or the possible discussion that ensued, is available. Kling might be referring to Muench's pro-German and anti-Jewish pastoral letter, *One World in Charity*, which circulated widely in Germany during the fall of 1947.

40. Enclosure authored by Karl Lüssenhop, Wiesbaden, sent to Muench, Kronberg, 29 November 1946. HM 37/127/7, ACUA.

41. Letter from Muench, Kronberg, to Carl Zietlow, c/o OMGUS, 13 April 1948. HM 37/14/9, ACUA.

42. Letter from Muench, Bad Godesberg, to a "Sister Manuela," 3 January 1957. HM 37/38/5, ACUA.

43. Letter from Muench, Kronberg, to Carl Zietlow, c/o OMGUS, 13 April 1948. HM 37/14/9, ACUA.

44. The Stratton bill, introduced to Congress in April 1947, proposed to allow 400,000 (Jewish and non-Jewish) displaced persons into the United States over the next four years. See Dinnerstein, *America and the Survivors of the Holocaust* (New York: Columbia University Press, 1982), 132–33. For Muench quote, see letter from Muench, Kronberg, to Mulloy, Covington, 27 June 1947, HM 37/7/1, ACUA.

45. Letter from Bishop Albert Stohr, Mainz, to Captain Kenny, OMGUS-Wiesbaden, 6 August 1947. HM 37/141/3, ACUA.

46. Ibid.

47. Letter from Sister Ant. Reifsmeier, Josefsheim, Bad Wörishofen, to Muench, Kronberg, 20 June 1947. HM 37/37/1, ACUA.

48. Letter from Muench, Kronberg, to General Clarence Huebner, Frankfurt, 28 June 1947. HM 37/124/5, ACUA.

49. Letter from Lieutenant General C.R. Huebner, Chief of Staff-USFET, to·Muench, Kronberg, 11 July 1947. HM 37/37/1, ACUA.

50. Letter from Robert Deubel to Muench, 14 July 1947. HM 37/37/1, ACUA.

51. For a discussion about the case of Philipp Auerbach, an Orthodox German Jew and survivor of Auschwitz, Gross-Rosen and Buchenwald, see Brenner, *After the Holocaust*, 135–37.

52. Letter from Sister Fernanda Weip, Kneippianum, Bad Wörishofen, to Muench, Kronberg, 20 July 1947. HM 37/37/1, ACUA.

53. Letter from Weip to Muench, 3 August 1947. HM 37/37/1, ACUA.

54. Letter from Sisters Serva Riedl and Edgarda Haiden, Josefsheim, to Muench, Kronberg, 10 October 1947. HM 37/55/6, ACUA.

55. Letter from Muench, Kronberg, to Huebner, Frankfurt, 27 October 1947. HM 37/55/6, ACUA.

56. Letter from Bishop Dr. Ferdinand Dirichs, Limburg an der Lahn, to Muench, Kronberg, 4 July 1948. HM 37/141/1, ACUA.

57. Letter from Muench to Dirichs, 9 July 1948. HM 37/141/1, ACUA.

58. Brenner, *After the Holocaust*, 94; and letter from Father Rupp, Frankfurt-Zeilsheim, to Muench, Kronberg, 19 April 1948. HM 37/128/5, ACUA.

59. Muench diary entry dated 6 January 1947, vol. 5, p. 43.

60. Memorandum from Major General W. A. Burress to Chief of Staff, Frankfurt, 9 January 1947 (document 10), in folder 6, box 117, OAG-GC, REO, RG 260-OMGUS, NARA.

61. Letter from an unnamed priest, Frankfurt, to Father Rupp, 15 January 1947. Rupp sent the letter to Muench in Kronberg. HM 37/69/6, ACUA.

62. Letter from Father Rupp to Muench, 24 November 1948. HM 37/128/8, ACUA.

63. Brenner, *After the Holocaust*, 13.

64. Letter from Father Brim, co-signed by sixteen Zeilsheim Catholics, to Muench, Kronberg, 21 January 1947. HM 37/127/9, ACUA.

65. Letter from Muench, Kronberg, to General Joseph T. McNarney, Berlin, 15 January 1947. HM 37/124/3, ACUA.

66. Letter from Rupp to Muench, 19 April 1948. HM 37/128/5, ACUA. "Mammon" is a common term in rabbinical literature denoting "money, goods, or wealth." In parts of the New Testament, "Mammon" is also personified as an "object of false devotion."

67. Brenner, *After the Holocaust*, 94.

68. Letter from Rupp to Muench, 24 November 1948.

69. Memorandum entitled "Zeilsheim" from Robert Deubel to Muench, Kronberg, 4 July 1949. HM 37/128/12, ACUA.

70. Letter from Father L. A. Fritsch, Chicago, to Muench, Kronberg, 30 November 1946. HM 37/55/2, ACUA.

71. Muench diary entry dated 15 July 1951, vol. 14, p. 59.

72. Letter from Father James "Boots" Nellen, Milwaukee, to Muench, Kronberg, 9 July 1949. HM 37/13/6, ACUA.

73. Letter from Muench, Kronberg, to Nellen, Milwaukee, 13 August 1949. HM 37/13/6, ACUA.

74. Muench diary entry dated 13 October 1946, vol. 6, pp. 87–88. The reference to the bishop is unclear. Muench may have meant Bishop Henry Joseph O'Brien, auxiliary bishop of Hartford (1940–45), diocesan bishop of Hartford (1945–53), and archbishop of Hartford (1953–68). More likely in view of Muench's extensive connections in the Midwest, he may instead have meant Bishop William David O'Brien, auxiliary bishop of Chicago (1934–62).

75. Letter from Fasnacht, Chicago, to Muench, Kronberg, 9 December 1950. HM 37/140/5, ACUA. Fasnacht suspected Jews of plotting against Catholics, as shown in the "Fulda Affair." Fasnacht (and Muench) suspected an American man, whom they set out to prove was Jewish, of attempted extortion. The German bishops' conference at Fulda was the attempted target. For documentation of this incident, see letter from Bishop Johannes Dietz, Fulda, to Muench, Kronberg, 22 July 1950 (HM 37/140/5, ACUA); letter from Muench, Kronberg, to Fasnacht, Chicago, 26 July 1950 (HM 37/140/5, ACUA); letter from "Investigator" to Fasnacht, 2 August 1950 (HM 37/140/5, ACUA); letter from Fasnacht to Muench, 6 August 1950 (HM 37/140/5, ACUA); letter from Muench to Fasnacht, 12 August 1950 (HM 37/140/5, ACUA); letter from Fasnacht to Muench, 13 October 1950 (HM 37/140/5, ACUA); and letter from Fasnacht to Muench, 25 November 1950 (HM 37/140/5, ACUA).

76. Phayer, *Catholic Church and the Holocaust*, 180–81.

77. Ibid., 181.

78. Letter from Cardinal Samuel Stritch, Chicago, to Nuncio Amleto Cicognani, Washington, 26 October 1946, CC/C, Archdiocesan Archives Chicago.

79. The "restrictionist" senators were committee chair Alexander Wiley (Republican, Wisconsin), William Chapman Revercomb (Republican, West Virginia), E. H. Moore (Republican, Oklahoma), James Eastland (Democrat, Mississippi), Patrick McCarren (Democrat, Nevada), and Forrest C. Donnell (Republican, Missouri). The "liberal" senators on the Senate Judiciary Committee were John S. Cooper (Republican, Kentucky), J. Howard McGrath (Democrat, Rhode Island), Homer Ferguson (Republican, Michigan), Harley Kilgore (Democrat, West Virginia), Warren Magnuson (Democrat, Washington), and J. William Fulbright (Democrat, Arkansas). See Dinnerstein, *American and Survivors of the Holocaust*, 164–65.

80. Ibid., 165–66. An ardent anti-communist, Senator Langer compared the twelve Nuremberg successor trials with "Stalinist show trials," claiming that "communists" employed the war crimes trials in occupied Germany for the purpose of "destroying property rights." His stance included intervention on behalf of Martin Sandberger, commander of *Einsatzkommando* 1a and commander of the Security Police and *Sicherheitsdienst* in Estonia (December 1941 through the fall of 1943). A defendant in the *Einsatzgruppen* case (*U.S. v. Ohlendorf et al.*), Sandberger received the death penalty. Langer placed pressure on the Truman administration and OMGUS officials, and though historian Frank Buscher acknowledges that it "is impossible to determine exactly how much Langer's lobbying impacted the decision," in January 1951 John J. McCloy commuted Sandberger's death sentence to life. See Frank M. Buscher, "To Punish and Reeducate: U.S. War Crimes Policy in Germany After the Second World War," manuscript, 10–11.

81. Letter from Senator William Langer, Washington, to Muench, Fargo, 13 November 1946. HM 37/4/1, ACUA. The letter was forwarded from Fargo to Kronberg.

82. Letter from Muench, Kronberg, to Langer, Washington, 18 January 1947. HM 37/125/11, ACUA.

83. See letter from Father G. P. Aberle, Dickinson (ND) to Muench, Kronberg, 30 September 1946. HM 37/148/1, ACUA. Aberle's mother, four sisters, two brothers, and two sisters-in-law were among those German-Russians sent first to Saxony and then to Siberia.

84. Letter from Muench, Kronberg, to Aberle, Dickinson, 29 October 1946. HM 37/148/1, ACUA.

85. Letter from Muench, Kronberg, to Senator William Langer, Washington, 30 November 1946. HM 37/148/1, ACUA.

86. Dinnerstein, *America and the Survivors of the Holocaust*, 163. Dinnerstein obtained these statistics from the *Report of the Senate Committee on the Judiciary Pursuant to Senate Resolution 137*, or Revercomb Report (Report No. 950), issued during the 80th Congress, 2nd Session, 2 March 1948.

87. Letter from Muench, Kronberg, to Langer, Washington, 28 March 1947. HM 37/148/1, ACUA.

88. Aloisius Muench, "Interview with President Truman," 8 February 1949, p. 2. HM 37/29/3, ACUA.

89. Helmreich, "Against All Odds," 751.

90. Dinnerstein, *America and the Survivors of the Holocaust*, 174–75.

91. Ibid.

92. Letter from William Langer, Washington, to Robert Murphy, Berlin, 3 August 1948. Folder: "Aux-L," box 10 (1948: Correspondence with Congressmen), CGCPA, OPAG-B, RG 84-State Department, NARA.

93. Dinnerstein, *America and the Survivors of the Holocaust*, 176.

94. Helmreich, "Against All Odds," 751.

95. Letter from Muench, Kronberg, to Monsignor Luigi Ligutti, Des Moines, Iowa, 22 November 1948. HM 37/26/1, ACUA.

96. Dinnerstein, *America and the Survivors of the Holocaust*, 171.

97. If Murphy referred to Jews incarcerated in concentration camps, his impressions of Dachau and Buchenwald as sites of Jewish habitation were accurate only in late 1944–45. Through most of their existence, Dachau (1933) and Buchenwald (1937), located near Munich and Weimar respectively, were concentration camps largely reserved for "political" enemies of Nazism. But the imprisoned included some Jews, considered "racial" enemies of the Third Reich. Between the end of December 1944 and liberation in April 1945, thousands of inmates (including many Jews) were forcibly marched from camps in the East to Buchenwald, Dachau, and other German camps. Hence, when American troops liberated Dachau and Buchenwald in April 1945, they found many Jewish prisoners. See Yahil, *Holocaust*, 534–39.

98. Letter from Robert Murphy, Berlin, to Judge H. Freeman Matthews, Washington, 12 October 1945. Folder 5: "August 1947," box 6 (June–September 1947), CGCPA, OPAG-B, RG 84-State Department, NARA.

[Au: state or D.C?]

99. "Excerpts from Speech of Senator Langer," included in letter from chairman of the *Volksverein* United Action Committee for Expellees, Chase F.

Gerhard, Philadelphia, to Aloisius Muench, Kronberg, 2 September 1949. HM 37/25/3, ACUA. See also Congressional Record for 25 August 1949, 12448-12449.

100. Bendersky, *"Jewish Threat,"* 364.

101. Ibid., 367.

102. Muench diary entry dated 14 November 1949, vol. 11, p. 44–45.

103. Muench diary entry dated 12 March 1947, vol. 5, p. 87.

104. Muench diary entry dated 11 July 1947, vol. 6, p. 28.

105. Muench diary entry dated 4 May 1952, vol. 15, pp. 4–5.

106. Letter from Muench, Bad Godesberg, to Howard Smith, Fargo, 18 March 1954. HM 37/63/13, ACUA.

107. Muench diary entry dated 23 August 1954, vol. 20, pp. 116–17.

108. Muench diary entry dated 8 February 1947, vol. 5, pp. 61–63. Tellingly, this was only two months before Clay issued a directive to remove those army officers "naturalized since 1933."

109. Muench diary entry dated 17 January 1948, vol. 7, p. 52.

110. Muench diary entry dated 16 September 1947, vol. 6, p. 66.

111. Muench diary entry dated 22 November 1946, vol. 5, pp. 19–20. Aradi was the former Hungarian cultural attaché to Italy in Milan (1941–43) and part of the Royal Hungarian Legation to the Holy See (1943–44). He worked for army intelligence in Heidelberg probably due to his language skills, which included English, German, Italian, Hungarian, French, and Slovak. He became an employee of the State Department and a consultant to Voice of America. Aradi was a prolific writer of historical texts, articles, and biographies. He settled in New York City after the war and maintained contact with Muench as late as 1957. See correspondence between Muench and Aradi, HM 37/14/10 and HM 37/15/1; Muench diary entry dated 16 July 1954, vol. 20, p. 93 and diary entry dated 7 September 1957, vol. 22, p. 37.

112. Muench diary entry dated 16 October 1948, vol. 9, pp. 18-19. Aradi complained that "Jews" were now in power in his native Hungary, a fact which "alarmed good Jews."

113. Muench diary entry dated 12 August 1946, vol. 4, pp. 48–49.

114. Bendersky, *"Jewish Threat,"* 366–67.

115. Letter from Parker Buhrman, Munich, to Robert Murphy, Berlin, 11 January 1946. Folder 86: "Ambassador Murphy files for January 1946," box 2 (January–April 1946). Classified General Correspondence of the Political Advisor, 1944–1949 (hereafter CGCPA), Office of the United States Political Advisor to Germany-Berlin (hereafter OPAG-B), Record Group 84: United States Department of State Foreign Service Posts (hereafter RG 84-State Department), NARA.

116. Letter from Parker Buhrman, Munich, to Robert Murphy, Berlin, 21 March 1946. Folder 88: "Ambassador Murphy files for March 1946," box 2 (January–April 1946), CGCPA, OPAG-B, RG 84-State Department, NARA.

117. Letter marked "personal and confidential" from Parker Buhrman, Munich, to Robert Murphy, Berlin, 26 March 1946. Folder 88: "Ambassador

Murphy files for March 1946," box 2 (January–April 1946), CGCPA, OPAG-B, RG 84-State Department, NARA.

118. Muench diary entry dated 28 May 1948, vol. 8, p. 36.

119. According to intelligence officers, 108 graves in fifteen different cemeteries were reported desecrated to the German police in the state of Bavaria between January and June 1948. Each had to be verified by the German police, whom State Commissioner Philipp Auerbach described as "not free of anti-Semitism." German police "verified" 31 (of 108) cases between March and June 1948. More than 200 incidents of grave desecration occurred in the state of Hesse, also home to a number of partially Jewish displaced persons camps, in 1950. See Zietlow, Bad Nauheim, to Muench, Bad Godesberg, 4 January 1951 (HM 37/21/6, ACUA). For Auerbach on the German police in Bavaria, see "Protokoll der dritten Sitzung des zivilen Ausschusses des Gesellschaft für christlich-jüdische Zusammenarbeit: Rede von Herrn Generalanwalt Dr. Auerbach," Munich, 26 April 1949. In folder entitled "Religious Affairs Miscellaneous," box 163 (RA, ECR, RG 260-OMGUS, NARA).

120. A great deal of tension existed between Jewish DPs and Allied-approved German police, who conducted overzealous raids on Jewish DP camps accompanied by German shepherd dogs. In Stuttgart, a German policeman shot a member of the Jewish camp police, causing a riot in March 1946. See Brenner, *After the Holocaust*, 53. Also, crime in general was often blamed on displaced persons, which, in this context, was a coded phrase for Jews. See Stern, *Whitewashing of the Yellow Badge*.

121. In his speech to the ICCJ in Munich, Auerbach denied the validity of German "collective guilt" just as he denied the "collective" charge that all Jewish DPs were black marketers. Nor was Auerbach above criticizing conditions in Jewish DP camps. In 1947, he wrote a report to Robert Murphy criticizing the DP Central Committee, the survivors' organization and principle representative body for Jewish DPs with strong Zionist overtones. The Committee was officially recognized by the Americans as the authorized representative of Jewish DPs in the American zone and had offices in Munich's *Deutsche Museum* (German Museum). Auerbach told Murphy, "I accuse the Central Committee of being guilty of the black market bargains made by Jewish citizens . . . because it did not allow the proper distribution of goods among the 25,000 Jewish DPs placed in towns and communities. He called the Central Committee a "state within a state" that supported Zionist party interests and created dissension among Jewish DPs. See report entitled "The Position of the Jewish DPs" by State Commissioner Philipp Auerbach, 23 June 1947, folder 4 (no title), box 6 (June–September 1947), CCGPA, OPAG-B, RG 84-State Department, NARA.

122. "Report on Efforts to Combat Acts of Anti-Semitism" by Herbert J. Gauerke, Religious Affairs deputy chief, 23 June 1948, in folder entitled "Jews and Christians Council," box 165 (RA, ECR, RG 260-OMGUS, NARA). The report does not further identify officer Moeller.

Notes to Appendix A

1. Rolf Hochhuth, *Der Stellvertreter: Ein christliches Trauerspiel* (Reinbek: Taschenbuch Verlag, 1967).

2. Saul Friedländer followed with the first major scholarly criticism of the pope in *Pie XII et le IIIe Reich* (Paris: Editions due Seuil, 1964).

3. Pierre Blet, Robert A. Graham, Angelo Martini, and Burkhart Schneider, eds., *Actes et Documents du Saint Siège relatifs à la seconde guerre mondiale* (Vatican City: Libreria Editrice Vaticana, 1965–81). Incidentally, Father Graham was acquainted with Muench and wrote to him in 1948 while working on the editorial staff of *America.* They exchanged views about U.S. Chamber of Commerce president Daniel R. McDonald, who sought Muench's intercession in obtaining an appointment to the administration of the European Recovery Program (ERP, the Marshall Plan). "If you know of a good economist of repute with the Catholic slant on social policy he would be better than McDonald," wrote Graham. Muench responded, "ERP needs men who have vision not beclouded by war propaganda, ill will or hatred. The world needs peace. Morgenthauers can not make it." Graham to Muench, 8 April 1948 (HM 37/9/4, ACUA) and Muench to Graham, 26 April 1948 (HM 37/9/4, ACUA).

4. David Alvarez and *Actes* editor Robert A. Graham, S.J., *Nothing Sacred: Nazi Espionage Against the Vatican, 1939–1945* (London: Frank Cass, 1997); *Actes* editor Pierre Blet, S.J., *Pius XII and the Second World War: According to the Archives of the Vatican,* translated by Lawrence J. Johnson (New York: Paulist Press, 1999); Robert A. Graham, S.J., "How to Manufacture a Legend," *Pius XII and the Holocaust: A Reader* (1963; reprint, Milwaukee: Catholic League for Religious and Civil Rights, 1988); Pinchas Lapide, *The Last Three Popes and the Jews: Pope Pius XII Did Not Remain Silent* (New York: Hawthorne, 1967); Margherita Marchione, *Pope Pius XII: Architect for Peace* (Mahwah, N.J.: Paulist Press, 2000); and Ronald Rychlak, *Hitler, the War, and the Pope* (Huntington, Ind.: Our Sunday Visitor Press, 2000).

5. James Carroll, *Constantine's Sword: The Church and the Jews* (Boston: Houghton Mifflin, 2000); John Cornwell, *Hitler's Pope: The Secret History of Pius XII* (New York: Penguin Books, 2000); Heinz Hürten, *Pius XII und die Juden* (Cologne: J.P. Bachem, 2000); Uki Goni, *The Real Odessa: Smuggling the Nazis to Peron's Argentina* (London: Granta Books, 2002); Robert Katz, *The Battle for Rome: The Germans, the Allies, the Partisans, and the Pope, Summer 1943–June 1944* (New York: Simon & Schuster, 2003); David Kertzer, *The Popes Against the Jews: The Vatican's Role in the Rise of Modern Antisemitism* (New York: Knopf, 2001); Ernst Klee, *Persilscheine und falsche Pässe: Wie die Kirchen den Nazis halfen* (Frankfurt am Main: Fischer Verlag, 1991); John F. Morley, *Vatican Diplomacy and the Jews During the Holocaust, 1939–1943* (New York: Ktav Publishing House, 1980); Michael Phayer, *The Catholic Church and the Holocaust, 1930–1965* (Bloomington: Indiana University Press, 2000); Carol Rittner and John K. Roth, eds., *Pope Pius XII and the Holocaust* (London: Leicester University Press, 2002); and Susan Zuccotti,

Under His Very Windows: The Vatican and the Holocaust in Italy (New Haven, Conn.: Yale University Press, 2000).

6. José M. Sánchez, *Pius XII and the Holocaust: Understanding the Controversy* (Washington, D.C.: Catholic University of America Press, 2002), 80.

7. Ibid., 37, 173.

8. Cornwell, *Hitler's Pope;* Daniel Jonah Goldhagen, *A Moral Reckoning: The Role of the Catholic Church in the Holocaust and Its Unfulfilled Duty of Repair* (New York: Alfred A. Knopf, 2002).

9. Phayer, *Catholic Church and the Holocaust;* Peter C. Kent, *The Lonely Cold War of Pope Pius XII: The Roman Catholic Church and the Division of Europe, 1943–1950* (Montreal/Kingston: McGill-Queen's University Press, 2002).

10. Sánchez, *Pius XII and the Holocaust,* 177.

11. Ibid., 63.

12. David Kertzer, *Popes Against the Jews.*

13. Sánchez, *Pius XII and the Holocaust,* 107; Kent, *Lonely Cold War of Pope Pius XII.*

14. Susan Zuccotti, "Pope Pius XII and the Rescue of Jews During the Holocaust," in Rittner and Roth, *Pope Pius XII and the Holocaust,* 210.

15. Richard Rubenstein, "Pope Pius XII and the Shoah," in Rittner and Roth, *Pope Pius XII and the Holocaust.*

16. Ibid., 187.

17. Ibid., 195.

18. Phayer, *Catholic Church and the Holocaust,* 47.

19. John T. Pawlikowski, "The Papacy of Pius XII: The Known and the Unknown," in Rittner and Roth, *Pope Pius XII and the Holocaust,* 58.

20. Pawlikowski, "Papacy of Pius XII"; Michael Marrus, "Pius XII and the Holocaust: Ten Essential Themes," in Rittner and Roth, *Pope Pius XII and the Holocaust,* 49.

21. Rittner, Carol, Stephen D. Smith, and Irena Steinfeldt, eds., *The Holocaust and the Christian World* (New York: Continuum, 2000), 22.

22. Ibid., 23.

23. Sergio I. Minerbi, "Pius XII: A Re-Appraisal," in Rittner and Roth, *Pope Pius XII and the Holocaust,* 92.

24. Sánchez, *Pius XII and the Holocaust,* 5–6.

25. Zucotti, "Pope Pius XII and the Rescue of Jews," 211–13.

26. Antonio Gaspari, "New Letter Shows Pius XII Opposed Hitler," *Inside the Vatican News* (4 March 2003).

27. Ludwig Volk, ed., *Akten Kardinal Michael von Faulhaber, 1917–1945,* Band I, VKZ A-17 (Mainz: Matthias Grünewald Verlag, 1975), 318–20. Volk's source is Archdiocesan Archive of Munich: Faulhaber Papers (Nachlass), Nr. 7229, *Schriebmaschinabschrift.*

28. *Bayerische Kurier,* Nr. 309, dated 6 November 1923. From the *Archiv des Erzbistums Muenchen und Freising,* Karmeliterstrasse 1, 80333 Muenchen; Dr. Peter Pfister, Archivdirektor.

29. Peter Godman, *Hitler and the Vatican: Inside the Secret Archives that Reveal the New Story of the Nazis and the Church* (New York: Free Press, 2004); Gerhard Besier (with Francesca Piombo), *Der Heilige Stuhl und Hitler-Deutschland: die Faszination des Totalitären* (Munich: Deutsche Verlags-Anstalt, 2004).

Notes to Appendix B

1. As reproduced from the Military Government Report "Religious Affairs," dated August 1946 (Basic Documents, box 158, RA, ECR, RG 260, NARA, pp. 24–25).

Notes to Appendix C

1. Jeremiah 6:3.
2. David Lawrence, quoted in the *Brooklyn Tablet,* 15 December 1945.
3. Exodus 21:24; Leviticus 24:20.
4. Matthew 5:38–48.
5. Luke 6:36.
6. Psalm 85:15.
7. Psalm 144:8.
8. Psalm 129:4.
9. Psalm 39:12.
10. Psalm 118:77.
11. Psalm 144:9.
12. Matthew 18:28.
13. Editorial, *Life* (24 December 1945).
14. Matthew 7:2.
15. Editorial, *Life,* (24 December 1945).
16. Alexander Boeker, "The Nativity," *Human Events* (19 December 1945).
17. II Kings 24:14.
18. Russell Hill, *New York Herald-Tribune.*
19. Quoted, *Congressional Record,* 5 December 1945, p. A5688.
20. *Life* (27 March 1944).
21. Pius XI, *Principles for Peace,* 834–38.
22. Colmer Congressional Committee.
23. Ecclesiastes 11:1.
24. Proverbs 25:21–22.
25. Ecclesiastics 28:1–4.
26. Psalm 7:5–6.
27. Luke 6:27–34.

28. Romans 12:17–21.

29. Letter, "Feeding the Germans," *Congressional Record,* 18 December 1945, p. A6027.

30. Letter, "Charity Should Begin at Home," ibid., p. A6053.

31. *Life,* 3 December 1945.

32. C. L. Sulzberger, European correspondent, *New York Times,* 13 November 1945.

33. Colmer Committee on Postwar Economic Policy.

34. "Between War and Peace," Statement of American Hierarchy, 18 November 1945.

35. Lithuanian-American Congress, "Policy Declarations and Resolutions," *Congressional Record,* 13 December 1945, p. A5911.

36. Pius XII, "Christmas Message 1945."

37. Proverbs 20:9–10.

38. Pius XII, "Christmas Message 1945."

39. Ibid.

Bibliography

Primary Sources

Private Papers Consulted

Aloisius Cardinal Muench Papers. Archives, Catholic University of America (ACUA), Washington, D.C.
   The papers of Cardinal Aloisius J. Muench, who acted as Pope Pius XII's papal visitor (July 1946–January 1947), mission head of papal relief at Kronberg (February 1947–September 1949), regent (October 1949–February 1951), and nuncio to Germany (March 1951–December 1959). He was Pope Pius XII's main liaison between the Holy See in Rome and German Catholicism. Muench also served as liaison representative between German Catholicism and the Office of Military Government, United States Zone between July 1946 and the end of occupation in summer/fall 1949. These papers provide the bulk of the primary source material for this book.

John O. Riedl Papers. Archives, Marquette University, Marquette Memorial Library, Milwaukee, Wisconsin.
   John O. Riedl worked for the Religious Affairs Division of the Office of Military Government, United States Zone (OMGUS) between 1946 and 1949. In his capacity as religious affairs officer, Riedl interacted with Muench when he was U.S. liaison representative. Only a portion of his papers reflect

his interactions with Muench, and most are available in Record Group 260 (OMGUS), National Archives II, College Park, Maryland.

Francis J. Cardinal Spellman Papers. Archives, Archdiocese of New York Archives, Saint Joseph's Seminary, Yonkers, New York.

Samuel Cardinal Stritch Papers. Archives, Archdiocese of Chicago's Joseph Cardinal Bernardin Archives & Records Center, Chicago, Illinois.
Cardinal Samuel Stritch served as archbishop of Milwaukee and of Chicago. He first met Muench in Milwaukee and became his mentor. Stritch was the impetus behind Pius XII's selection of Muench as the Holy See's representative in Germany. Only a portion of the Stritch papers mention Muench.

Official Papers Consulted

Records of the United States Department of State. Record Group 84, National Archives II, College Park, Maryland.
A portion of this collection contains interaction between Muench and political advisor Robert Murphy.

Records of the Office of Military Government, United States Zone. Record Group 260, National Archives II, College Park, Maryland.
This vast collection is a necessary complement to the Muench Papers, providing documentation of Muench's interactions with military government officials. The records of the Religious Affairs Division and the Information Control Division, among others, contain multiple references to Muench.

Records of the United States Army, European Command. Record Group 338, National Archives II, College Park, Maryland.
This collection contains records related to the U.S. war crimes trials program, specifically to all post-trial activities between 1945 and 1957.

Newspapers and Periodicals Consulted

Catholic Action News. A Monthly Publication of the Diocese of Fargo, North Dakota. 1940–46.
"Eine Welt in der Liebe," Parts 1–5. *Nord Dakota Herold* (Dickinson, N. D.). March–August 1946.
Muench, Aloisius. "Father Coughlin's Money Program." *Salesianum* 30, 2 (April 1935): 8–21.

Booklets and Pamphlets Consulted

No author listed. *A Tribute on the Occasion of the Silver Jubilee of Aloisius Joseph Cardinal Muench: Episcopal Consecration, 1935–1960*. Diocese of Fargo, N.D., 1960.

No author listed. "Eulogy of His Eminence Cardinal Muench." *In Memory of His Eminence Aloisius Joseph Cardinal Muench*. Rome: Arti Grafiche Scalia, 1962.

Muench, Aloisius. "The Outstretched Hand of Communism." Saint Louis, Mo.: Central Bureau Press, 1938.

Muench, Aloisius, and Vincent J. Ryan. "The Church, Fascism, and Peace." Huntington, Ind.: Our Sunday Visitor Press, 1944.

Secretariat for Ecumenical and Interreligious Affairs and National Conference of Catholic Bishops, eds. *Catholics Remember the Holocaust*. Washington, D.C.: United States Catholic Conference, September 1998.

Secondary Sources

Books Consulted

Adam, Stephan. *Die Auseinandersetzungen des Bischofs Konrad von Preysing mit dem Nationalsozialismus in den Jahren 1933–1945*. Saint Ottilien: EOS, 1996.

Allen, Michael Thad. *The Business of Genocide: The SS, Slave Labor, and the Concentration Camps*. Chapel Hill: University of North Carolina Press, 2002.

Arendt, Hannah. *Eichmann in Jerusalem: A Report on the Banality of Evil*. New York: Penguin Books, 1964.

Avella, Steven. *Milwaukee Catholicism: Essays on Church and Community*. Milwaukee, Wis.: Knights of Columbus, 1991.

———. *This Confident Church: Catholic Leadership and Life in Chicago, 1940–1965*. Notre Dame, Ind.: University of Notre Dame Press, 1992.

———, ed. *St. Francis Seminary: Sesquicentennial Essays*. St. Francis, Wis.: Saint Francis Seminary, 1997.

Bacharach, Walter Zwi. "The Catholic Anti-Jewish Prejudice, Hitler, and the Jews." In Baulcier, ed., *Probing the Depths of German Antisemitism*.

Bankier, David, ed. *Probing the Depths of German Antisemitism: German Society and the Persecution of the Jews, 1933–1941,* New York: Berghahn Books, 2000.

Barry, Colman, O.S.B. *American Nuncio: Cardinal Aloisius Muench*. Collegeville, Minn.: Saint Johns University Press, 1969.

Bauer, Fritz, ed. *Justiz und NS-Verbrechen: Sammlung deutscher Stafurteile wegen national-sozialistischer Tötungsverbrechen 1945–1966*. 22 vols. Amsterdam: University Press, 1968-81.

Bauer, Yehuda. *Out of the Ashes: The Impact of American Jews on Post-Holocaust European Jewry*. Oxford: Pergamon Press, 1989.

Baumann, Ulrich. *Zerstörte Nachbarschaften: Christen und Juden in badischen Landgemeinden, 1862–1940*. Hamburg: Dölling und Galitz, 2000.

Bendersky, Joseph W. *The "Jewish Threat": Anti-Semitic Policies of the U.S. Army*. New York: Basic Books, 2000.

Berenbaum, Michael, and Abraham J. Peck, eds. *The Holocaust and History: The Known, the Unknown, the Disputed, and the Reexamined.* Bloomington and Washington, D.C.: Indiana University Press in association with the United States Holocaust Memorial Museum, 1998.

Bergen, Doris L. *Twisted Cross: The German Christian Movement in the Third Reich.* Chapel Hill: University of North Carolina Press, 1996.

Bergmann, Werner, and Rainer Erb. *Anti-Semitism in Germany: The Post-Nazi Epoch Since 1945.* Translated by Belinda Cooper and Allison Brown. New Brunswick, N.J.: Transaction, 1997.

Blackbourn, David. *Marpingen: Apparitions of the Virgin Mary in Nineteenth-Century Germany.* New York: Alfred A. Knopf, 1994.

Blaschke, Olaf. *Katholismus und Antisemitismus im Deutschen Kaiserreich.* Göttingen: Vandenhoeck und Ruprecht, 1997.

Boberbach, Heinz, ed. *Berichte des SD und der Gestapo über Kirchen und Kirchenvolk in Deutschland, 1934–1944.* Mainz: Grünewald Verlag, 1971.

Boehling, Rebecca. *A Question of Priorities: Democratic Reform and Economic Recovery in Postwar Germany.* Providence, R.I.: Berghahn Books, 1996.

Bracher, Karl Dietrich. "Problems of the German Resistance." In *The Challenge of the Third Reich,* ed. Hedley Bull. Oxford: Clarendon Press, 1986.

Brenner, Michael. *After the Holocaust: Rebuilding Jewish Lives in Postwar Germany.* Translated by Barbara Harshav. Princeton, N.J.: Princeton University Press, 1997.

Browning, Christopher R. *Ordinary Men: Reserve Police Battalion 101 and the Final Solution in Poland.* New York: HarperCollins, 1992.

Broszat, Martin, et al. *Bayern in der NS-Zeit.* 6 vols. Munich: Oldenbourg, 1977–83.

Bücker, Vera. *Die Schulddiskussion im deutschen Katholismus nach 1945.* Bochum: Studienverlag Brockmeyer, 1989.

Buscher, Frank M. *The U.S. War Crimes Trial Program in Germany, 1946–1955.* New York: Greenwood Press, 1989.

Büttner, Ursula. "The Jewish Problem Becomes a Christian Problem: German Protestants and the Persecution of the Jews in the Third Reich." In Baulcier, ed., *Probing the Depths of German Antisemitism.*

Carpenter, Ronald H. *Father Charles H. Coughlin, Surrogate Spokesman for the Disaffected.* Westport, Conn.: Greenwood Press, 1998.

Carroll, James. *Constantine's Sword: The Church and the Jews.* Boston: Houghton Mifflin, 2001.

Conway, John. *The Nazi Persecution of the Churches, 1933–1945.* New York: Basic Books, 1968.

Cornwell, John. *Hitler's Pope: The Secret History of Pius XII.* New York: Penguin Books, 1999.

Deats-O'Reilly, Diana. *The Bishops of Fargo: Biographical Sketches of the Shepherds of the Diocese of Fargo, 1889-1985.* Grand Forks, N.D.: Diana Deats-O'Reilly, 1985.

Dietrich, Donald J. *God and Humanity in Auschwitz: Jewish-Christian Relations and Sanctioned Murder*. New Brunswick, N.J.: Transaction, 1995.

Dinnerstein, Leonard. *America and the Survivors of the Holocaust*. New York: Columbia University Press, 1982.

Donat, Alexander. *The Holocaust Kingdom: A Memoir*. Reprint. Washington, D.C.: United States Holocaust Memorial Museum, 1999.

Earl, Hilary Camille. "Accidental Justice: The Trial of Otto Ohlendorf and the Einsatzgruppen Leaders in the American Zone of Occupation, Germany, 1945–1958." Ph.D. dissertation, University of Toronto, 2002.

Ellis, John Tracy. *American Catholicism*. Second Edition. Chicago: University of Chicago Press, 1969.

Frei, Norbert. *Vergangenheitspolitik: Die Anfänge der Bundesrepublik und die NS-Vergangenheit*. Munich: Beck Verlag, 1996.

———. "Von deutscher Erfindungskraft oder: Die Kollektivschuldthese in der Nachkriegszeit." In *Hannah Arendt Revisited: Eichmann in Jerusalem und die Folgen*, ed. Gary Smith. Frankfurt am Main: Suhrkamp Verlag, 2000.

Friedlander, Henry. *The Origins of Nazi Genocide: From Euthanasia to the Final Solution*. Chapel Hill: University of North Carolina Press, 1995.

Friedländer, Saul. *Pie XII et le IIIᵉ Reich*. Paris: Editions due Seuil, 1964.

Fulbrook, Mary. *The Divided Nation: A History of Germany, 1918–1990*. New York: Oxford University, 1992.

Gellately, Robert. *Backing Hitler: Consent and Coercion in Nazi Germany*. Oxford: Oxford University Press, 2001.

Glaser, Hermann. *The Rubble Years: The Cultural Roots of Postwar Germany*. Translated by Franz Feise and Patricia Gleason. New York: Paragon House, 1986.

Gleason, Philip. *The Conservative Reformers: German-American Catholics and the Social Order*. Notre Dame, Ind.: University of Notre Dame Press, 1968.

Goldhagen, Daniel J. *Hitler's Willing Executioners: Ordinary Germans and the Holocaust*. New York: Alfred Knopf, 1996.

Gordon, Sarah. *Hitler, Germans, and the "Jewish Question."* Princeton, N.J.: Princeton University Press, 1984.

Griech-Polelle, Beth A. *Bishop Von Galen: German Catholicism and National Socialism*. New Haven, Conn.: Yale University Press, 2002.

Harris, James F. *The People Speak! Anti-Semitism and Emancipation in Nineteenth-Century Bavaria*. Ann Arbor: University of Michigan Press, 1994.

Heilbronner, Oded. *Catholicism, Political Culture, and the Countryside: A Social History of the Nazi Party in South Germany*. Ann Arbor: University of Michigan Press, 1998.

Heimannsberg, Barbara, and Christoph J. Schmidt, eds. *The Collective Silence: German Identity and the Legacy of Shame*. Translated by Cynthia Oudejans Harris and Gordon Wheeler. San Francisco: Jossey-Bass, 1993.

Helmreich, Ernst Christian. *The German Churches under Hitler: Background, Struggle, and Epilogue*. Detroit: Wayne State University Press, 1979.

Helmreich, William B. "Against All Odds: Survivors of the Holocaust and the American Experience." In Berenbaum and Peck, eds., *Holocaust and History*.

Hennesey, James, S.J. *American Catholics: A History of the Roman Catholic Community in the United States*. Oxford: Oxford University Press, 1981.

Henry, Frances. *Victims and Neighbors: A Small Town in Nazi Germany Remembered*. South Hadley, Mass.: Bergin & Garvey, 1984.

Herbrich, E. *Alois Kardinal Muench: Ein Lebensbild*. Limburg: Pallottinerdruck, 1969.

Herf, Jeffrey. *Divided Memory: The Nazi Past in the Two Germanys*. Cambridge, Mass.: Harvard University Press, 1997.

Hilberg, Raul. *The Destruction of the European Jews: Revised and Definitive Edition*. 2 vols. New York: Holmes & Meier, 1985.

Hockenos, Matthew D. *A Church Divided: German Protestants Confront the Nazi Past*. Bloomington: Indiana University Press, 2004.

Hodgson, Godfrey. *America in Our Time: From World War II to Nixon, What Happened and Why*. New York: Vintage Books, 1976.

Höpfl, Bernhard. *Katholische Laien im Nationalsozialistischen Bayern: Verweigerung und Widerstand zwischen 1933 und 1945*. Veröffentlichungen der Kommission fuer Zeitgeschichte, Reihe B: Forschungen Band 78. Paderborn: Ferdinand Schöningh, 1997.

Hürten, Heinz. *Deutsche Katholiken*. Munich: Schöningh Verlag, 1992.

Kaplan, Marion. *Between Dignity and Despair: Jewish Life in Nazi Germany*. New York: Oxford University Press, 1998.

Kater, Michael H. *The Nazi Party: A Social Profile of Members and Leaders, 1919–1945*. Cambridge, Mass.: Harvard University Press, 1983.

Klee, Ernst. "Der Umgang der Kirche mit dem Holocaust nach 1945." In Steininger and Boehler, eds. *Der Umgang mit dem Holocaust*.

———. *Persilscheine und falsche Pässe: Wie die Kirchen den Nazis halfen*. Frankfurt am Main: Fischer Taschenbuch Verlag, 1991.

Knappe, Siegfried. *Soldat: Reflections of a German Soldier, 1936–1949*. New York: Dell Publishing, 1992.

Kochavi, Arieh J. *Post-Holocaust Politics: Britain, the United States, and Jewish Refugees, 1945–1948*. Chapel Hill: University of North Carolina Press, 2001.

Kogon, Eugen. *Der SS Staat: Das System der deutschen Konzentrationslager*. Munich: Karl Alber Verlag, 1946.

———. *The Theory and Practice of Hell: The German Concentration Camps and the System Behind Them*. Translated by Heinz Norden. London: Secker and Warburg, 1950.

Koonz, Claudia. "Between Memory and Oblivion: Concentration Camps in German Memory." In *Commemorations: The Politics of National Identity*, ed. John R. Gillis. Princeton, N.J.: Princeton University Press, 1994.

Krausnick, Helmut, Hans Buchheim, Martin Broszat, and Hans-Adolf Jacobsen. *Anatomy of the SS State*. Translated by Elizabeth Wiskemann. New York: Walker and Company, 1968.

Kuropka, Joachim, ed. *Clemens August Graf von Galen: Neue Forschungen zum Leben und Wirken des Bischofs von Münster*. Muenster: Regensberg, 1999.

Kuropka, Joachim, and Maria-Anna Zumholz, eds. *Clemens August Graf von Galen: Sein Leben und Wirken in Bildern und Dokumenten*. Cloppenburg: G. Runge, 1992.

Laliberte, Robert. "Muench as Bishop: Actions and Words." In *Scattered Steeples: The Fargo Diocese, a Written Celebration of its Centennial*, ed. Jerome D. Lamb, Jerry Ruff, and Father William Sherman. Fargo, N.D.: Burch, Longergan and Lynch, 1988.

LaFarge, John. *The Manner Is Ordinary*. Garden City, N.Y.: Image Books, 1957.

Lewy, Guenther. *The Catholic Church and Nazi Germany*. New York: McGraw-Hill, 1964.

Lipstadt, Deborah. *Beyond Belief: The American Press and the Coming of the Holocaust, 1933–1945*. New York: Free Press, 1986.

Löhr, Wolfgang, ed. *Dokumente deutschen Bischöfe: Hirtenbriefe und Ansprachen zu Gesellschaft und Politik 1945–1949*. Würzburg: Echter Verlag, 1985.

MacLean, French L. *The Camp Men: The SS Officers Who Ran the Nazi Concentration Camp System*. Atglen, Pa.: Schiffer, 1999.

Martin, Marko. *"Eine Zeitschrift gegen das Vergessen." Bundesrepublikanische Traditionen und Umbrüche im Spiegel der Kulturzeitschrift "Der Monat."* New York: P. Lang, 2003.

———. *Orwell, Koestler und all die anderen: Melvin J. Lasky und "Der Monat."* Asendorf: Mut-Verlag, 1999.

Megargee, Geoffrey P. *Inside Hitler's High Command*. Lawrence: University of Kansas Press, 2000.

Meinecke, Friedrich. *Die deutsche Katastrophe; betrachtungen und erinnerungen*. Zürich: Aeo-Verlag, 1946.

Merrit, Richard L. *Democracy Imposed: U.S. Occupation Policy and the German Public, 1945–1949*. New Haven, Conn.: Yale University Press, 1995.

Moeller, Robert. *War Stories: The Search for a Usable Past in the Federal Republic of Germany*. Berkeley: University of California Press, 2001.

Naasner, Walter. *SS-Wirtschaft und SS-Verwaltung: Das SS-Wirtschafts-Verwaltungshauptamt und die unter seiner Dienstaufsicht stehenden wirtschaftlichen Unternehmungen und weitere Dokumente*. Düsseldorf: Droste Verlag, 1998.

Nowak, Kurt. *Geschichte des Christentums in Deutschland*. Munich: Beck Verlag, 1995.

Oppitz, Ulrich-Dieter. *Medizinverbrechen vor Gericht: das Urteil im Nürnberger Ärzteprozess gegen Karl Brandt und andere sowie aus dem Prozess gegen Generalfeldmarschall Milch*. Erlangen: Palm & Enke, 1999.

Owings, Alison. *Frauen: German Women Recall the Third Reich*. New Brunswick, N.J.: Rutgers University Press, 1993.

Passelecq, Georges, and Bernard Suchecky. *The Hidden Encyclical of Pius XI*. Translated by Steven Randall. New York: Harcourt Brace, 1997.

Pawlikowski, John T., O.S.M. "The Catholic Response to the Holocaust: Institutional Perspectives." In Berenbaum and Peck, eds., *Holocaust and History*.

Phayer, Michael. "Die Katholische Kirche, der Vatikan und der Holocaust 1940-1965." In Steininger and Boehler, eds., *Der Umgang mit dem Holocaust*.

————. *The Catholic Church and the Holocaust, 1930–1965*. Bloomington: Indiana University Press, 2000.

Repgen, Konrad. "Die Erfahrung des Dritten Reiches und das Selbstverständniss der deutschen Katholiken nach 1945." In *Die Zeit Nach 1945 als Thema kirchlicher Zeitgeschichte*, ed. Victor Conzemius, M. Gneschat, and H. Kocher. Göttingen: Vanderhoeck und Ruprecht, 1988.

Riechert, Karen. "Der Umgang der Katholischen Kirche mit Historischer und Juristischer Schuld Anlässlich der Nürnberger Kriegsverbrecherprozesse." In *Der Rolle der Katholische Kirche in Deutschland nach 1945*, ed. Joachim Kohler and Damian van Delis. Stuttgart, 1998.

Rittner, Carol, and John K. Roth, eds. *Pope Pius XII and the Holocaust*. London: Leicester University Press, 2002.

Ross, Robert. *So It Was True: The American Protestant Press and the Nazi Persecution of the Jews*. Minneapolis: University of Minnesota Press, 1980.

Ross, Ronald J. *The Failure of Bismarck's Kulturkampf: Catholicism and State Power in Imperial Germany, 1871–1889*. Washington, D.C.: Catholic University of America Press, 1998.

Schulte, Jan Erik. *Zwangsarbeit und Vernichtung: das Wirtschaftsimperium der SS: Oswald Pohl und das SS-Wirtschafts-Verwaltungshauptamt, 1933–1945*. Paderborn: F. Schöningh, 2001.

Schwartz, Thomas Alan. "John J. McCloy and the Landsberg Cases." In *American Policy and the Reconstruction of West Germany, 1945–1955*, ed. Jeffrey M. Diefendorf, Axel Frohn, and Hermann-Josef Rupieper. Washington, D.C.: German Historical Institute and Cambridge University Press, 1993.

Sereny, Gitta. *Into That Darkness: An Examination of Conscience*. New York: Vintage Books, 1983.

Smith, Helmut Walser. *German Nationalism and Religious Conflict: Culture, Ideology, Politics, 1870–1914*. Princeton, N.J.: Princeton University Press, 1995.

Southern, David W. *John LaFarge and the Limits of Catholic Interracialism, 1911–1963*. Baton Rouge: Louisiana State University Press, 1996.

Sperber, Jonathan. *Popular Catholicism in Nineteenth-Century Germany*. Princeton, N.J.: Princeton University Press, 1984.

Spicer, Kevin. *Resisting the Third Reich: The Catholic Clergy in Hitler's Berlin*. DeKalb: Northern Illinois University Press, 2004.

Spotts, Frederic. *The Churches and Politics in Germany*. Middletown, Conn.: Wesleyan University Press, 1973.

Standifer, Leon C. *Binding Up the Wounds: An American Soldier in Occupied Germany, 1945-1946*. Baton Rouge: Louisiana State University Press, 1997.

Steininger, Rolf, and Ingrid Boehler, eds. *Der Umgang mit dem Holocaust. Europa-USA-Israel.* Vienna: Boehlau Verlag, 1994.

Stember, Charles Herbert, ed. *Jews in the Mind of America.* New York: Basic Books, 1966.

Stern, Frank. *The Whitewashing of the Yellow Badge: Antisemitism and Philosemitism in Postwar Germany.* Translated by William Templer. Oxford: Pergamon Press, 1992.

Stoltzfus, Nathan. *Resistance of the Heart: Intermarriage and the Rosenstrasse Protest in Nazi Germany.* New York: W.W. Norton, 1996.

Stücken, Wolfgang, *Hirten unter Hitler: Die Rolle der Paderborner Erzbischöfe Caspar Klein und Lorenz Jäger in der NS-Zeit.* Essen: Klartext Verlag, 1999.

Tent, James F. *Mission on the Rhine: Reeducation and Denazification in American-Occupied Germany.* Chicago: University of Chicago Press, 1982.

Vollnhals, Clemens. *Evangelische Kirche und Entnazifierung, 1945–1949: Die Last der nationalsozialistischen Vergangenheit.* Munich: R. Oldenbourg, 1989.

Warren, Donald. *Radio Priest: Charles Coughlin, the Father of Hate Radio.* New York: Free Press, 1996.

Weingartner, James J. *A Peculiar Crusade: Willis J. Everett and the Malmedy Massacre.* New York: New York University Press, 2000.

Wiesel, Elie. *Night.* Translated by Stella Rodway. New York: Avon Books, 1969.

Wistrich, Robert. *Antisemitism: The Longest Hatred.* New York: Pantheon Books, 1991.

Wollasch, Hans-Josef. *Betrifft, Nachrichtenzentrale des Erzbischofs Gröber in Freiburg: Die Ermittlungen der Geheim Staatspolizei gegen Gertrud Luckner, 1942–1944.* Konstanz: UVK, 1999.

Yahil, Leni. *The Holocaust: The Fate of European Jewry.* Translated by Ina Friedman and Haya Galai. New York: Oxford University Press, 1990.

Zahn, Gordon. *German Catholics and Hitler's Wars.* New York: E.P. Dutton, 1969.

Ziemke, Earl F. *The U.S. Army in the Occupation of Germany, 1944–46.* Army Historical Series. Washington, D.C.: United States Army Center of Military History, 1990.

Zöller, Michael. *Washington and Rome: Catholicism in American Culture.* Translated by Steven Rendall and Albert Wimmer. Notre Dame, Ind.: University of Notre Dame Press, 1999.

Zuccotti, Susan. *Under His Very Windows: The Vatican and the Holocaust in Italy.* New Haven, Conn.: Yale University Press, 2000.

Articles Consulted

Barry, Colman, O.S.B. "Cardinal Muench: Mission of Charity." *American Benedictine Review* 19, 4 (December 1968): 403–26.

Bartov, Omer. "Defining Enemies, Making Victims: Germans, Jews and the Holocaust." *The American Historical Review* 103, 3 (June 1998): 770–816.

Besier, Gerhard. "Anti-Bolshevism and Anti-Semitism: The Catholic Church in Germany and National Socialist Ideology, 1936–1937." *Journal of Ecclesiastical History* 43 (July 1992): 447–56.

Buscher, Frank. "The Great Fear: The Catholic Church and the Anticipated Radicalization of Expellees and Refugees in Postwar Germany," *German History: The Journal of the German History Society* 21, 2 (2003): 204–24.

Buscher, Frank, and Michael Phayer. "German Catholic Bishops and the Holocaust, 1940–52." *German Studies Review* 11, 3 (October 1988): 163–85.

Gushee, David. "Many Paths to Righteousness: An Assessment of Research on Why Righteous Gentiles Helped Jews." *Holocaust and Genocide Studies* 7, 3 (winter 1993): 372–401.

Hamilton, Richard F. "The Rise of Nazism: A Case Study and Review of Interpretations—Kiel, 1928–1933." *German Studies Review* 26, 1 (February 2003): 43–62.

Hardtwig, Wolfgang. "Political Religion in Modern Germany: Reflections on Nationalism, Socialism, and National Socialism." *German Historical Institute Bulletin* 28 (spring 2001): 3–27.

Mann, Michael. "Were the Perpetrators of Genocide 'Ordinary Men' or 'Real Nazis'? Results from Fifteen Hundred Biographies." *Holocaust and Genocide Studies* 14, 3 (winter 2000): 331–66.

McNutt, James E. "Adolf Schlatter and the Jews." *German Studies Review* 26, 2 (May 2003): 353–70.

Mitchell, Maria. "Materialism and Secularism: CDU Politicians and National Socialism, 1945–9." *Journal of Modern History* 67 (June 1995): 278–308.

Moeller, Robert. "War Stories: The Search for a Usable Past in the Federal Republic of Germany." *American Historical Review* 101, 4 (October 1996): 1008–48.

Phayer, Michael. "The Catholic Resistance Circle in Berlin and German Catholic Bishops during the Holocaust." *Holocaust and Genocide Studies* 7, 2 (fall 1993): 216–29.

———. "The German Catholic Church after the Holocaust." *Holocaust and Genocide Studies* 10, 2 (fall 1996): 151–65.

———. "Pope Pius XII, the Holocaust, and the Cold War." *Holocaust and Genocide Studies* 12, 2 (fall 1998): 233–56.

———. "The Postwar German Catholic Debate over Holocaust Guilt." *Kirchliche Zeitgeschichte* 8, 2 (1995): 426–39.

Smith, Helmut Walser. "The Learned and Popular Discourse of Anti-Semitism in the Catholic Milieu of the Kaiserreich." *Central European History* 3 (1994): 315–28.

Stambolis, Barbara. "Nationalisierung trotz Ultramontanisierung, oder, Alles für Deutschland, Deutschland aber für Christus. Mentalitätsleitende

Wertorientierung deutscher Katholiken im 19. Und 20. Jahrhundert," *Historische Zeitschrifte* 269 (1999): 57–97.

Volk, Ludwig. "Der Heilige Stuhl und Deutschland 1945–1949." *Stimmen der Zeit* 194 (1976): 795–823.

———. "Bilanz einer Nuntiatur 1946–1959: Schlussbericht des ersten Nuntius in der Nachkriegszeit." *Stimmen der Zeit* 195 (1977): 147–58.

Webster, Ronald. "Opposing 'Victors' Justice': German Protestant Churchmen and Convicted War Criminals in Western Europe after 1945." *Holocaust and Genocide Studies* 15, 1 (spring 2001): 47–69.

Westermann, Edward B. "Ordinary Men or Ideological Soldiers? Police Battalion 310 in Russia, 1942." *German Studies Review* 21, 1 (February 1998): 41–68.

Index

SUZANNE BROWN-FLEMING
is senior program officer in the University Programs Division of
the United States Holocaust Memorial Museum's Center for
Advanced Holocaust Studies in Washington, D.C.